TRAVELLER'S GUIDE TO EAST AFRICA AND THE INDIAN OCEAN

A complete travel companion to
Comoros, Djibouti, Ethiopia,
Kenya, Madagascar, Mauritius,
Reunion, Seychelles, Somalia, Sudan,
Tanzania and Uganda

Seventh edition

TRAVELLER'S GUIDE

TO

EAST AFRICA

AND THE INDIAN OCEAN

an iC publication

Introduction and Acknowledgements

Africa is a volatile continent constantly on the move politically, socially and economically. Despite frequent communications and transport difficulties and escalating economic problems in many parts of Africa, the continent as a whole is receiving more visitors than ever before.

The urge to travel leads people further and further afield in search of exotic and remote destinations, and Africa has enough to offer every brand of traveller – mountains, forests, deserts, unspoilt beaches, abundant wildlife, historic sites, cultural festivals, excellent crafts and the attraction of many sophisticated cities.

The *Traveller's Guide to East Africa* edited by Alan Rake has been entirely revised and updated, following the total sell-out of the sixth edition.

The *Traveller's Guide to East Africa* is a companion volume to the *Traveller's Guide to West Africa*, the *Traveller's Guide to Central and Southern Africa*, and the *Traveller's Guide to North Africa*. Readers familiar with the *Traveller's Guides to Africa* will recognise the format of these new regional guides which now provide an expanded coverage of each area in a handier pocket-size volume. The Traveller's Guides provide essential coverage of the history, economy and cultural life of the continent as well as offering a mass of practical up-to-date travel information and a hotel reference guide for each country. Our books are aimed at a wide variety of travellers – holidaymakers, businessmen, students, researchers and the independent traveller in search of adventure. We have included a number of background chapters on different aspects of each region which we hope will be of interest.

For those who can find the money, the opportunity and especially the time, we hope this book will be an encouragement to see more of Africa, to explore beyond the beaten tourist tracks, to meet and make contact with the people and to come to some understanding of the rich cultural life that Africa offers.

Our thanks go to the many contributors who have assisted us in providing the latest travel information. The editors also wish to acknowledge Roma Beaumont, Kathryn Hopkirk and Gorden Reynell who prepared all the maps included in this guide.

Publisher	Ahmed Afif Ben Yedder
Editor	Alan Rake
Published by	IC Publications Ltd **London Office** P.O. Box 261 69 Great Queen Street, London WC2B 5BN Telephone 01-404 4333 Cables Machrak London WC2 Telex 8811757 **US Office.** IC Publications Ltd Room 1121, 122 East 42nd Street New York, N.Y. 10168 Telephone (212) 867 5159 Telex 425442
US Edition published by	Hunter Publishing Inc 300 Raritan Center Parkway Edison, N.J. 08818
Typeset by	RSB Typesetters Bagshot Road Worplesdon, Surrey
Printed by	Page Bros (Norwich) Ltd.
Cover Photograph	Alan Rake

© 1990 IC Publications Ltd
ISBN 0905268-56-3
ISSN 0144-7653
ISBN 1-55650-230-3 (US) Hunter Publishing
Inc. $13.95

CONTENTS

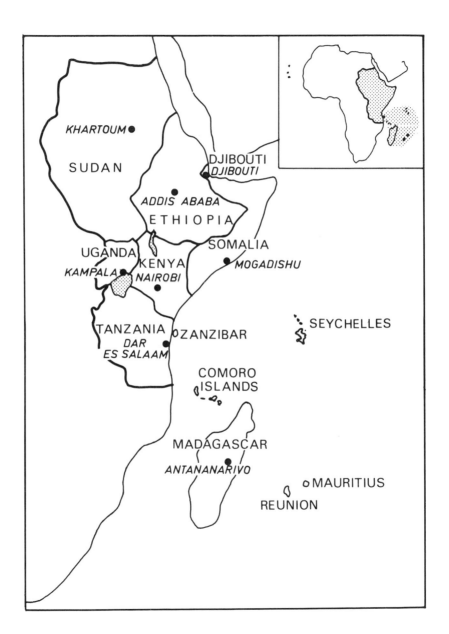

KHARTOUM ●

SUDAN

DJIBOUTI
DJIBOUTI

ADDIS ABABA ●

ETHIOPIA

UGANDA

SOMALIA

KAMPALA

KENYA

NAIROBI ●

MOGADISHU ●

TANZANIA ○ZANZIBAR

DAR
ES SALAAM

SEYCHELLES

COMORO
○ISLANDS

MADAGASCAR

ANTANANARIVO ●

○MAURITIUS

REUNION

8

Currency Table

COUNTRY	CURRENCY	£1 VALUE	$1 VALUE
Comoros	CFA Franc	481.00	284.00
Djibouti	Djibouti Franc	295.00	174.00
Ethiopia	Ethiopian Birr	3.47	2.05
Kenya	Kenya Shilling	36.40	21.50
Madagascar	Malagasy Franc	2200.00	1300.00
Mauritius	Mauritian Rupee	24.90	14.70
Reunion	French Franc	9.62	5.67
Seychelles	Seychelles Rupee	9.11	5.37
Somalia	Somali Shilling	693.00	409.00
Sudan	Sudanese Pound	19.30	11.40
Tanzania	Tanzania Shilling	325.00	192.00
Uganda	Uganda Shilling	631.00	372.00

Official values as at 12 February 1990.

Rainfall · Temperature

over 16 ins (over 400 mm) ■
8-16 ins (200-400 mm)
2-8 ins (50-200 mm)
0-2 ins (0-50 mm)

over 100°F (over 38°C)
80°-100°F (27°-38°C)
60°-80°F (16°-27°C)
Below 60°F (below 16°C)

Black areas denote maximum rainfall. Grey areas maximum temperature.

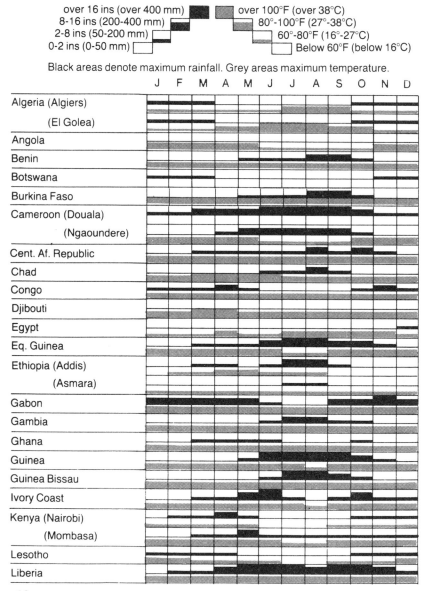

	J	F	M	A	M	J	J	A	S	O	N	D
Algeria (Algiers)												
(El Golea)												
Angola												
Benin												
Botswana												
Burkina Faso												
Cameroon (Douala)												
(Ngaoundere)												
Cent. Af. Republic												
Chad												
Congo												
Djibouti												
Egypt												
Eq. Guinea												
Ethiopia (Addis)												
(Asmara)												
Gabon												
Gambia												
Ghana												
Guinea												
Guinea Bissau												
Ivory Coast												
Kenya (Nairobi)												
(Mombasa)												
Lesotho												
Liberia												

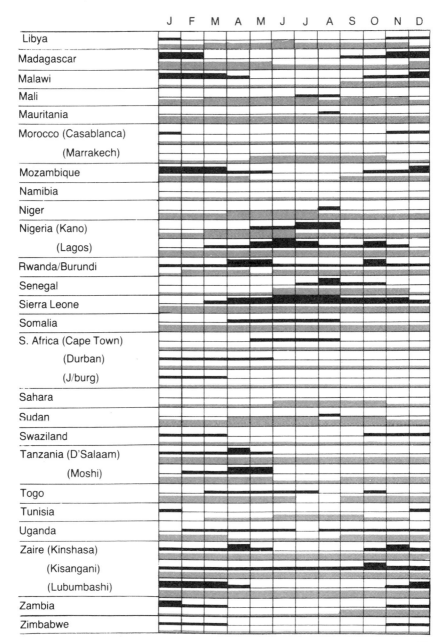

	J	F	M	A	M	J	J	A	S	O	N	D
Libya												
Madagascar												
Malawi												
Mali												
Mauritania												
Morocco (Casablanca)												
(Marrakech)												
Mozambique												
Namibia												
Niger												
Nigeria (Kano)												
(Lagos)												
Rwanda/Burundi												
Senegal												
Sierra Leone												
Somalia												
S. Africa (Cape Town)												
(Durban)												
(J/burg)												
Sahara												
Sudan												
Swaziland												
Tanzania (D'Salaam)												
(Moshi)												
Togo												
Tunisia												
Uganda												
Zaire (Kinshasa)												
(Kisangani)												
(Lubumbashi)												
Zambia												
Zimbabwe												

11

Do's and Don'ts

Whenever you enter or leave a country, you are likely to be required to fill out several forms – memorising your passport number and date of issue helps expedite these formalities. If you do not have a fixed address before you arrive, give the name of one of the big hotels or your embassy. Similarly when completing the 'occupation' section, don't announce yourself as a journalist or television researcher, if you could as easily be something less controversial. Don't get irritated with long bureaucratic procedures – it only makes things worse.

On arrival should your vaccination certificate not be in order, request that any injections required be provided by a qualified medical person.

If you intend travelling from one country to another by car, make sure you have 1) a triptyque or carnet de passage 2) a green card or other proof of insurance cover 3) licence plates with a national symbol 4) an international and/or national driver's licence. If you intend crossing the border in a taxi check that the driver and vehicle have all the proper documents. It is not possible to cross from one country to another in a hired car.

On the Subject of Money

Many countries request that visitors fill in currency declaration forms issued on arrival – it is obligatory to declare how much foreign currency you are bringing into the country and then note each time you exchange money or travellers cheques. The forms are then presented to customs officials on departure. Take this procedure seriously as you do not want to be accused of selling money on the black market. Don't be lured into black market currency deals – you often come off worst and the penalties are severe. On the other hand, on arrival or departure you may be approached by an official who suggests that your documents or baggage are not in order, but that a small cash handout may rectify the situation. Do not be intimidated into paying but ask to see the director of customs or immigration.

Besides banks, it is possible to exchange travellers cheques and currency at most airports and big hotels (although usually at a less favourable rate of exchange). Exchange only what money you think you may need on a daily basis so that you can avoid having to change back into foreign exchange or accumulate worthless notes. If travelling overland try and obtain a little of the currency of each country before you arrive if possible, as at some small border points there is nowhere to change money at all.

Always have your money and passport somewhere close to your body to protect them from pickpockets. A small pouch which you can hang around your neck or wear under your shirt strapped to your body is a good idea. If your passport or travellers cheques are lost or stolen, report this to the local police and to your embassy or consulate.

If you are forced to take a taxi from the airport to town because of lack of airport services, negotiate the price before you leave.

Enjoy Your Stay

Once in Africa it becomes useless to plan the details of your stay closely; throw away your watch and enjoy the unhurried tempo of life: 'African time' is the antithesis of Western clock watching and inflexible planning will only cause frustration. You may want to stay longer in one place or you may be invited to visit the local people in the country or to visit a local festival. Carefully made travel plans are especially bound to go awry. If you're flying from one country to another allow yourself a full day to include the likely chance of delays and lengthy arrival and departure formalities.

Arabic, English and French are probably the three most widely spoken languages in Africa, while Swahili is the first language for many millions in East Africa. Wherever you are the pleasure and response evoked from local people by using a few simple words and phrases in the indigenous language will amply repay the small effort involved. Learn at least how to greet people, to say please, thank you and goodbye.

Do not be paternalistic; waiters and hotel staff should be addressed in the approved local manner. (In East Africa, the word to use when calling for service is 'rafiki', meaning friend in Kiswahili).

Remember in Muslim countries Islamic customs often differ markedly from Western customs. Always respect this difference. Ask permission before entering any mosque and always remove your shoes.

CLAUDIO MUÑOZ

Try to deviate from the beaten tourist track – you haven't really been to Africa unless you've experienced some rural life. A chance acquaintance with someone you meet, be it a student or taxidriver may bring you in contact with his family in the countryside. Don't miss the opportunity. It is in these areas that you are likely to enounter authentic dance, (rather than the versions provided by local package tours) hear real traditional drumming and music and see genuine works of African arts and crafts.

If you are lucky enough to be invited into an African family remember that their ideas of correct behaviour may differ markedly from yours. Always show respect to the elders of the community or family; it is disrespectful to call old people by their first names. You should shake hands with everyone in the room when you are introduced even if you do not know them. Most rural Africans are poor, hospitality is of the utmost importance and reciprocity in gifts is part of the code. If you're invited to an African village or home bring along a few small items as gifts. As most of these people live largely outside the money economy, they value things according to their usefulness or novelty. A penknife or a cheap cigarette lighter and a few packs of cigarettes would always be welcome as would bottled drinks and fruit for the children. A polaroid camera is also popular – and overcomes the problem of the promised photographs never sent. Another way to repay hospitality is to do odd practical jobs or engine repairs; offer your services as best you can.

CLAUDIO MUÑOZ

When you arrive in Africa don't photograph the airport, harbour, soldiers or anything which could be regarded as a military installation. This includes railways and bridges. Be polite and always ask before taking anyone's photograph – this applies particularly to the many Muslim people, especially women who do not like being photographed. Sometimes the donation of an instant polaroid photo can overcome initial reluctance but it is also likely that a small fee will be requested for the privilege. Pay up or don't go ahead!

Be warned that in some countries the authorities do not welcome people who can be labelled 'hippies' and who are considered as Western degenerates. To avoid being harassed it costs little effort to keep one's hair relatively short and appearance tidy. Women or girls travelling alone should be quite safe if they do not wear provocative clothing. In many African countries there are also heavy penalties and strong hostility to the smoking of marijuana.

Don't walk alone after dark in unfrequented places in major cities. As in any big Western city it is dangerous. However, petty thieving from your room or vehicle is more likely than getting mugged, so take sensible precautions.

Motoring

If you intend renting a car inspect your car thoroughly before you accept it. Check that it has proper documents, spare tyres (you will be driving on rough roads if you leave the city), tyre changing equipment, and a tool kit. Check the rental contract for responsibility for cost of repairs (especially broken windshields, common from flying stones), breakdown and towing, and accidents. Attempt to get this in writing. Remember that although driving is one of the best ways to see Africa, there are few good roads such as you may be used to, and distances are enormous. Always carry extra petrol in rural areas, petrol stations are few and far between. Drive carefully – there is a high accident rate in Africa. Don't be afraid to use your hooter on bends and in market areas where there are lots of pedestrians and when passing another vehicle. If you do have an accident, especially one involving a pedestrian, it is advisable to go immediately to the nearest police station. If you need repairs done to your vehicle negotiate the price before work begins.

If you are planning a long overland expedition by car – remember that Western commodities are imported and tend to be expensive so take plenty of basic supplies from home.

Desert Travel

Crossing the desert should not be attempted by hitchhikers. A four-wheel drive vehicle in good order is essential. Always carry spare parts, extra water, food and petrol, a first aid kit and a compass. Don't overload the vehicle. Desert travel should be in convoy with other vehicles. In the event of a breakdown or loss of direction, passengers should remain with the vehicle and inside the car during the heat of the day. Anyone seeing a parked car in the desert will stop, assuming you need help. It is advisable to give local authorities a precise route plan before setting out. This makes rescue easier in case of difficulties.

Stay Healthy

Don't swim, wash or even paddle in slow moving water, bilharzia, carried by small water-snails, is endemic throughout the continent. If you contract

dysentry make sure you seek treatment immediately; it is debilitating and can cause dehydration if left untreated. If you are far away from any big town, bush hospitals or mission stations will treat you.

More common stomach upsets can have several causes – change of routine, exposure to a different diet or the reaction to a new virus strain. However, attacks are frequently caused by food that has been improperly cooked or that has been cooked in unhygienic circumstances, or by impure water. Avoid foods that have been prepared in advance and left standing. Always use water purifying tablets outside major cities and try to wash fruit and vegetables in purified water. Don't eat salad unless you know it has been carefully washed. Pasteurised milk is available in Kenya – elsewhere it is advisable to drink powdered milk. Most of these stomach disorders can be cleared up with drugs.

Try and eat in reasonable restaurants when possible, although don't be extreme and be put off trying local foods or risk being impolite by being over-cautious if offered hospitality in some remote village. It would be a great shame to eat only uniform hotel food when there is often interesting African fare to be sampled. Each country has its own specialities, and although East African cooking may not be as exotic as on the west coast, there is plenty of unusual tropical fruit, excellent seafood and freshwater fish.

It is very easy to forget how strong the sun is in Africa. Wear a hat and sunglasses, use a sunscreen (rather than a suntan) lotion or cream, and stay out of the sun during the hottest part of the day. Take time to acclimatise to very hot weather, drink plenty of liquids, take salt tablets and don't undertake any strenuous activities in the middle of the day.

Shopping

Haggling over prices in street markets is normal procedure and also in many shops where prices are not displayed. Bargaining is not bad manners – it is expected and it is a good idea to check prices on items in the shops and expect to do about 25-50% better by bargaining in the market. Your starting price should be about half of what you would be prepared to pay. Don't be rude or aggressive or feel pressed for time. You do not do the trader down, bargaining is a ritual requiring patience and a sense of humour.

If you do not enjoy haggling in market places, purchasing directly from a craftsman probably ensures the best quality and price. Many shops will arrange to ship things home for you but these will be at a higher price. Some shops allow discount for purchases made with travellers cheques.

When you buy hides, skin goods and ivory in shops, you should be given Game Department Certificates. Customs require these when you leave – this is to discourage the sale of poached skins. Be cautious when game skins are offered at low prices – they may not have been properly cured. Traditional sculpture survives but you will have difficulty finding genuine 'antiques' and should be prepared to pay the expected price as well as meeting government export licence requirements. When you purchase gold jewellery, ivory or rugs look for government seals or stamps endorsing the quality.

In the Game Parks

Firearms and domestic pets are prohibited in parks. Warning notices must be taken seriously. When notices warn you to stay in your car don't get out because you feel no animals are near; nature camouflages them well. Don't make the mistake of thinking of small, furry looking wild animals as pets. Always travel slowly, otherwise you frighten the animals and see very little. Leave radios behind in the camp and don't blow your horn. If watching animals which are close by, don't talk loudly. Remember that the big cats can be the most dangerous animals because they can see you in the car – all the other animals see only the vehicle. Don't hop out of the car just to get that perfect shot from 10ft nearer! Carry a good pair of binoculars with you and a good reference book describing the wildlife you are likely to meet.

Taking Photographs

Most modern cameras and film are capable of giving excellent results in countries where the lighting is harsh. Remember to make allowances in your exposure meter readings for bright sand or strongly lit white buildings. Try close-up photographs in the shade and use the bright reflected light from the ground or a wall to give soft lighting.

Suggested films: Kodachrome 64 (slides), Ektachrome II (colour prints), Tri-x (black and white).

Suggested lenses: telephoto, wide-angle (for single lens reflex cameras). A powerful telephoto is essential for photographing wildlife.

Suggested filters: (either gel or glass) polarised against reflected glare, or daylight filter for a cool tint. Both give richer sky colour and cut out glare.

It is also very important to remember if you have an automatic electric exposure meter or flash gun to carry spare batteries. **Never** leave a camera or film in bright sunlight for long. Film is stored best over long periods in a cool refrigerator if this is possible, but wait until it has reached room temperature before opening the containers.

Ready, Steady, Go

Planning a trip to Africa can be time consuming and harassing; there seem to be endless travel arrangements to make, documents to put in order, and mental notes of essential items to remember. We have compiled a brief list of ideas and reminders to make all this simpler. The idea of a trip to Africa need not be a daunting one – by taking sensible precautions and opening yourself to experiencing a totally different culture, Africa is probably one of the most exciting and enjoyable places to travel anywhere in the world.

Before You Go

A good introduction for your forthcoming trip to Africa is to read something about the country. An introduction to the history, culture, people, food specialities, wildlife and major places of interest can only make your trip more enjoyable and provide you with a much richer experience.

Novels written by indigenous authors often give added valuable insight into the people and their cultural and social values. Similarly, if you are interested in music, it is also worth listening to some of the many available recordings of traditional and urban African music before you leave. This may help you to choose from the many performances available.

Planning your trip: Even if you do not like an organised schedule when travelling, there are certain things which if thought about beforehand are always an advantage. Book your charter flight well in advance and pay attention to dates when off-season rates go into effect for both hotels and charter flights – a week one way or the other can make all the difference to your budget. It is also worthwhile considering local holidays and festivals which may make travelling or accommodation difficult and expensive. On the other hand, you may like to plan a trip around a major cultural or religious festival of a particular region. Even if you are naturally opposed to dealing with travel agents, using one frequently saves time, aggravation and even money (remember there is no charge for booking and reservation services) as some of the package deals available may incorporate your basic requirements and cost less than individual arrangements. It is worthwhile shopping around for an agent – ask friends or colleagues who have had similar travel needs to recommend one who has done a good job for them.

When planning travel in the East African region, you will find a copy of Thomas Cook Overseas Timetable invaluable. The timetable, which is published every two months, gives schedules and sample fares for all the major rail, bus and ferry services throughout the area. You can get a copy by post from Thomas Cook Ltd., (Dept. TPO/ICH), PO Box 36, Peterborough, England, PE3 6SB for £6.40 (including postage in UK) and in North America from Forsyth Travel Library, PO Box 2975, Shawnee Mission KS 66201, USA, for US$22.45.

Make sure you have good maps

Documents: Once you have purchased your ticket check to see that dates, times, and destinations have been filled in correctly. Always telephone to confirm international flights. Ensure that your passport is still valid and that you have all the necessary inoculations (see under Entry Regulations in the General Information section of this guide for the requirements of each individual country). Check that the latter have been correctly noted in your International Certificate of Vaccination. Make sure you obtain visas for countries where these are required well in advance. Although it is possible to get visas while travelling, it is infinitely more time consuming and troublesome.

When ordering traveller's cheques, it is advisable to request small denominations so that you can reduce the quantity of local currencies that you carry around with you. The rates for changing money back into foreign exchange are highly unfavourable, and most African currencies are worthless outside their own borders. For entry into some countries the authorities may demand evidence that you can pay your way out again. Sufficient proof of this is a valid return air ticket, a guarantee from your bank at home, or a guarantee from your national embassy.

If you intend hiring a car it is essential to obtain an International Driving Licence before leaving home. This is valid for one year and is recognised by most African countries. Your national driving licence is also useful for identification if you lose your passport or misplace your international licence. If you belong to an automobile association, your membership card often facilitates service from partner clubs abroad.

Student identity cards allow students special rates on trains and buses, and access to hostels and university dormitories. As a card-carrying member of the YMCA/YWCA, similar facilities would be available.

Check with the embassy, consulate or national airline of the country concerned if there are specific regulations or licences required for special equipment or sporting gear (guns, aqualungs etc) you plan to take with you.

Try to get introductions to family or business friends before you leave for Africa. One introduction usually leads to others and it is only by interacting with the people who live there that you will really get to know a country.

It is always advisable to take out health insurance. There are schemes available which are specifically for travel. Health insurance can also be part of a wider insurance policy which would cover loss of baggage, and insure against flight cancellation. The latter is advisable if flying with a charter organisation, while baggage insurance is almost essential, as the enormous distances and frequent air traffic confusion increase the chance of baggage loss.

Medical Precautions: Always pack a small supply of medicines to take along (see check list). Although in most big towns medical facilities are available, you may be in a remote area where medical help and drugs are difficult or impossible to obtain. The two main common health problems likely to be incurred in Africa are either some form of stomach upset or gastro-enteritis or sunburn and, even more severely, sunstroke. (See Do's and Don'ts for how best to avoid these complaints once you get there). Before you leave ask your doctor to prescribe the correct drug to combat diarrhoea or stomach upsets. Ask for a sulphur based drug.

Besides the other statutory inoculations it is advisable to have a gamma-globulin injection as it helps to prevent hepatitis and other infections. If you intend travelling in any region host to malaria, it is important to remember to begin a course of malaria prophylactics two weeks before you leave, and to continue taking them once you arrive. If you suffer chronic ill-health, contact your doctor before you leave, take an adequate supply of necessary medication and any prescriptions that may need to be made up. It is a good idea to carry a card stating your blood type and any chronic health problems or allergy to drugs which you may have. If your visit is likely to be a long one, have a dental checkup before you leave. Travellers who wear glasses or contact lenses should carry an extra pair and the prescription.

For a small charge, it is possible to secure a booklet listing all participating English-speaking doctors, clinics and hospitals around the world from the International Association of Medical Assistance to Travellers (IAMAT). The booklet includes a climate chart and inoculation information for every country in the world. Write to IAMAT, 350 5th Ave, Room 5620, New York, NY 10001, USA.

What to Pack

Clothing: For African travel you always need far less than you think, and this really depends on what you intend doing rather than where you are going – ie

20

will you be on safari, mountain-climbing, lying on the beach or staying in sophisticated hotels? Rather than be fashionable you should concentrate on good boots for hiking and the other basics not easily obtainable in Africa.

It is easy to rinse out cotton shirts and skirts as they dry very quickly, and always remember that cotton is preferable to synthetic clothing, as the latter combined with the heat can irritate your skin. Even in summer a sweater or jacket is often necessary in the evening. Be able to dress in layers so that with the dramatic temperature changes that frequently occur, clothing can be added or removed as required. Cotton T shirts and light woollen sweaters are ideal for this. Long sleeved cotton shirts and long socks are also useful to keep arms and legs covered while walking in the bush. A widebrimmed hat and sunglasses are essential, while a pair of canvas shoes for walking on coral are also useful. Coral is very sharp and can cause cuts to turn septic.

Consult the Climate and What to Wear sections in the individual country chapters in this guide for more specific advice and for advice on dress for visitors to Muslim countries or countries with conservative outlooks.

Miscellaneous items: If you intend travelling overland at all, or exploring beyond the usual tourist areas, make sure you have good maps with you. These may be easier to obtain before you leave; the most accurate and exhaustive of the available maps of Africa are the Michelin 'red' maps (No. 153 for North and West Africa, 154 for North East Africa and 155 for Central, East and Southern Africa including Madagascar). These maps contain details which include distances, road surfaces, seasonal road conditions, accommodation, rainfall and temperature. If you intend going on a safari or you are particularly interested in wildlife, it is certainly worth investing in a good pair of binoculars and buying a good book on the birds,

Wear clothing suitable to the occasion

CLAUDIO MUNOZ

21

animals, flora and fauna of Africa.

It is worth carrying as much of your own film with you as possible – colour and black and white film are available in Africa, but both are expensive. A lens hood is a good idea, while an ultraviolet filter cuts down glare.

Take a few empty plastic bags with you – they may be scarce in out of the way places and are always useful to keep things wet, dry or dustproof, eg to protect your camera lens from sand and dust, or to keep a spare set of clothes dry when hiking etc.

Leave large heavy beach towels at home and buy one of the all purpose strips of local coloured cloth or fabric found all over Africa. This can be used as a beach towel and has the advantage of not collecting grains of sand and of drying very quickly. It also doubles as a wrap around skirt, a picnic cloth and a ground sheet. It is very light and folds away to nothing, and makes an attractive table cloth when you get home!

All countries have their cheap hotels but if you intend staying out of towns, it is best to have rudimentary camping equipment – a lightweight warm sleeping bag should be sufficient, while a small lightweight tent and light mosquito net for the tropics would also be useful.

Checklist

Documents
valid passport
visas where required
international certificate of vaccination
air tickets
extra passport photographs
traveller's cheques
international driving licence
student identification card
youth hostel card
credit cards (Diner's Club, American Express)
card carrying address and telephone number of whom to contact in the case of an emergency
any necessary prescriptions for glasses or medication
insurance certificates

Medical kit
salt tablets
vitamin tablets
sun protection cream
antiseptic cream
plasters
crepe bandage
mosquito repellent
malaria preventives
water sterilising tablets
aspirin
antibiotic ointment
anti-histamine cream/tablets (this relieves allergies to grasses, pollens and dust and gives relief from bites and skin rashes)
an anti-diarrhoeal drug (sulphur based if possible)
disposable syringes (for use off the beaten track – re-usable needles not properly disinfected can cause hepatitis)

Miscellaneous items
needle and thread
candles
torch
batteries
penknife
bottle opener
plastic bags
binoculars
maps
reference books
camera (telephoto lenses)
film
sleeping bag
lightweight plastic mac

East Africa Holiday

by Linda Van Buren and Alan Rake

A guide to package tours

So you are thinking of taking your first holiday in Africa this year, but you are not sure. You may have heard about the big-game safaris and the idyllic beaches, and you may book your East African holiday, as well over half a million people do every year, on the strength of those features alone. Names like Serengeti, Maasai Mara, Ngorongoro, Amboseli, Kilimanjaro, Zanzibar and Diani Beach beckon you, and seeing the film *Out of Africa* has only made you want to go to Africa even more.

On the other hand, what of the evening news and the anti-apartheid riots and famine in the Sahel, and what of the horror story your cousin's cousin once told you about appalling chaos at some African airport? Which of these images is the real Africa?

The answer is that they both are Africa, in the same sense that both Covent Garden and Brixton are London or both Disneyland and Watts are Southern California. Africa is larger and arguably less culturally homogeneous than Europe is, and Nigeria is as different from Kenya as Greece is from Scotland. Even within the East African region, conditions and culture vary tremendously from place to place.

You may be a veteran East Africa traveller out to discover yet another layer of its profound fascination, or you may be a first-timer slightly apprehensive about taking on too much of the unknown or a little worried that you might have to give up creature comforts to come to Africa. Whichever you are, or if you are somewhere in between, East Africa has a holiday that is right for you. This book will help you put it all in perspective. You are very likely to feel as one 11-year-old American boy did at the end of his three-week East Africa holiday: "It wasn't like I thought it would be. It was even better."

This is the year for Africa

East Africa is set for its biggest tourism year yet this coming season. Package tour operators are featuring Kenya more prominently than ever before in their global brochures. Many brochures devote 10-15 pages to Kenya, more than any other destination in the world. Mauritius and Seychelles are also on most tour operators' agenda, and Tanzania too gets the nod from several, especially in two-centre holidays, in combination with another destination.

Other destinations – Madagascar, Comoros, Djibouti – will require a more extensive search to arrange holidays there. Still others with plenty of attractions well worth seeing and experiencing are virtually off limits to tourists at the present time, either for security reasons or because extreme economic difficulties make it impossible to maintain an adequate tourism infrastructure. Among these are Ethiopia, Sudan and Uganda. Somalia too is not prepared to receive tourists.

Kenya – as you like it

Kenya, long established on the world tourism market, has become even more popular today. It has not only a wealth of interesting features to see and experience but also a well-developed tourism infrastructure from which to enjoy them.

Best known are its big-game safaris, with the emphasis now on photography and conservation rather than on hunting, and its Indian Ocean beach resorts. All these can be seen from accommodation providing absolute comfort, of course. But Kenya has many lesser-known attractions not covered in the global brochures, all of which can also be seen without leaving the tourism infrastructure, thus making them within the reach of a wide range of visitors without special qualities of fitness or endurance. Here are a few of them:

* **Lake Victoria.** Africa's largest lake, it is shared by Kenya, Tanzania and Uganda. Lakeside residents grow maize and sugar cane, sing their own brand of modern African music and are blessed with a "gift of the gab". You can dine on Nile perch and tilapia fresh from the lake, taste *ugali* (made from maize or corn meal) or stick with strictly Western fare – all over Kenya, the choice is yours. You can see hippos, a wealth of bird life and spectacular sunsets over the lake from the comfort of well-equipped international-standard hotels.

* **Lake Naivasha.** Here modern Kenya indulges those who have a nostalgic wish to relive the colonial era, with G&Ts on a veranda wreathed in bougainvillea overlooking the lake, immaculately manicured gardens and an easily accessible path for lakeside strolling. Popular with retired tourists as well as younger ones, the lake's shores also nurture the vineyards of Kenya's nascent wine industry.

* **Lake Nakuru.** If you thought a sky pink with flamingoes could be found only in dreams, come to Lake Nakuru. At charming Lake Nakuru Lodge, you sleep in spotless octagonal huts with Dutch doors and all mod cons, dine on a buffet of Kenyan cookery (and even Ugandan *matoke*, or green banana) as well as Western dishes, swim in the pool or just relax on the veranda with binoculars at the ready, gazing out across the game park and the lake itself.

* **Lake Turkana.** Situated in the stark surroundings of the Kenyan north, here is a very different aspect of Kenya. It was in Kenya that Louis S. B. Leakey in 1961 at Fort Ternan discovered man's oldest known ancestor, *Kenyapithecus wickeri*, who lived 14 million years ago in the Upper Miocene period. Leakey's son Richard, working in the late 1960s and early 1970s at

Koobi Fora on the eastern shore of Lake Turkana, discovered *Homo erectus*, who lived 3 million years ago and is regarded by some authorities as the earliest human remains yet found. The Leakeys are Kenyan citizens, and in fact Richard is the only white member of parliament in this country of full majority rule.

You can visit Koobi Fora from Lake Turkana Lodge (as well as from camping holidays), and while you are in the area you can meet the Turkana people as they herd their camels or fish with harpoons from *doum* palm rafts, or you can watch El-Molo fishermen cast their round nets, or you can try your own hand at fishing (one Nile perch fished out of Lake Turkana is said to have weighed 236 lbs!), or you can keep an eye peeled for tawny eagle, sacred ibis, white stork, malachite kingfisher, Egyptian goose or any of the other 300 species of birds found on the lake.

* **Swahili coastal history.** At Jumba la Mtwana, north of Mombasa, you can see how coastal peoples lived in the 1400s. At Gedi, a 45-acre site inland from Malindi, you can see remnants of the Golden Era of Islamic culture dating from the 15th century. The Mnarani ruins, on a bluff above Kilifi Creek, also date from the 15th century. And right in Mombasa, you can explore Fort Jesus, the oldest fortress built by a European power in Africa – built in 1593 by the Portuguese. Lamu island is a world apart from the Kenyan mainland, and from there you can take a lateen-rigged *dhow* to the uninhabited Manda island nearby for a visit to the Takwa ruins, dating from the 16th century and covering 12 acres. Huts are available so that visitors can camp overnight among the ruins.

* **Mount Kenya.** At 17,058 feet (5,199 metres), this is Africa's second-highest mountain (after Kilimanjaro), and snow stays on it all year round above 15,000 feet even though it is right on the equator. Its jagged peaks shelter 12 glaciers. Although the intrepid take delight in scaling the peak right to the top, Mount Kenya's lower slopes provide excellent hiking country. Plants grow here that grow nowhere else on earth. Wrap up warmly. The area is great for camping holidays, but at nearby Nanyuki you can enjoy Mount Kenya from one of the world's top hotels, at the Mount Kenya Safari Club. En route from Nairobi, you can see Kenya's fine Arabica coffee growing.

* **Kericho.** This is the centre of one of Kenya's main tea-growing areas and much of the tea is grown by smallholders to the highest standards. You will have enjoyed Kenyan tea throughout your stay in Kenya, since every year a given percentage of each grade of tea is held back from the world market for local consumption inside Kenya, and this is enjoyed not only in tourist facilities but in Kenyan homes as well. It is served to you English-style – but if you ask for it Kenyan-style (brewed directly in the milk, sometimes flavoured with spices), you are very likely to be served it by someone who is delighted that you asked.

These are all things you can see in addition to the wild animals and the beaches. Kenya has 13 national parks, the best-known of which are Amboseli, Tsavo and Mount Kenya, and seven national reserves, the best known of which is the Maasai Mara. Animals abound, especially in the Maasai Mara, and visitors almost always see far more animals than they expected. Coastal hotels are sited on the North Coast and on the South Coast (Diani Beach), where there is plenty of unspoilt open beach between hotels, with a coral reef rich in marine life and with sand as white as table salt. You can choose hotels with entertainment and nightlife frequented by the local smart set, or you can bask in complete seclusion and quiet, away from the traffic, but not away from high standards of comfort and service.

You may opt for a self-catering holiday, or a self-drive holiday with the big-name international car hire groups, or you can take the train from Nairobi east to Mombasa or west to Kisumu. You can cocoon yourself in your hotel complex if you want, or you can branch out if you want – the choice is yours.

Nairobi, Mombasa and the other larger towns have a choice of restaurants outside the hotels, and a popular restaurant guide, *Eating Out in Kenya*, provides a ratings guide to 300 restaurants.

Tourism in Kenya, unlike that in many Third World countries, is a self-sustaining endeavour. It is an important source of foreign exchange, all the more so because most of what the tourist consumes while he is in Kenya is produced locally. Keeping hotels supplied with paper products, blankets, wood furniture and other necessities provides jobs for Kenyans in local industry, and virtually everything a tourist eats or drinks is produced locally, including beer, wine, spirits, meat and even the extras like mushrooms. Kenya is one of the few places anywhere on the equator with a viable dairy industry, producing fresh milk and a variety of cheeses, yoghurt etc. Kenyan farmers grow everything from the papayas and mangoes you would expect to apples, asparagus and rhubarb, which you might not expect. You can enjoy

Rhino: one of East Africa's wildlife attractions

TANZANIA HC TOURIST OFFICE

Kenya in the full knowledge that you are contributing to, not draining, the country's scarce financial resources.

And, for those who are wondering, the electricity works, water flows from the taps, the Flying Doctors are on call and can reach you even when you are in a tent far from any town, the minibuses have enough petrol, the beer is properly chilled, the food is familiar and varied, and the planes usually run on time. If Kenya Airways has confirmed you a seat on a flight, then it is yours. (This is true in other African countries besides Kenya, of course, but alas in *some* African countries it is not true.) In Kenya, even when you are sleeping in a tent, someone makes sure your shower water is hot.

Global tour operators offering Kenya holidays are too numerous to mention them all, but a typical company like *Thomson Worldwide* offers a 14 day stay in July or August 1990, on the beach (Africana Sea Lodge) from £826 and safari beach combined (Samburu game park and Lagoon Reef) from £1,046. There are many other more expensive combinations. Novelties available include a camel safari (*Silk Cut Faraway*) and game-viewing from hot-air balloons (most operators, and locally available).

It is quite easy to arrange your own holiday in Kenya. You can fly in on any of more than 30 international airlines, book hotel space through major chains like Hilton or Inter-Continental or by telexing any of the hotels listed in the Kenya section of this book, and arrange a safari after you arrive by going to any of the Nairobi offices of local tour operators that are members of the Kenya Association of Tour Operators. Christmas is high season, with July/August second-highest.

Seychelles – beaches unique by a thousand miles

East Africa's second-most prominently featured destination in international brochures is Seychelles. The string of 86 islands boasts some of the world's best beaches, and the tourism infrastructure is up to very high – and often very luxurious – standards. The focus of most recent development for tourism has been the largest island, Mahe, but it is possible to visit other islands such as Praslin, La Digue, Aride, Denis and Bird.

A glance at any Seychelles brochure will show you why its beaches are renowned for their beauty, but there is more to see than snow-white coral strands. Seychelles has unique birds and plants, including the Coco-de-Mer nut, which is the world's largest seed, though it is better known for its suggestive shape. Sightseeing conveyances include small airplanes, bicycles, ox-carts and various types of boats.

The Seychelles Tourist Board in London (PO Box 4PE, 50 Conduit Street, London W1A 4PE, UK, telephone 01-439 9699, telex 21236 SEYCOM G) is very efficient, and you will find it to be one of the most helpful tourist boards you've ever dealt with, if you want to arrange your own holiday in Seychelles. Air Seychelles flies on weekends from London and Paris, fitting in conveniently with holidaymakers' needs. Kenya Airways, Air France and British Airways also fly to Seychelles.

Among the tour operators doing the Seychelles are *Speedbird Beachcombers, Thomson Worldwide, Jet Tours, Kuoni Worldwide, Silk Cut Faraway, Tradewinds Faraway, Intasun Leisure Group's Select. Jet Tours* offer 14 days in July or August 1990 at the Meridien Barbarons Beach, Mahé and at Paradise Hotel, Praslin from £1,340. *Thomson* offers 14 days at the Reef Golf Club, Mahé from £1,234. Better hotels and more interesting combinations are more expensive.

Although most food is imported, the government is trying to encourage more local food production, and you can enjoy good locally caught fresh fish. All the hotels feature lavish spreads of food worthy of an ocean liner. Most Seychellois speak a Creole language, but English and French are both official languages, and both are widely spoken. As a conservation measure, shell-collecting is discouraged, but most tourists report that just seeing the exotic marine life is reward enough.

Craft stalls in Victoria attract the tourists

Mauritius – the most cosmopolitan island in the sun

Mauritius, like Seychelles, is a tropical island in the Indian Ocean with gorgeous white sand beaches. But the two countries are really much more different from each other than most tourists would realise from just looking at brochures. Mauritius has four times as much land area, yet it is primarily a single island; Mauritius is volcanic, while the Seychelles islands are granitic or coral. The Seychellois number 65,000, while there are a million

Mauritians.

For the tourist, Mauritius combines beautiful scenery and beaches with a fascinating culture which represents one of the most complex linguistic and ethnic mixes in the world. English and French are the official languages and are widely spoken in urban and resort areas, but English is the mother tongue for only one Mauritian in 500. Hindi ranks first, spoken by a third of the population, while another one-quarter of the population speak a Creole tongue that is a mixture of French, Malagasy and Bantu languages. Others speak Urdu, Tamil, French, Telugu, Chinese, Marathi and Gujarati. Uninhabited until the 1700s, Mauritius is a microcosm of Indian Ocean peoples and others who journeyed even farther to find the island.

Some 30 magazines and newspapers are published in several of these languages. Mauritius claims one of the highest literacy rates in the world.

Whatever time you go to Mauritius, you are likely to be able to enjoy one or another festival, since almost every holiday under the sun is celebrated there, from Christmas to the Hindu Cavadee and Mahashivaratree to the Muharram to the Chinese New Year (see chapter on Mauritius for complete listing).

Sport fishermen catch wahoo, yellow fin tuna, blue marlin, black marlin (Mauritius claims the world record), jackfish, barracuda and sea bass; sophisticated boats, equipment and tackle are available tax free. Shell collecting is permitted. Deep-sea divers are attracted by the exotic marine life and by the more than 50 shipwrecks in Mauritian waters, including the *Saint-Géran,* lost on a reef off Amber Island in August 1744. Advance planning is recommended for any diving expedition, however. Mountain peaks include Le Pouce ("The Thumb"), Les Trois Mamelles ("The Three Breasts") and the "Vest-Pocket Matterhorn".

Not surprisingly, the cuisine of Mauritius is as cosmopolitan as its people. It combines local fish, fruits, vegetables and meat with imports to come up with sumptuous buffets. The chef suggests freshly caught oysters, shrimps, crayfish, crabs or giant prawns served with *sauce rouge* and accompanied by *coeur de palmiste* (the heart of a seven-year-old palm tree), known as "millionaire's salad". Mauritian rum is also a favourite; sugar cane is the principal export crop.

Mauritius Government Tourist Offices are in France (8 villa des Sablons, F-92200 Neuilly-sur-Seine), West Germany (22 Goethestrasse, D-6000 Frankfurt am Main), Italy (Corse Monforte 15, I-20122 Milano), Switzerland (Werbe AG, Kirchenweg 5, CH-8632 Zürich), the UK (49 Conduit Street, London W1R 9FB) and the US (Jeremy Pask Associates, 401 Seventh Avenue, 18th Floor, New York, NY 10001).

Air Mauritius links the island to London, Paris, Zürich, Rome, Nairobi, Bombay, Singapore, Johannesburg and Durban. Regional links serve Antananarivo in Madagascar and Moroni in the Comoros, as well as the French island of Réunion. Also flying to Mauritius are Air France, British Airways, Kenya Airways, Lufthansa, South African Airways, Singapore

Airlines, Air India, Air Malaŵi and Air Madagascar.

With so much flight space available, it is worth remembering that Mauritius has 28 beach hotels with 3,600 beds and 15 hotels in towns with 860 beds. If all these flights arrive full, they can bring well over twice as many people in any one week. If you resort to a cheap flight through a bucket shop, you should be certain that you have a place to stay after you get to Mauritius, and this can be difficult in some peak periods, when the major tour operators through package holidays have already staked out most of the beach hotel beds.

In London, some travel agencies specialise in "discount" flights to Mauritius. They will quote prices on the telephone for package trips including flight, airport transfers and half board accommodation at various Sun hotels (see below) for prices similar to those of the established tour operators, but they say that if you come in in person they can offer a lower price. Travellers are advised to use their own judgment, and tourists who like to feel sure about what they are getting are advised to stick with familiar names.

The newest of the main beach hotel complexes is the Royal Palm, located on Grand Baie, north coast. It has 60 rooms and is described as the "most deluxe in the Indian Ocean". It is 100% owned by the Beachcomber group. It opened in December 1985.

The three Sun properties – the La Pirogue Sun, the Saint-Géran Sun and the Touessrok Sun – are all owned by the South African group Sun International. The big-name global tour operators do rely heavily on these three, but tourists who prefer not to stay at hotels with South African links can stay at any of several other hotels of comparable quality. The Merville beach, for example, is part-owned by the Lonrho-affiliated Metropole group, with Mauritians holding the majority share. It is on Grand Baie, north coast, and is used by package operators *Sovereign*, *Holiday Planners* and *Twickers World* (see below for addresses).

Sunset Travel Ltd (306 Clapham Road, London SW9, telephone 01-622 5466) is an all-Mauritian company specialising in package holidays of all types to Mauritius. They use Air Mauritius, British Airways and Air France and offer tourists the choice of all hotels, private bungalows and self-catering. They even provide two-centre holidays which include Seychelles.

Among the tour operators are *Sovereign Worldwide* (c/o British Airways, P.O. Box 10, London Heathrow Airport, Hounslow, Middlesex TW6 2JA, telephone 01-897 1336). *Twickers World* (22 Church Street, Twickenham, Middlesex TW1 3NW, telephone 01-892 7606, telex 25780 TWICKTRAV G). *Holiday Planners* (Broughton House, 6/8 Sackville Street, London W1X 1DD, telephone 01-439 7755).

Other tour operators include *Thomas Worldwide*, *Thomas Cook*, *Kuoni Worldwide*, *Jet Tours*, *Tradewinds Faraway* and *Silk Cut Faraway*. *Jet Tours* offer 14 days in July/August at Le Cannonier Hotel for £1,476. *Speedbird*, 14 days at Island View Hotel for £1,185. Better hotels are more expensive.

The clean, golden beaches of Mauritius

Tanzania – Land of Kilimanjaro

Tanzania is also the land of Serengeti and Ngorongoro – and lays claim to having even more big game animals than Kenya. Wildlife enthusiasts regard a visit to the Serengeti Plain or the Ngorongoro crater as a thrill of a lifetime. Mount Kilimanjaro, at 5,895 metres, is Africa's highest mountain, and its rounded, snow-capped peak can be seen for miles around in both Tanzania and Kenya. But unlike the jagged peaks of Mount Kenya, Mount Kilimanjaro can be climbed by any physically fit person; it has been climbed by an 11-year-old and by a 74-year-old. Ascent can also be made by alpinists using much more challenging routes.

Serengeti (the name is Maasai for "extended place") is indeed extended, over almost 13,000 square kilometres. Game is extremely abundant. The Ngorongoro Crater is a collapsed volcano 259 square kilometres in area with walls 610 metres tall; the name is Maasai for "cold place". Tanzania also has other game parks such as Lake Manyara National Park, the Selous Game Reserve, the Ruaha National Park and Mikumi National Park.

The Olduvai Gorge in northern Tanzania has a treasure trove of fossils, and it was here that Mary Leakey in 1959 discovered a skull of *Zinjanthropus boisei* ("nutcracker man"), who lived in the Lower Pleistocene period about 1,750,000 BC. A year later her husband, Louis Leakey, discovered skull fragments of *Homo habilis*, of the same period. Nutcracker man's skull is in the National Museum in Dar es Salaam.

Also part of Tanzania are the Indian Ocean islands of Zanzibar and Pemba, rich in seafaring Arab culture and redolent with the smell of cloves, traditionally the principal cash crop.

Tanzania is rich in tourism potential, and many visitors even at the present time report that they thoroughly enjoyed their stay. However, owing to an extremely difficult economic situation going back over a number of years, the tourism infrastructure falls below the standard usually demanded by global tour operators and their market. While some hoteliers struggle to keep things running fairly well given the difficulties of keeping their operations supplied with fuel, food and other essentials, others are less successful. Although none of these problems occur all the time, tourists have reported such instances as power blackouts of some duration, temporary lapses in the flow of tap water to hotels, shortages of petrol that hinder the movements of their minibus vehicles to take them from their accommodation for game viewing, lack of variety in the food available (though they usually say the meals were prepared very nicely considering) and severe confusion on domestic flights by Air Tanzania.

If you are troubled when things do not run smoothly, perhaps Tanzania is not for you just yet. But those of you who don't mind things like this (I am among thousands who find there is plenty to be enjoyed even when the logistics are at their worst) should not be deterred – Tanzania will reward you with an outstanding complement of things to see and do, not to mention with a very warm and hospitable reception by the Tanzanian people.

Tanzania has tourist representatives in West Germany (Kaiserstrasse 13, D-6000 Frankfurt am Main), Italy (Palazzo Africa, Largo Africa 1, Milano), Sweden (Oxtorgsgatan 2-4, P.O. Box 7627, S-10394 Stockholm), the UK (Tanzania Tourist Office, 77 South Audley Street, London W1Y 5TA) and the US (201 East 42nd Street, 8th Floor, New York, NY 10017).

Although Air Tanzania does not fly to Europe or North America, 15 airlines do link Tanzania's two airports – Kilimanjaro, serving Arusha and the safari areas, and Dar es Salaam – to the country's primary tourism markets, including Kenya Airways and Ethiopian Airlines.

The Tanzania Tourist Office in London lists no fewer than 28 international tour operators which have Tanzania on their agendas, including some overland expeditions which carry their accommodation with them and two-centre holidays which include Tanzania. Among the tour operators are *Kuoni Worldwide, Thomson Worldwide, Speedbird World Wide* and *Silk Cut Faraway. Speedbird World Wide* offered a Tanzania Safari (Serengeti) and a Kenya coast holiday (Mombasa beach hotel) combined for 14 days in July/August from £1,400 upwards. Better hotels and other combinations are more expensive.

Untapped potential

Package tours to the remaining countries of East Africa are few and far between, since these countries have not been as extensively developed for tourism – but that is not to say that they are any less interesting. The chapters on Madagascar, Comoros and Djibouti describe the facilities available in these countries for tourists on an individual basis. Somalia is closed for tourism, embassy sources confirm.

Although Sudan, Ethiopia and Uganda are not at this stage ready to receive tourists, it is worth pointing out that all three possess great potential for package-holiday tourism in future. Sudan has the wonders of the ancient Nubian civilisation, for example, while Ethiopia has its own centuries-old unique culture, language and Christian faith, with marvels like the rock-hewn churches of Lalibela. Uganda has the Mountains of the Moon National Park, plus considerable potential for developing its Lake Victoria shore. Chapters in this book on these countries describe their potential in more detail.

It will be some time before development priorities in Uganda can restore the tourism sector to an internationally acceptable standard, though the security situation has greatly improved. Security is still a problem in parts of Sudan and Ethiopia, however, and both these are suitable only for seasoned travellers who are well up on the situations there. In time, they may again be open to the rest of us, for all three are, as the saying goes, well worth the journey.

Wildlife of East Africa

by Colin Willock

The wildlife of East Africa starts from the moment you get out of the plane. You cannot expect to see giraffes or antelope on the edge of the runway, but from the moment you arrive in the country, you will certainly see birds – strange beautiful and exciting birds.

Visitors are understandably so lion- or elephant-oriented that they forget that brilliantly coloured bird life is all around them, even in the garden of their hotel in the centre of Nairobi, Arusha, Addis Ababa or Dar-es-Salaam. In order to take advantage of this tremendous wildlife bonus the first essential is a good bird identification book. John Williams' *Field Guide to the Birds of East and Central Africa* (Collins) is the best all-round bet. The second essential is a good pair of binoculars, which you will need anyway for game viewing. Eight magnification is about right. Though they are expensive, a pair of folding Zeiss, which fit into a shirt pocket, are ideal for viewing all wildlife.

Birds that you cannot fail to see include the brilliantly iridescent sunbirds sipping nectar from blossoms; lilac-breasted rollers; long-tailed mousebirds, crested and querulous; bulbuls, drongos, glossy starlings; different species of shrikes sitting on telegraph wires looking for insect prey; circling vultures and even eagles. It is impossible even to suggest the diversity available just for the looking, practically anywhere you travel. Even for the inexperienced bird-watcher, the pleasure in spotting and identifying different birds is enormous.

Though large mammals are becoming increasingly scarce outside reserves and national parks, if you keep your eyes open, you are bound to see a fair amount of game simply when travelling by bus or car. There is a tremendous bonus to spotting your first game animals long before you reach a national park. In East Africa quite a number of the larger cattle ranches (such as those on the Athi plains a few miles south-east of Nairobi, or north of the city on the road to Lake Naivasha) still hold a surprising head of plains game. You may easily spot giraffe and certainly zebra or small herds of Thomson's gazelle, the elegant little antelope with the black side-stripe. Ostrich are fairly common in the grassland savannahs, too. Vervet monkeys with cheeky black faces are often to be seen in the acacia trees. You may come across troops of baboons foraging in trees or on the ground, though these are less generally distributed. Farmers do not take kindly to baboons. They are omnivorous and particularly partial to crops.

The great game areas of East Africa lie in or close to the Rift Valley. The Rift comes ashore, so to speak, in the Danakil Depression of Ethiopia via the Red Sea, which is itself part of the Rift. The Danakil country is inaccessible to the tourist and hostile to most forms of wildlife. Soon the Valley turns

Lobo Wildlife Lodge, Tanzania

inland and cleaves its way through the Ethiopian highlands. Almost at once, south of Addis Ababa, you reach the first of the Rift lakes which run in an unbroken chain all the way down to Tanzania and eventually to Malawi. Several of these lakes are remarkable for their waterbird life. But before setting out to visit them on a southward journey, it is necessary to make a digression, 480 km north of Addis, to one of the most striking reserves in Africa, the Simyen Mountains National Park.*

The Simyens are a breath-taking volcanic massif of gorges and peaks that are home to some unique mammals, including the Walia ibex, a very large mountain goat, the Simyen fox and great troops of Gelada baboons,

---

* Check first with your local Ethiopian embassy that chosen destinations are currently open to tourists, as many areas have been closed for security reasons.

distinguishable from savannah baboons by long shaggy hair that protects them against the cold at 3-4,000 m. The Simyens are a wonderful place to watch birds of prey, especially lammergeiers or bearded vultures who are said to break open bones to get at the marrow inside by dropping them on the rocks far below. A 60 km mule trek is necessary to reach the Park.

Back in the Ethiopian Rifts, a two hour drive south from Addis Ababa brings you to a series of large lakes. The most interesting of these are Shala and Abiata. Shala is isolated and its waters are subject to sudden storms, which for centuries disguised the fact that a large proportion of the Rift's great white pelican population nests on a tiny island about eleven miles out from the lakeside road. Previously, the whereabouts of the pelican nesting colony has been a mystery. The water of Shala has a high soda content and hence is unfriendly to all but small, specially adapted fish. The Shala pelicans commute to nearby Abiata by soaring on thermals of hot air over an intervening mountain. Abiata is a freshwater lake and full of large fish worthy of a pelican's appetite. Its waterbird life is remarkable.

Moving southward again, we come to Ethiopia's remote national park on the Omo River. Few visitors are likely to reach this, though they may well visit the great Kenyan lake into which the Omo River flows, Lake Turkana. Air travel has made Lake Turkana pretty accessible these days. You can land on the west shore at Ferguson's Gulf where there is a safari lodge perched out on the end of a sandspit. There is now a national park on the east shore at Marsabit. Lake Turkana was discovered as recently as 1887 and is one of the most fascinating wildernesses in East Africa. It is vast, around 200 km long and 40 km wide, and it is easy to be disappointed during a brief visit. The west shore is fairly barren of vegetation and animal life, but east Turkana is quite different.

Reeds and rushes fringe the lake. Dry country antelope such as oryx and topi come to drink. It is a great place for crocodiles though, happily, these do not seem to molest humans swimming in the vicinity of recognised camps. The crocodiles feed on tilapia, tiger fish, but more especially on the very large Nile perch (up to 90 kg) that are common in the lake. Many tourists come specially to fish for the perch with large spoons and plugs.

Any visit to Lake Turkana is likely to be made by light aircraft so it is as well to be able to recognise the strange terrain over which you are flying. There are three islands, North, Central and South. Central consists of several linked extinct volcanic craters, and is one of the main breeding grounds for the lake's very large crocodile population. The southern end of the lake is a volcanic wilderness with many small craters and the collapsed cone of Count Teleki's volcano. The flats in the Segutu Valley around this area are often flooded and home to many thousand flamingoes.

Flamingoes are one of the main wildlife wonders of East Africa and their lives are closely connected with the Rift system of lakes. Flamingoes depend on soda for their very existence. They feed mostly on blue-green algae and brine shrimps, which are produced by the soda lakes. The total population is somewhere in the order of two million, mostly lesser flamingoes, with a far smaller proportion of greaters. They move between the soda lakes of the Rift as feeding requirements and opportunities dictate.

The next lake you will overfly on a southward journey is Baringo. It is a freshwater lake and whatever else you see in the way of crocodiles and birdlife you will not see any flamingoes. Furthermore it is not a good place for mammals since the immediate countryside is overrun by tribal goats and cattle. Baringo was once a great place for waterbirds. Recently it appears to have declined in this respect.

Press on a little to the south and you next come to Lake Hannington, recently renamed Bogoria. This long narrow cleft in the Rift is heavily soda-saturated. Though flamingoes do not nest here it is not unusual to find half a million birds feeding.

The next lake southwards is the flamingo's traditional feeding grounds and a national park, well worth a visit for its birdlife and easily accessible by main road from Nairobi. Lake Nakuru National Park consists of a narrow strip along one shore of the lake. When the flamingo population is up to strength there, a million flame-pink birds can easily be seen. Continue on southwards and you come, within a few miles, to Lake Elementeita (a soda lake). Greater flamingoes sometimes nest there, but the shoreline is privately owned and hard to approach.

The next lake down the Rift is another freshwater lake, Lake Naivasha, which is well worth a visit for its sheer beauty. Some very shy hippos live among the purple lilies and floating papyrus islands. Small antelope suck as dikdik and duiker are a fairly common but secretive. Again, this is a wonderland for birdwatchers, with malachite and pied kingfishers, plentiful fish eagles, sacred ibis, lily-trotter, tree ducks, purple and goliath herons.

Dikdik

ELAINE WEEDON

If you fly on down the Rift south of Nairobi, within 120 km you will come to Magadi, a lake which is practically pure soda, and then eventually on to the weirdest and most unearthly lake of all – the hell's cauldron – Lake Natron. This is where the lesser flamingoes nest.

It is impossible to cover all East African parks in the space available and I suggest for full coverage of all the parks you get hold of Collins *Guide to the Parks of East Africa* by John Williams.

Since I first visited the parks of Uganda, Kenya and Tanzania a lot of good and bad has happened, to the three countries as well as to their conservation plans. From a conservation viewpoint, there is much to praise in both Kenya and Tanzania. Since the borders were opened in December 1983 it is possible to plan tours taking in the best of both countries.

Uganda

In the early 1960's, Uganda looked like the country most likely to settle down to a tranquil future. Its wildlife seemed reasonably secure with three well-run parks then called Murchison Falls, Queen Elizabeth and Kidepo National Parks. The first two have now been rechristened Ruwenzori and Kabalega respectively.

These are not the only changes, unfortunately. The dreadful regime of Idi Amin murdered countless thousands of people. When compared with this, the fate of Uganda's wildlife must rank as a minor tragedy but it is a tragedy, nevertheless. The glories of both Murchison and Queen Elizabeth, pre-Amin, were their huge mixed herds of plains game, especially, in the case of Murchison, its elephants. There is no doubt that the animals have been mercilessly shot for meat, skins, ivory and horn as the result of the anarchy that overtook Uganda during Amin's rule and in the liberation war that ended it.

Even before the end of Amin's reign of terror, the parks had largely run down due to sheer inertia and the fact that the machinery, both administrative and mechanical, did not exist to maintain them. At the moment of writing, Uganda is said to be encouraging tourists to its parks once again. The first thing they have to do is to guarantee the security of the visitors; the second, to ensure that there is enough wildlife for them to see when they get there.

Kenya

Kenya parks offer an enormously rich variety from mountain habitat to savanna. The Aberdares, a range of mountains forming part of the eastern wall of the Rift Valley, are lush and green and, of course, heavily forested. Animals are naturally secretive in this kind of environment. Night-time viewing lodges offer luxury opportunities for watching forest animals drink at water-holes made specially attractive with mineral licks. Elephants, leopards, rhinos, giant forest hog, bushback, buffalo, red duiker and suni (two of the smallest forest antelope) are night-time visitors that may be seen there.

The parks most visited are undoubtedly the savanna or grassland areas, as the sort of country gives the best opportunities for game viewing. You could do far worse than start at Nairobi National Park. You can even take a taxi there from the centre of town though it is probably best to be a thorough-going tourist and book one of the minibus day trips organised by many tour companies in the city. The remarkable thing about Nairobi National Park is that it is where it is, literally on the edge of the capital city's airport, and yet it remains totally wild. It is an excellent place to see most plains animals such as wildebeest, zebra and giraffe. Ostriches are also very plentiful as are Grant's and Thomson's gazelle. It is not so long since lions actually roamed the streets of Nairobi at night. That may not happen nowadays but there are plenty of lions to be seen in the park. In fact, don't look for lions, just look for cars. Wherever you find a 'pride' of cars, you can be sure there are lions nearby.

Grant's gazelle (left) and Thomson's gazelle (right)

Almost everyone who goes to Africa for the first time, puts lions at the top of their list. Though impressive, lions are, in fact, rather dull animals for most of their lives. During daylight hours they are most likely to be asleep under a bush or tree. Occasionally, you will be lucky enough to see a pride playing with cubs or on a kill and, even more rarely, making a kill. Lions, like most predators, and a good deal of their prey species, are most active at dawn and dusk or after dark. Thus, the best time for game viewing is early morning and late afternoon and evening when temperatures are falling and the direct sunlight is not nearly so powerful. It pays always to get up before dawn – which is around 0630 in equatorial Africa, all the year round – in order to see animals. By mid-morning most will have sought the shade. It is amazing how even a rhino or an elephant can disappear beneath the cover of a few trees.

Some of the greatest game parks in Kenya are well within a day's drive from Nairobi. Amboseli should not be missed, if for no other reason than that it is dominated by Africa's highest mountain, 5,900 m Kilimanjaro, about 35 km away.

Amboseli is renowned for the great clouds of white alkali dust thrown up by tourist minibuses. The presence of its two permanent swamps, the Simek and Longinye, guarantee remarkable game viewing within a quite small area. Amboseli's 500 elephants are some of the most amenable in Africa, though it goes without saying that no liberties can, or should, be taken with them. There are six prides of lions resident within the parks so that the chances of seeing lions on a kill are extremely good. As always, buffalo, wildebeest and zebra comprise the lions' main food supply. The tree savanna areas of the park contain fine herds of impala, the graceful, leaping antelope whose bucks have handsome back-curving horns. Impala thrive on the grasses that grow in woodland areas. Furthermore, Amboseli contains 17 species of antelope.

Amboseli currently has a problem in its acacia woodlands which are being killed off by volcanic salts brought to the surfce by recent years of excessive rainfall. Amboseli's other sadness is that it was once the best place to see black rhino in numbers. It is doubtful if any exist there at the moment of writing. The black rhino has a well-justified reputation for being liable to charge anything, including motor vehicles, on sight. Nevertheless it is easily killed, even by a determined hunter with a spear. Rhino horn continues to fetch huge prices as an alleged aphrodisiac and source of magic cures in the Near and Far East. As a result, the black rhino has virtually disappeared from most of Central and East Africa.

Tsavo National Park, a few hours out of Nairobi on the Mombasa road, should certainly be visited. It is a vast park but in drought conditions can be disappointing. In addition to the large mammals already mentioned it can offer: leopard, cheetah, lesser kudu, eland (the largest of the antelope), waterbuck, oryx, Coke's hartebeest and gerenuk, the antelope with the giraffe-like neck adapted for browsing off trees and bushes which other antelope cannot reach. The lava flows that occur in parts of the park offer a natural sanctuary for black rhino.

Tsavo was once literally a kingdom of elephants. Alas, ivory poaching, often condoned and even supported by businessmen and politicians, took place on a huge scale there in the late 'seventies. The poachers were mainly Somalis moving down from the north. Under President Moi's administration this evil has been very largely stopped. Nevertheless, the damage done to Tsavo elephants is such that it will take a very long time to repair. It is very doubtful whether the visitor will see Tsavo elephants carrying sustantial ivory. Because of recent harassment, Tsavo cow herds should be treated with great respect. Visitors please note: it is almost invariably the cows and not the bulls who are likely to press home a charge. Elephant society is matriarchal, not a patriarchal one; it is the adult cows who wear the trousers!

Any visit to Tsavo must take in Mzima springs. This clear water oasis receives its water supply from water filtering through through layers of volcanic ash, from the Chyulu hills outside the park. There is an underwater observation window from which it is possible to see fish (chiefly *barbus* species) and hippos. Mzima is a great place for hippo-watching; many of the

ELAINE WEEDON

Common waterbuck

great 'water horses' lie in the cool spring all days with just the tips of ears, 'eyebrows' and nostrils showing. You can get out of your car, as long as you keep to recognised tracks. It is as well to note that the hippo causes more deaths than any other African animal, usually because the human intruder gets between the animal and the water and cuts off its retreat to safety. However, this situation is not likely to arise on the controlled paths at Mzima.

Tanzania

Tanzania's parks are splendidly run and maintained and a great deal of scientific work is carried out there, notably at the Serengeti Research Institute. The plains of Serengeti stretch all the way from the Crater Highlands to Lake Victoria. The park covers 1,476,300 hectares. Though this vast area consists mainly of long and short grass plains, there are also hills, acacia woodlands and rocky outcrops as well as lakes. It provides the greatest wildlife spectacle in the world, the annual migration of one million plains animals.

At least half of the migrating animals are wildebeest and the migration is basically a circular movement in search of new grazing following the rains. It is worth consulting beforehand to see if it is possible to make your visit coincide with the area the migration has currently reached. In an area the size of the Serengeti, this is by no means easy. Nor do the wildebeest follow an entirely regular pattern but tend to ebb and flow and even backtrack. The easiest way to see the migration when it is really under way is from a light aircraft.

The Serengeti can produce practically everything in the way of big animals. Despite its size, it is difficult, even in Land Rover trips from one of the lodges, not to see a great many wildlife dramas. Predators, particularly, can put in a spectacular appearance, not only the Serengeti lions but also packs of hunting dogs and cheetahs chasing gazelle at up to 120 kms per hour.

Tanzania has other fine parks and conservation units, including the Selous Game Reserve and the Ruaha National Park, both nearly as large as Serengeti itself. Two more may be mentioned in detail and they are both on the road that climbs up through the Crater Highlands.

ELAINE WEEDON

Cheetah

The first is the Ngorongoro Conservation Unit. Scenically, Ngorongoro is one of the most beautiful places in East Africa, and it is one of the absolute musts of any visit to African game parks. Ngorongoro is the world's sixth largest caldera, the collapsed crater of an extinct volcano. It is big enough to hold the entire city of Paris. Inside its two thousand foot high walls lives a virtually self-contained community of plains animals. It is the one place where you can be sure of seeing black rhino. Ngorongoro has eleven prides of lions and a number of clans of hyenas both of whom are highly territorial and can therefore be relied upon to be found hunting inside a given area. When visiting the park you do not stay in the crater, but on lodges on its rim, making the trip down inside by vehicle.

As you descend from the Crater Highlands on the road towards Arusha, you come, at the very edge of the western wall of the Rift, to lake Manyara National Park. Once again, you cannot stay inside the park but in the hotel on the rim of the Rift. From there you look down on the large soda lake

ELAINE WEEDON

Black rhino

which makes up a good deal of the park. Along the nearer shore of the lake is a long, narrow, fertile strip some 40 km long which comprises the land part of the park. Lake Manyara Park is an African Eden that includes a lush ground-water forest with clear-running streams, acacia savanna, grassland savanna, lake shore, dry river beds and rock ravines. It is a wonderful place for elephants, antelope and buffalo, giraffe and lions. The Manyara lions have one great distinction: they are well-known for taking their siesta in trees. A tip for lion-watchers: if you want to find a lion sleeping in a tree, look for a bell-rope hanging down. It will probably turn out to have a lion on the end of it.

The Seasons for Visiting

When visiting the East African Game Parks it is worth bearing in mind that the seasons do not exist as we know them in temperature zones. Instead there are rainy and dry seasons. In the countries mentioned, these vary somewhat. They even vary in individual countries from year to year. In East Africa there are usually two rains, in October and again in February to March.

The coming of the rains affects wildlife in several ways. Everything, including insects and grazing, is more plentiful after them. Birds therefore tend to nest after the rains. Weavers, for example, build their coconut-shaped, woven grass nests so they can be found hanging from many trees following the rains. Many mammals give birth to their young at this time also.

In tall grass areas the rains can make game-viewing difficult if not impossible. Even elephants can disappear in the sea of grass within a few yards of the road. In some areas, notably those with black cotton soil, roads and tracks become impassable. Advice should be taken, therefore, before a trip is planned.

Accommodation in game-viewing lodges is usually booked well in advance. So reservations should be made early. However, the finest way to experience the African wilderness is under canvas. Camping safaris can easily be arranged and most parks have camp sites which are much cheaper.

Peoples of East Africa

by Jocelyn Murray

For hundreds – even thousands – of years East Africa has been a meeting place of peoples. One of the myths which the traveller must counter is that of 'unchanging Africa'. Not only is there the incredibly rapid social and industrial change of the late 20th century, and the changes of the comparatively short period of colonial rule, but in earlier centuries immigrants and invaders constantly entered and overcame or peacefully mingled with earlier inhabitants.

We now know that East Africa was one of the first homes of the human race. The intervening millennia cannot yet be bridged historically, but in the less distant past much of East Africa seems to have been inhabited by autochthonous peoples, probably hunters and gatherers, who live on in legend as dwarfs or goblins. Some stories speak of their living in holes in the ground, and there is archaeological evidence that sometimes this may have been the literal truth. They may also have been short people, the so-called pygmies, whose descendants are not now particularly different in appearance, and who survive in forests and other remote areas. In Kenya they are known as Dorobo, and they have become linguistically assimiliated to their neighbours, mainly Nandi and Kikuyu. In central Tanzania two groups survive who speak their own languages – the Hadza and the Sandawe.

Down the Great Rift Valley

One of the geographical features of the region which has facilitated the movement of peoples is the corridor of the Great Rift Valley. At some time in the past it allowed the incursion of peoples downwards from the highlands of what is now Ethiopia. These people spoke languages of the group known as Cushitic (Afro-Asiatic family) and brought with them many highly distinctive culture traits which were to be very influential in the culture of groups who emerged subsequently in the region. It is this Cushitic element which so radically distinguishes many of the peoples of the Kenya highlands and of the central Rift area of Northern Tanzania from their linguistically-related neighbours.

Groups who will speak Cushitic languages have all but disappeared from the scene. Northwest of Mount Kenya a tiny group known as Mogodogo Maasai retained their language till recently. In Tanzania several remnants speaking southern Cushitic languages survive (Burungi, Goroa, Iraqw, Mbugu). But most of the Cushitic-speakers were absorbed by later arrivals speaking Bantu or Nilotic languages; the former, however, passed on some particular and distinctive customs.

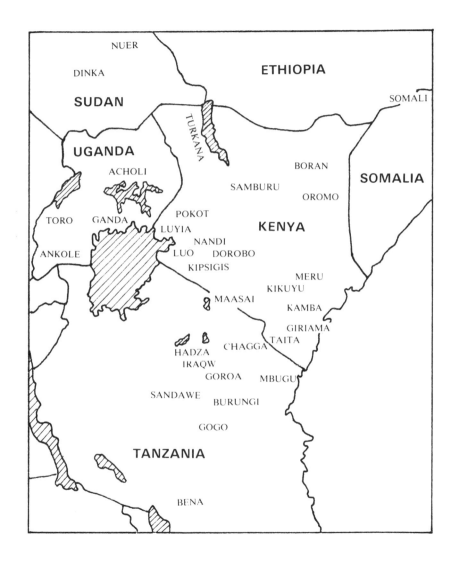

Continuing Customs

One such custom was of political and military organization through named age-sets into which the young men were initiated at puberty. The initiation included circumcision and the initiated men formed regiments which engaged in fighting and cattle-raiding. Later the whole group graduated to become junior elders who were free to marry, while a younger group took over the warrior role. The older group passed on to become senior elders and finally to retire from active participation in the affairs of the clan and residential unit. This type of organization was found among people speaking totally different languages, such as the Nilotic-speaking Nandi, Kipsigis and Maasai and the Bantu-speaking Kikuyu, Embu and Meru, to name just a few. Many other peoples who did not have named age-sets also circumcised at puberty – the Kamba, Taita and Chaga, for example. The young Maasi *moran* – and the word *moran* is itself from a Cushitic root – are the most famous surviving examples of the young initiated warriors.

An even more unusual custom which also seems to have derived from the Cushitic-speaking peoples is that of an initiation ceremony for girls parallelling that for boys. It includes female circumcision, or more correctly, excision or clitoridectomy. Although not as severe as the operation of infibulation performed on young girls in Somalia, parts of Ethiopia, Egypt and the northern Sudan (pharonic circumcision), the operation can have dangerous physiological and psychological results. It has been dropped by many Western-educated families in recent decades. People who circumcise both boys and girls are found throughout the Kenya highlands and the Rift Valley into central Tanzania, the most southerly being the Gogo and Bena. The Nilotic-speaking peoples of western and northwestern Kenya, northern Uganda and the southern Sudan – Luo, Acholi, Dinka, Nuer, Turkana and others – initiate young men with bodily scarifications or teeth removal, but they do not circumcise nor do they form named age-sets.

Amongst Highlands-Rift peoples speaking related languages, those who have been subject to Cushitic influences can be distinguished by the observance of certain less striking customs. For example, they carry on Cushitic traditions by neither burying their dead, nor holding elaborate wakes at the time of death. There is a belief in a high god, to whom sacrifices are made, but comparatively little emphasis on ancestor reverence and witchcraft. On the other hand, the Cushitic link also helps to explain why people who speak totally unrelated languages, like the Kikuyu and Maasi, and who follow completely different modes of life (agricultural as against herding) are yet alike in many important aspects of their culture.

Language Families in East Africa

We have mentioned the different language families represented in East Africa, and it is worth noting that all the language families found in the rest of Africa are also found in this region. Bantu languages which are part of the huge Niger-Congo family, are spoken from Cameroon to South Africa, and in Kenya and Uganda reach their northern limit in the east. Bantu speakers are in two main groups which entered at different periods. Those in the west probably came in from the south-west; those in the central highlands and along the coast came from the south and south-east to a dispersal point on the northern Kenya coast, whence they later scattered west and south again. Nilotic speakers appear to have entered from the north and north-west while late incomers have been the Somali and Oromo (Galla) peoples from the Horn of Africa. Their languages belong to the Semitic group, which like the Cushitic languages, are part of the Afro-Asiatic family. The Sandawe and Hadza of Tanzania speak languages thought to be connected with the Khoisan languages of South Africa.

A further and important incursion of new peoples came from the coast. The regular monsoon winds had long been used by sea travellers across the Indian Ocean and early in the Islamic era Persian and Arab seafarers settled along the coast and mixed with the local black population so that new ethnic and religious identities developed. Since the rulers of the Islamic city-states established along the coast of what is now Kenya and Tanzania, and on the off-shore islands – Lamu, Pemba, Zanzibar – were literate, the growth of these states has been well-documented for many centuries back, and historical chronicles have survived. But Islam did not spread at all widely outside the town until the end of the 19th century; even despite their contact with Islam, those peoples living close to the cities stayed faithful to their traditional beliefs.

The language which developed along the coast, Swahili, has become a *lingua franca* throughout East Africa and as far west as Zaire. Contrary to what is sometimes stated, it is not a hybrid nor even a pidgin language. In form and structure it is closely related to other coastal Bantu languages. But it has a large vocabulary of Arabic-derived words, which makes it extremely rich and flexible. It was formerly written in Arabic script, which was not as suitable to express its vowels as the Roman script now more commonly used. A number of dialects exist, and those of Mombasa and Zanzibar have become the basis of official Union Swahili.

Political Systems

East African peoples have preserved sharp contrast in their political systems and everything from tiny dispersed bands of hunter-gatherers to highly centralized kingdoms, can be located. In the minds of many people the word 'chief' is associated with Africa, and they were sought by the early colonial administrators when they first tried to control their new and alien subjects. They found chiefs, and even kings, in southern Uganda, Rwanda, Burundi and western Tanzania and, to some extent, western Kenya. But in all the rest of the region nothing really corresponding to a chief could be found.

Highly structured centralised kingdoms like those of Buganda, Ankole and Toro developed in the area around Lake Victoria, and to the west and south of it. These kingdoms were typically controlled from the central court, where the king – in Ganda the *Kabaka* – had an entire cabinet of officials under him. In much of this area the staple food was banana, which was easily cultivated with minimal labour. Thus many men were free to carry out other tasks which helped in creating a highly developed state. Early European visitors were amazed at the Kabaka's court at Mengo where beautifully dressed courtiers in barkcloth robes attended the monarch, and there were large buildings, fleets of canoes, and good roads. This was very different from what they had encountered further east and south. The sophistication of such centralised kingdoms, however, did not prevent the perpetation of cruelties on a grand scale.

Outside the kingdoms, organisation was on a much smaller scale. People who spoke the same languages and followed the same customs were conscious of their basic unity, but were unconnected in any formal way. Where age-sets existed they provided a link across geographically dispersed peoples, and sometimes large-scale rituals held at certain times brought the people together. But day-to-day affairs were in the hands of local elders who were judges, councillors and juries all in one. In times of danger a war-leader might emerge, or a religious functionary take on a wide role. Such people were less well able to resist the colonial intruders when they came, although some did so in a remarkable way. The colonial officials picked out natural leaders as so-called chiefs, and used them as assistants in tax-collecting and maintaining order. Many of these men acquired wealth and lands from their position, and a new class emerged which had not existed earlier.

Religion and Education

Islam has been mentioned as an influence along the coast, and it was and still is the religion of the Horn of Africa, of the Northern Sudan and of parts of Ethiopia. In the late 19th century it spread widely to parts of Tanzania, but in most of Kenya and Uganda Muslims are found only in the towns and in the far north.

Christian missionaries first arrived in East Africa in the mid-19th century and until the colonial period there were few Christians. But the role of the missions in education has made a great mark on all the countries of the region, and the visitor from Europe should be prepared to find the churches important and influential in much of the region. Both Christians and Muslims often take their religious observances very seriously, and though young educated Africans may be very critical of such religious practices and of what they term 'outside influences', they do not always reflect the popular view.

African children are increasingly likely to acquire at least a primary school education. Many are taught English (English also being the language of instruction) from their first year in school, and if the visitor is stuck for language in an isolated spot, he will usually find a bright schoolboy or girl only too happy to act as a translator. (In Tanzania Swahili is stressed, however, and there it may be necessary to find a secondary-school student as interpreter.)

In upcountry Kenya visitors may be puzzled when they see African men wearing a long white robe or *kanzu* and often a white turban like those worn by Punjabi Indians. Such men are often accompanied by women wearing long dresses and white headcloths. These people are easily mistaken for Muslims, but they are Christians, belonging to various indigenous churches, and often a red cross is part of their garb. They follow their own interpretation of the Bible, without Western teachers, and are strongest among the Kikuyu, Embu and Meru of central Kenya, and among the Luyia and Luo of the west. In Nairobi, Nakuru or Kisumu you may see them on a Sunday morning, singing in the open air to the beat or drums, or carrying banners in a procession to an open air meeting. They are often nicknamed 'spirit people'. There are other so-called independent churches which are not so conspicuous, including some affiliate to the Orthodox Church. Such churches exist elsewhere in East Africa, but not in the numbers and strength found in Kenya.

Dress

Along the coast the Muslim may often be recognised by his or her dress – men wear a *kanzu* and a red embroidered cap (*kofia*) on their heads. Few Muslim women in East Africa are veiled, but many wear the *buibui*, a black cloth covering head and shoulders. Breasts and legs are generally covered, and the bare-breasted Giriama women on the Mombasa hinterland (who wore a pleated cotton skirt and little else) were ordered to add a blouse when they came to town. A common and practical dress for women, along the coast and through much of Tanzania, is made from two large rectangles of brightly printed cotton cloth (*shuka*). One is wound around the body under the arms and forms a dress; the other covers the head and face when necessary, or acts as a shawl for a baby. Men often wear a long checked cotton skirt, like a sarong – a more sensible garment in humid heat than trousers.

In Ethiopia and the Northern Sudan robes of white cotton were worn, and in the 19th century cotton cloth became widely valued as trade goods. Unbleached cotton cloth is still called *amerikani*, since it came through American merchants sailing to Zanzibar. In the Lakes region of Uganda people dressed in barkcloth garments or clothing of dressed leather skins although in much of the region few clothes other than ornaments were worn. As such garments are not very practical for school pupils and employees, it is not surprising that cotton dresses, khaki drill shirts and trousers were soon adopted. Village women usually wear cotton dressed with a kerchief on the head, or the *shuka*.

In Uganda long sashed robes with puffed sleeves have become a traditional dress. In the rural areas the older men and women often dress in cotton cloths (or blankets) draped like the former skin garments, and with earrings and necklaces of wire and beads. But year by year these ornaments become rarer, outside of the most remote areas. Local people can tell a city woman's origin by the way she ties her headcloth, or a man by the Western clothes he wears.

Now, however, in nearly all East African towns and cities, the height of European fashion may be seen, and the visitor will not usually be able to distinguish people of different ethnic groups.

Africa Misconceived

In the cities of East Africa, among the luxuries of modern hotels, good food and air conditioning, or crossing busy city streets through the traffic, surrounded by well-dressed African civil servants and businessmen, the visitor may well feel that the old Africa has completely disappeared. Yet, a few hundred miles away, sitting in a safari camp at night, listening to the drum-beats and singing from a nearby African village, he may well feel nothing at all has changed. Neither scene is a wholly accurate picture of present day Africa and the truth lies in the co-existence of both the old and the new, a mixture of traditional and modern Africa.

In the same way that our civilisation and culture has changed and taken in different aspects from many cultures over the centuries, so it is in Africa. The past and the present meat naturally in the university educated professional man who returns to his parents' for a funeral and observes traditional rites, or in the tribesman who finds no paradox in going to church on one Sunday and to a traditional ceremony on the next. Similarly, the modern African sees nothing odd in a tradition dance performed by 'tribesmen' wearing spectacles and tennis shoes, nor any contradiction in consulting a medical specialist trained in America, as well as the local herbalist.

Thus, perhaps the best course for the alert and interested visitor is to rid himself of any romantic, preconceived ideas about African culture and African peoples as they once might have been, and to open himself to the Africa and the Africans of today.

From Cairo to the Cape

To span an entire continent is a great experience for any traveller. In Africa the vision was first mapped out by Cecil Rhodes in his plan to build a railway from Cairo to the Cape that would provide a political and economic backbone for the British empire in Africa. The railway was never built, but the idea of spanning the continent has survived.

The latter-day 'Cairo to the Cape' vision of a journey that begins beside the monuments of ancient Egypt, continues up the Nile from Islamic culture into traditional and Christian cultures, past the 'White Caps' of Mount Kenya and Kilimanjaro, through herds of elephant and giraffe that abound on the East African plains, across the Great Rift Valley, down past the surging waters – 'the smoke that thunders' – of the Victoria Falls, skirting the Kalahari Desert, home of the few surviving Bushmen, and so through the South African veld to the slopes of Table Mountain.

Such is the dream, but what are the realities of such a journey? At one time the obstacles that travellers faced were mainly physical, but now they are political. Africa has indeed been 'opened-up' in the sense that roads and railways have been built and rivers charted. There are now few sections of our Cairo to Cape journey that are made impassable because of the vagaries of geography or climate. The real obstacles have become borders that are closed between nations that are politically at odds, countries that become inhospitable or unsafe for travellers because of internal conflict, and visas that become unobtainable and flights that no longer operate because of diplomatic fractures. In any sensible view these problems must be regarded as more than passing inconveniences unreasonably brought about by temperamental and jingoistic African politicians. They form part of an historical and economic process in which those in the 'developed' world are also involved, and would-be travellers will do well to spend a little time studying the countries they intend to visit in order to have a slightly broader view of the difficulties they may encounter.

The fact remains, however, that many of the practical problems of the journey from Cairo to the Cape are now determined by political events. The border between Uganda and Sudan was officially opened to normal traffic in January 1980 and the road from southern Sudan to Nairobi which passes through Uganda is open to travellers but safety in Uganda though improved, is still not totally guaranteed. However, beyond Nairobi, the border between Kenya and Tanzania was reopened in 1983. Further south, the war in Zimbabwe has happily come to an end, but South Africa itself is outlawed by much of black Africa because of the system of apartheid that it perpetuates, and visitors with South African stamps in their passports may well find difficulty in returning to countries further north.

So our route, although an obvious and long-established one, now threads its way rather tenuously from Egypt, through Sudan, Kenya, Tanzania,

Zambia and Botswana, into South Africa. Malawi can easily be included and officially Uganda too, although travelling in Uganda is still not recommended owing to the possibility of banditry and to the increasingly serious food shortages in the northern regions. Mozambique, whose borders have been closed to visitors until now is also dangerous because of the Renamo guerillas. It is difficult to cross the Zambian border into Mozambique and the Malawian borders can only be crossed by rail. Visas for Mozambique take more than three months to be processed. For current information on travel in Mozambique it is advisable to write to the Centre of Information and Tourism, CP 614, Maputo, Mozambique. Zimbabwe, formerly only accessible via its lifelines from the south, now has an open border with Zambia and is welcoming visitors. Angola, however, does not yet welcome travellers at her borders. Ethiopia's borders are effectively closed, especially at the main road and rail crossings from Sudan, into Eritrea. Southern Zaire has been chaotic since the invasions of Shaba province and travelling there is still very hazardous.

For the dedicated and inventive overlander the full 5,000-mile trek from Cairo to the Cape remains possible, if unpredictable. It is not necessary to join an overland group package tour and spend 16 weeks in the back of a truck with a dozen others in order to do so. That may be one of the safer and more convivial ways to cross the Sahara and to bash one's way through the dense Central African Republic and the remoter parts of northern Zaire. But, in my view, ordinary public transport offers a cheaper and better way to get to know the more accessible parts of Africa. It also promises you more in the way of encounters with ordinary Africans, because your travel options then become the same as theirs.

The journey does not have to be a trial of endurance. Physical discomfort may result from the extremes of an unfamiliar climate, or from long hours cramped on a hard seat, or from miles of unguided trudging with a heavy backpack. It is the first of these that can make the others virtually intolerable, and that is one reason why a lot of travelling is best done in the cool, dry season – from about June to September for most of the countries concerned. Sudan is likely to be hottest, with no real 'cool' period, and the long train and boat journey along the upper reaches of the Nile, especially in third class, can be a gruelling experience that some comfort-lovers may wish to avoid. If you can afford such extravagance, this can be most simply achieved by hopping onto an aeroplane, or the journey can be more drastically simplified by cutting it in half and starting from Nairobi or Dar es Salaam. The southern half of the journey undoubtedly poses fewer physical problems.

The first step of any journey will be getting to Africa. By aeroplane the youth fare from London to Cairo is still low. If you are over 26 the local airlines (Egypt Air, Sudan Air, etc) will usually offer the best 'deals'. If you are not quite so impatient to get to Africa, there are numerous cheap ways of getting to the Mediterranean, and thence by boat from Venice or Athens to

Alexandria. If you want to take Nairobi or Dar es Salaam as your starting point, then you can take advantage of either youth or 'Apex' fares – but there is the restriction of early and very rigid booking requirements, limited stay, and draconian cancellation and no-show penalties. Through some travel agents – and here it is always worth shopping around – it is possible to get full, open-dated return tickets from non-IATA airlines such as Aeroflot – often with the unique advantage of a stopover in Moscow, but otherwise very inflexible: other airlines may well laugh if you present them with an Aeroflot ticket.

But with all cheap deals you are sacrificing flexibility for the sake of economy. If you have the money there is nothing better in the world of air travel than an unrestricted, full-fare ticket bought from a major airline. With that, especially on a long-haul, you can re-route, stopover, and change airlines almost endlessly. In connection with an overland journey through Africa, the best options for air travel will depend mostly on how you want to get home.

Flying from South Africa to Europe is expensive; taking a boat is more expensive but better value for money. Turning round and going back overland to Cairo may not seem an attractive option after several months on the road, although if you've started in East Africa the prospect is less daunting. In this case visas and passport stamps will need to be carefully juggled: Tanzanian immigration officials will need much persuading before even thinking about letting in a visitor with South African stamps in his passport. There are good political reasons for this: if you think about them you may decide to stop short of South Africa. Alternatively, many consciences are salved by arguing that apartheid is best judged by observing it. The decision is yours.

If you have a yet further-flung destination, such as Sydney or Rio, then you can do all sorts of ambitious and money-saving things with a carefully constructed air ticket. For example it is cheaper to get an economy ticket from London to Sydney, routed via Nairobi and Johannesburg, and not use the middle section (which you will travel overland), than it is to buy one ticket from London to Nairobi and another from Johannesburg to Sydney. In the same way it may well be worthwhile getting an excursion (return) ticket from London to Johannesburg with a stopover in Nairobi, again discarding the middle section for your overland trip, and then flying back to Europe from Johannesburg. The possibilities are endless. Travel agents, like many 'professionals', try to preserve a monopoly of the knowledge and expertise which, they claim, is necessary to make sense of multitudinous fare and route options. This isn't true: if you can lay your hands on an ABC 'World Airlines Guide', which every travel agent uses, you can do it yourself.

Cairo to Khartoum

Cairo is more a European or Middle-Eastern city than an African one, and reveals little of what lies further south. The tourist industry is vast and unbridled, and intimate exploration of the city's ancient environs is no longer easy. For the journey south to Luxor and Aswan there is a choice of rail, road or boat. The railway is usually favoured, because driving can be perilous and riverboats are either expensive or very slow. Tickets for all sections of the line can be bought at the station in Cairo, with student reductions available on production of a card. 2nd Class sleepers with air conditioning are quite cheap and quicker than 3rd Class. There are overnight trains between Cairo and Luxor, where you can explore for a day or two the temple of Karnak and the Valley of Kings, before continuing overnight again to Aswan.

The 8 km journey between the town of Aswan and the High Dam, which was built by the Russians in the early 1960's, can be made either by bus or taxi. Taxis are more convenient, but make sure you negotiate a price before you start. The High Lake Steamer takes you as far as Wadi Halfa on the border with Sudan, where it meets the train for Khartoum. Sudanese trains tend to be extremely slow, and the combined boat and train journey from Aswan to Khartoum will take at least four or five days.

Khartoum to Nairobi

Khartoum lies at the junction of the Blue and the White Nile, with the different coloured waters visibly merging there. Highly decorated buses and trucks, bound for most destinations, can be found in the main market place. However roads throughout Sudan are generally very bad, and petrol is often in short supply. The main route south is up the river from Kosti to Juba. This can be an uncomfortable twelve day journey, for which you must buy your own food supplies at Kosti and again at Malakal. For student reductions on the train to Kosti you will need to get a permit from the Ministry of Youth, which is near the People's Palace in Khartoum. From Juba the main road runs through Uganda to Nairobi. Sudan's border with Kenya is a couple of hundred miles to the east, and is an adventurous route even in a well-equipped vehicle. The British are in the process of building a road here, but while Uganda has been so unpredictable many travellers have been obliged to take advantage of the Wednesday morning flight from Juba to Nairobi.

Within Kenya the main roads are all tarred and there is usually plenty of traffic on them. You can hitch-hike, although it is often safer and more effective to catch trucks and cars where they are stationary and ask their drivers for a ride, rather than stand pleadingly by the side of an open road – the principle is almost universal. If you are white it is an almost inescapable reality that white people are more likely to stop for you. When an African stops, regardless of the vehicle he is driving, it is quite likely that you will be expected to pay for the ride. Throughout Africa transport is scarce, and these informal (and sometimes illegal) 'bus' services operate everywhere. Whenever you see a pick-up with a dozen people clinging to the back, you can be sure they are paying for the service. You will be expected to do likewise.

Nairobi epitomises the modern African city. Its old colonial buildings are now overshadowed by skyscraping offices and international hotels, and surrounded at a distance by the squatter settlements and shanty towns that are a by-product of rapid urbanisation. For a long time it has been the centre of East African tourism, offering wildlife safaris on the one hand, and the sun-bleached beaches of the Indian Ocean on the other. You can expect to meet a great variety of overland travellers and low-cost *bons viveurs* both in the city and at the coastal resorts. It seems that a lot of people take Kenya as their jumping-off point because of its relative accessibility, develop a liking for its neo-colonial lifestyle, and don't get a great deal further. Others, travelling northwards, get stuck in Nairobi while applying for visas and are a valuable source of up-to-date information about what lies ahead.

Nairobi, epitome of the modern African city

CAMERAPIX

Nairobi to Dar es Salaam

The border between Kenya and Tanzania was opened in December 1983 and it is now possible to cross. Alternatively it is possible to fly to Dar es Salaam or Lusaka in Zambia.

The choice of transport is yours

Dar es Salaam to Lusaka

After Nairobi, Dar es Salaam seems a colourful and unpretentious city. The Muslim influence is ancient and still very strong, contrasting with the decaying architectural relics of German occupation which overlook the harbour. There is plenty of cheap, if basic, hotel accommodation. For a taste of the high-life and chance encounters with fellow travellers the patio bar of the New Africa Hotel is a favourite spot. In the 'downtown' areas you can expect to be approached by people offering to change money at rates maybe 50% better than those you've been getting at the bank. This is the currency black market, and you will come across it in every country you visit. The disparity between the official and the black market rate will depend on how strong the local currency is and how eager residents are to get their wealth out of the country. Thus in Kenya the black market has slumped since the coffee boom, while in Zambia the market has been curbed by the introduction of the system by which firms can buy foreign currency in auctions.

Governments do their best to stop illegal currency dealing. That is why you have to fill in a currency declaration form when you enter a country, get it officially stamped whenever you change money, and produce it as proof of bona fide dealing when you leave. The stringency with which these rules are enforced varies enormously from time to time and place to place. If you want to take the psychological stress out of your dealings with officials, then you should always stick meticulously to customs and immigration rules. If you are a gambler and you like a fast buck, or perhaps feel that the official rates are a rip-off, then you will probably find a bit of black market dealing too attractive to miss. And don't be surprised when customs officials start offering to change money too.

For the journey out of Tanzania the Chinese built 'Tanzam' railway is almost a must. There is a tarred road down which large trucks thunder on the traditional 'hell-run' to the Zambian Copperbelt, but the railway has surpassed it in terms of economy and variety. The thousand-mile journey from Dar es Salaam to Kapiri Mposhi (midway between Lusaka and Ndola) takes about 36 hours and is cheap for a 2nd Class sleeper (double for 1st Class, half for third). There are three fast and three slow trains a week. If you pick a noon-time departure, then several hours outside Dar es Salaam the train winds slowly along the northern edge of one of the best wildlife reserves in Africa, and from your compartment window you will be able to see elephant, kudu, zebra and much more. The trains run impressively to time, but the restaurant car tends to be amiably chaotic and beer sells out very quickly, so you would be well advised to cater for yourself. The railway and the road intersect repeatedly and it is very easy to combine the rail journey with stops in some of the towns, and spells of bussing or hitch-hiking. The slower train stops at remote places in the middle of the night and picks up women with small babies and bags of maize. Travelling third class is good fun if you're feeling gregarious, but the hard benches are almost impossible to sleep on: one night spent repeatedly nodding forward and jerking awake is usually enough.

If you want to branch off into northern Malawi, then you should get off at Nakonde on the Zambian border. The road from there to Chitipa is normally passable only in the dry season and the weekly bus service is rather erratic. Transport on the Malawian side is better. If you cross to Karonga you can choose between the Lakeshore road or the 'Ilala' lake steamer which departs every Wednesday for its three day journey from Monkey Bay to Karongo at the southern tip of the 300-mile-long Lake Malawi. There are good bus services from there to Blantyre and Lilongwe, and thence via Mchinji and the Great East Road to Lusaka.

If you stay on the Tanzam railway right through to Kapiri Mposhi, you will need to walk half a mile to the main road in order to catch a bus to Lusaka, or a bit further to the old railway line for a train – there are two a day in each direction, the continental-style coaches contrasting nicely with the rather quaint functionalism of the Chinese design.

Lusaka to Gaborone

Zambia's copper boom financed the extravagant multi-storey buildings that give Lusaka its angular skyline. It also created the inexorable drift of young job-seekers away from traditional agriculture into the towns. The boom is now over; Zambia drifted into severe economic problems and suffered serious food shortages during the Zimbabwean war and Lusaka has been left with thousands of unemployed. There are frequent shortages of basic commodities and an alarming incidence of petty crime. Destructive raids into Zambia by Smith's forces have kindled some anti-white feeling, and the Zimbabwean guerrillas who 'policed' some areas treated unwary – and sometimes foolhardy – travellers very harshly. All this led to an increasing exodus of expatriates.

Essentials for overland travel

Despite this catalogue of ills, many aspects of life in Zambia remain quite normal, and it is still possible to travel safely through the country. Hitchhiking anywhere near the border with Zimbabwe is still not advised nor is taking photographs of anything. But the train from Lusaka to Livingstone runs normally, and the Victoria Falls are still open to visitors. From Livingstone to the Kazangula Ferry and on to Francistown in Botswana there is no public transport. You will have to fix a ride, and probably pay for it, with one of the truck drivers at the main layby on the road out of Livingstone. The ferry itself is never 100% reliable: it sunk several times during the latter part of the Zimbabwean war. On the Botswana side you should not wander too far without transport because you are right on the edge of the Chobe Game Reserve. The road to Nata is recently constructed, and from there to Francistown it is tarred.

Francistown is an old colonial town and a major staging post between Zimbabwe and the south. There is now a large refugee camp nearby, and a major Botswana Defence Force barracks. The Zimbabwe Railways train with its splendid wooden coaches still comes daily across the border from Bulawayo, arriving in Francistown at about 18.00 and continuing overnight to Gaborone. The train arrives in Gaborone just before dawn, and you can take advantage of a cheap flat rate fare in a shared taxi in order to get to the centre of town.

Gaborone to Cape Town

Gaborone was planned as Botswana's capital city but is no bigger than a large town. The goods in the shops and names of the businesses reflect Botswana's continuing economic dependence on South Africa. This is in sharp contradiction to Botswana's political affiliation to the other 'frontline' states, and you will probably come across the rather uneasy balance of feelings towards the South African refugees who continue to cross into Botswana.

The final stage of the journey from Cairo to the Cape is the easiest of all: the train from Francistown to Gaborone continues over the border to Mafeking, and from there directly to Cape Town. By road there is a lot of traffic in both directions. White South Africans come to do business and to gamble in the Holiday Inn casino. This, and the massive migration of labour to the mines in South Africa, add to the feeling that the border between Botswana and South Africa is merely a rather fine political one. Yet to cross that border is to experience apartheid, for only in South Africa can you walk – or not walk – through a door which says 'Whites Only'.

Fishing craft near Dar es Salaam

TANZANIA HC TOURIST OFFICE

Country
by
Country

COMOROS

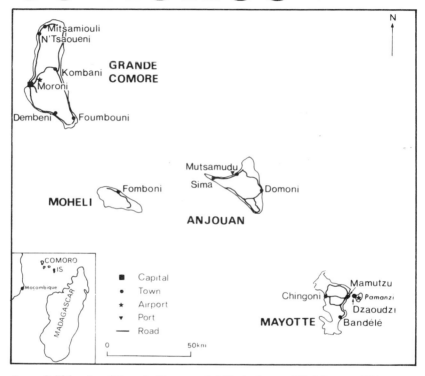

Area: 2,236 sq km (Grande Comore, 1,148; Anjouan 424; Mayotte 374; Moheli 290)
Population: 445,000 (1989 estimate)
Capital: (Grande Comore)

A string of beautiful islands of volcanic origin, surrounded by coral reefs, the unspoilt Comoro Islands stretch across the north of the Mozambique channel between Madagascar and East Africa. The archipelago comprises the four islands of Grande Comore, Anjouan, Moheli and Mayotte. The French continue to hold on to Mayotte as a naval base.

The special atmosphere of the Comoros is attributable both to the beautiful scenery and to the unique racial mixture, which reflects the successive invasions of sea-faring people in this part of the world: Arabs,

Persians, Malays, Malagasy and Africans. The strongest influences are Arab and African and for this reason the main religion is Islam and the predominant language is a variant of Kiswahili.

The mainstay of the islands' economy is plantation agriculture, producing perfume oils, copra, spices and vanilla, but many Comorians have to go to East Africa or France to find employment.

A big attraction of the Comoros to visitors is the scope for fishing – tuna, barracuda, shark, grouper, scad and, occasionally, the coelacanth.

History

The Comoro Islands have over the centuries been inhabited by people of great racial diversity. Malayo-Polynesian people were probably living in the islands by the 6th century AD. Africans and Arabs settled later, and the islands became a centre for slaves and spice trading. While no political stability or unity was achieved before French rule, Islam was a constant factor that came to dominate all aspects of social life for ten centuries.

In 1841 the French landed on Mayotte and the sultan was persuaded to cede his island to France. The rulers of the other three islands followed his example one by one, and in 1912 Les Comores was proclaimed a French colony. Two years later the islands became subject to the authority of the Governor-General of Madagascar. The Comoros thus became a minor appendage of a much larger, culturally very different and historically separate country. The islands were neglected and remained virtually in their pre-colonial conditions for most of the 20th century.

French administration benefitted only the foreign companies, the ruling nobility or the administration themselves. While Comorians continued in their traditional subsistence activities, cash crops (vanilla, cocoa, etc.) were developed for export by French companies and landowners for profits in which few Comorians shared. France, furthermore, maintained a situation of political absolutism where any political organisation and any press were banned.

In 1946, the Comoros were separated from Madagascar and became financially and administratively autonomous. A law of December 1961 conferred internal autonomy on the territory although the French High Commissioner still retained considerable powers. After a student strike in 1968, which was violently repressed by French paratroopers, the French government made concessions and allowed the first political parties to be formed in the country.

1971-73 were years of extreme political unrest. In general elections of December 1972 the pro-independence union had an overwhelming majority and Ahmed Abdallah Abderemane of the Union Démocratique des Comoros was elected President of the Council of Government. The new Chamber of Deputies adopted a 'resolution for independence', and an agreement was signed in Paris in July 1973 which included certain special conditions – viz a five-year delay before independence and a referendum on an island-by-island basis.

There was popular reaction against the document, but a referendum was nevertheless held in December 1974; there was a 96% vote in favour of independence but in Mayotte 64% reportedly voted against independence. The French government consequently applied pressure on the Comorian Government to propose a constitution for the islands which would allow a large measure of decentralisation and if any island twice rejected constitutional proposals it would not be included in the independent state – this was aimed at allaying the fears of the population of Mayotte.

In a bid to prevent the referendum plan being put into effect Ahmed Abdallah announced a unilateral declaration of independence on 6 July 1975. However, Mayotte's deputies in the Comorian parliament cabled the French government and placed themselves under the latter's protection. Abdallah was elected Head of State and the OAU admitted the Comoros into membership on 18 July 1975.

Abdallah faced opposition from the United National Front (FNU), a group of parties opposed to Abdallah's personal power and who favoured a more conciliatory policy towards Mayotte and France, and he was deposed on 3 August in a coup led by Ali Soilih. On 12 November the Comoros were admitted to the UN as a unified state. France did not oppose their admission but continued with preparations for a referendum on independence in Mayotte. In December, France formally recognised the independence of Grande Comore, Anjouan and Moheli but all relations between France and the Comoros had effectively ceased.

On 2 January 1976 Soilih became Head of State and the elected National Assembly was replaced by a Revolutionary Council of State. The revolution, however, found little willing acceptance outside the 'Revolutionary Youth' and the army, and its aim of changing colonial and feudal attitudes to progressive and socialist ones within two years, proved beyond the bounds of the possible. The economy remained in a site of chaos and the failure of the 1977 harvest as a result of drought caused chronic food shortages.

In December 1976, after two referendums, the French Senate decided Mayotte should become a 'collectivité particulière' (territorial community) – a status between a department and an overseas territory. In the meantime the Comorian government expelled all French citizens and nationalised French property.

Opposition to Soilih remained throughout this period and he survived four attempted coups. However, in May 1978 he was ousted by a coup led by an ex-Katanga white mercenary, Bob Denard, who also apparently had helped install Soilih himself in power in 1976.

A politico-military Directorate was formed and Soilih was placed under house arrest. He was shot dead on 29 May during what the authorities said was a 'rescue attempt'. Ahmed Abdallah, invited to return from exile, became co-President of the Directorate with his deputy Muhammad Ahmed (who had been with him in exile in France).

The name of the state changed to the Federal and Islamic Republic of the Comoros on 1 October 1978, and a policy of rapprochement with France was instituted. The French participated in the drawing up of the federal constitution whereby each island is expected to be fairly autonomous. It was hoped that this arrangement might help solve the Mayotte question. However, the leaders in Mayotte appeared to be in no hurry to join the Republic.

Abdallah has reversed the social and religious reforms introduced by Soilih. Nationalised property has been handed back to expropriated owners, Islamic forces have re-asserted themselves and women, who were compulsorily deveiled by Soilih's teenage supporters, are now under strong pressure to wear veils again. The re-emergence of the conservative face of Islam has stood Abdallah in good stead in attracting aid from the Arab oil states.

There is still considerable opposition to President Abdallah's rule, both within the country and outside it. Political consciousness has been growing among the youth in favour of the ideas of Soilih and although Bob Denard was expelled from the Comoros in September 1978, his associates still operate there much to the displeasure of neighbouring countries and the OAU.

On 8 March 1985 disgruntled elements in the Presidential Guard tried to seize power. They failed after three had been killed and many more injured. 68 people were later charged over the coup attempt.

Economy

The Comorian economy is one of the poorest and most under developed in the world and is based on agriculture for subsistence, and for export of crops such as copra, vanilla, ylang-ylang, coffee, cocoa and cloves. Most of the export and import trade is handled by French-owned companies and a handful of local entrepreneurs.

Much of the land is in the hands of foreign-owned companies – including the most fertile and best-watered areas – with only about 40% of land left to the Comorians and most of this is in the hands of the traditional ruling families. Land for subsistence needs is so short that 50% of the island's annual budget is spent on food.

There has been a major drive on road building in recent years, so each island now has a ring road and there were 400 km of tarmac roads at the end of 1985. Kuwait is presently giving aid for road building. The health situation is poor; there are three 'hospitals', but only one in Moroni warrants the name, and there is only a very limited number of trained medical staff. In the field of education, the colonial pressure was tremendous and the first secondary school was only opened in the late 1960's. High school graduates go abroad for further education. There is no library and no newspaper in the country.

The high rates of illiteracy and unemployment and the lack of land caused the early heavy emigration of Comorians to Madagascar, Reunion, Kenya and Tanzania. The first news magazine *Al Wattwany* was published on the 10th anniversary of independence on 4 July 1985. Although the islands have varied and beautiful scenery, the tourist industry has not yet been fully developed.

Comoro women in traditional robes.

CAMERA PRESS

General Information

Government

Presidential system. Federal Islamic Republic since 1 October 1978, with a people's assembly.

Languages

French and Arabic are the official languages; but the lingua franca is the Comorian variant of Kishwahili.

Religion

Islam of the Shafi sect – except for three Catholic families (totalling 152 people) on Mayotte.

How to Get There

By air: There is an international airport on Grande-Comore; the other three islands of Anjouan, Moheli and Mayotte have small airports. Air France, Air Madagascar and Air Mauritius serve the Comoros. Air Comores has regular services between the three islands, Dar es Salaam, Mombasa and Antananarivo.

By sea to Moroni and Mutsamudu: No regular service but occasional lines mostly via Madagascar, Reunion, Mauritius or East Africa. Baraka-Belinga line from Comoros to France.

Entry Regulations

Entry visa for Comoro Islands can be bought on arrival at the airport. The entry visa is valid for three months' stay.

An international certificate of vaccination is required showing immunisation against yellow fever and cholera if the traveller is arriving from an infected area.

Customs Regulations

Personal effects and restricted amounts of tobacco and alcohol are admitted free of duty.

There is no restriction on the amount of foreign currency taken into the Comoros, but a declaration must be made and the amount not used may be taken out again. the same applies to travellers' cheques.

Any amount of local currency may be taken into the Comoros but only 50,000 CFA francs may be taken out again, unless one is travelling direct to another franc zone country.

Climate

The most pleasant period for the Comoros extends from May to October. November and December are best for deep-sea fishing, and August and September are best for diving. The coasts swelter in the austral summer (December to March) although the rains at this time of year bring some relief – as well as the occasional cyclone. Higher points on the islands are cooler, especially at night, but the hills also attract greater rainfall.

What to wear: If you are climbing the Karthala or M'Tingui Mountains, you will need sweaters, thick trousers for protection against thorns, and a rainproof hat. Sturdy shoes are invaluable for walking anywhere on Grande Comore's hard-lava surface. Otherwise bring light clothing with little concern for formality. Women should remember general Muslim objections to the over-exposure of the female body – although French residents and tourists usually dress as they please.

Health Precautions

Precautions against malaria are essential. Medical facilities are scarce on the Islands. There is only one proper hospital in Moroni. Vaccination against cholera and yellow fever is recommended.

Banks and Currency

Banque Centrale des Comores (Central Bank)
Banque Internationale des Comores, Moroni, tel: 73 15 88
Banque Francaise Commerciale, Dzaoudzi, Mayotte, tel: 269.40.10.16
Currency: Comoro Franc divided into 100 centimes. 100 Comoro Francs = 2 French Francs. (Exchange rates p.9)

Business Hours

Banks: Monday-Thursday 0700-1200; Friday 0700-1130.
Offices and Shops: closed daily between 1200 and 1500.
Offices are closed on Saturday afternoons.

Public Holidays

Ascension of the prophet*, 2 February 1990
Start of Ramadan*, 27 March 1990
2nd Coup d'Etat, 13 May
Eid al-Fitr*, 26/28 April 1990
Independence Day, 6 July
Eid al-Adha*, 3/6 July 1990
Hijra*, 23 July 1990
Ashoura*, 2 August 1990
Prophet's birthday*, 2 October 1990
Admittance to UNO, 12 November
Christmas Day, 25 December
New Year's Day, 1 January
The dates of the Muslim holidays, marked with an asterisk, are only approximate as they depend on sightings of the moon.

Embassies in Moroni

Diplomatic representation is in the process of being established in Moroni.

At the present France and China have ambassadors resident in Moroni and the US has an embassy.

Transport

By road: Travellers depend on the all-purpose *taxi-brousse* (bush taxi), hired vehicles or private cars to circulate on the islands. Grande Comore and Anjouan have a network of tarred roads, but four-wheel-drive vehicles are advisable for the outlying islands and the interiors, especially in the rainy season.
By air: Each island has an airfield served by Air Comores' scheduled and charter flights; there are four weekly connections between Moroni, Moheli and Anjouan; and twice weekly between Moroni and Dzaoudzi.
By sea: Travellers can hire motorboats, sailing craft or canoes (*pirogues*) in port villages and towns; a boat can be especially useful for Moheli, where the road system is improving. Mayotte, Pamanzi and Dzaoudzi are linked by a regular ferry service.
Car Hire: Moroni-Omar Cassim and Sons, BP 700, tel: 2382. Hotel Itsandra in Grande Comore also hires out cars.

Accommodation and Food

Many hotels on grande Comore, Anjouan and Mayotte handle the needs of travelling businessmen, Government officials and other visitors. There are simple shelters (*gites*) on Mayotte and on the slopes of the Karthala.

The restaurants serve good food with local spiced sauces, rice-based dishes, cassava, plantain and couscous, barbecued goat meat and plentiful seafood.

Tourist Offices

Société Hotélière et Touristique des Comores at Itsandra Hotel, and Air Comores, BP 544 Moroni, tel: 2268. In **Paris:** Ambassade des Comores, 15 Rue de la Néva, 75008 Paris, Tel: (1) 47 63 81 78, Telex: 642390.

Hotels

NAME	ADDRESS	TELEPHONE	TELEX
GRANDE COMORE			
Ylang-Ylang (Novotel)	BP 404, Moroni	73 02 40	238
Le Coelacanthe	BP 404, Moroni	73 05 75	238
Hotel Itsandra	BP 1162, 7km north of Moroni	73 07 65	
Le Karthala	BP 53	73 01 88	
Maloudja	BP 404, Mitsamiouli	323	238
ANJOUAN			
Hotel al Amal	BP 19, Mutsamudu	365	238
MAYOTTE			
Village N'Goujat	BP 7, Dzaoudzi	40 14 19	
Hotel Le Rocher	BP 42, Dzaoudzi	42	
MOHELI			
Relais de Moheli	Fomboni (Moheli)		238

Grande Comore

Moroni, the territorial capital, has a quiet, whitewashed charm not unlike that of Zanzibar. A few broad squares and a modern government complex are surrounded by narrow winding alleys with a picturesque market place, several handsome mosques, a sleepy port of dhows and *boutres*, and villas and gardens on the Karthala's slopes.

There is a fine view from the top of the Vendredi Mosque. Important marriages and neighbourhood festivals often bring out a steady, stately sense of ceremony in the Comorians; drumming is sometimes 'in the air', and the dances of the men are dignified, contemplative and rhythmic.

A climb up the Karthala and a descent into its crater can be made with one

overnight stop. Ask the Tourist Office about guides, provisions and transport to and from the point of ascent.

The Tourst Office often commissions dance performances by the men of Itsandra, a rugged fishing village with rough lava walls and a fine beach 6 km from Moroni. Comorian products can be purchased at Moroni: these include jewellery in gold, pearls and shells, woven cloth, embroidered skull-caps (*koffia*) and slippers, carved chests, panels and portes-Cran (*lecterns*), pottery and basketry. Most items can be purchased in the villages where they are made – particularly the boat models carved at Iconi.

Travellers should stop at Bangoua Kouni Mosque, a pilgrimage site at Lac Sale; the attractive northern town of Mitsamiouli where Comorian dancing reaches its peak of elegance; the Trou au Prophete in Mitsamiouli for diving; the fishing villages of Chindini and Foumbouni.

Restaurants: Apart from the restaurants in the htoels there are the Al Islam in Magoudjou, Moroni; Cafe du Port also in Moroni; the Fakhri near Radio Comroes in Moroni; and Pouserlande in Mbachile beach at Iconi. Also La Grillade and Chez Babon.

Anjouan

With its waterfalls and luxuriant vegetation, Anjouan lures visitors from Moroni for a day or two at least. Its town, Mutsamudu, is an epitome of Swahili-Shirazi style, with 17th century houses in serpentine alleyways, carved doors, mosques, conical-shaped tombs, a citadel and a dash of colour in the gowns of its veiled women.

Restaurants: The Chez Nous in Domoni, the Charkani near Ouari and the Moya.

Mayotte

Mayotte is a place of the sea, with its neighbour Pamanzi and the rock-town of Dzaoudzi between them. Here are beaches, streams, coral reefs, excellent skin-diving and an occasional *pirogue* race. The island is surrounded by a coral reef, forming one of the most beautiful lagoons in the world.

Pamanzi is a lush, scented forest islet, 5 km across the straits from Mayotte with the lovely Dziani lake at its centre. Dzaoudzi has some fine old fortifications. There is a beach sports centre with bungalows on Mayotte.

DJIBOUTI

Having remained closely controlled by France until 1977, this country's birth into the family of independent nations at such a late stage is proving difficult, particularly with the continuing insecurity in neighbouring Ethiopia. The recent political unrest in the area does seem to be somewhat calmer at present, but it is advisable to consider the situation before planning a visit to Djibouti for a holiday. However, as an important port at the mouth of the Red Sea, the city of Djibouti will clearly continue to be cosmopolitan in its contacts after the present uncertainty has evaporated.

The Land and the People

The hinterland of Djibouti is a barren strip of land around the Gulf of Tadjoura, varying in width from 20 km to 90 km, with a coast line of 800 km, much of it fine white sand beaches. The land is semi-desert, with thorn-bush steppes and volcanic mountain ranges.

Millions of years ago this part of the world was ocean-floor. Submarine volcanic activity caused the contorted rock and lava formations that stand there today. Even now part of the territory is below sea level. Evaporation has left vast deposits of salt; this is collected by the Afar people who still distribute it as currency throughout the region.

The total population is small and until the recent influx of Issa refugees from the Ogaden region in Ethiopia, divided almost equally into Afars and Issas. The Issas now form about 60% of the population. Both Afars and Issas are Muslim-Cushitic speaking peoples with a traditionally nomadic economy and close cultural affinities. The Afar who have strong Ethiopian links inhabit the northern part of the country and the Issa, a Somali group, inhabit the southern part. Both populations extend across the artificial frontiers separating Djibouti from Ethiopia and Somalia. Since the development of the port of Djibouti at the turn of the century, the Issas have been joined by immigrants from the adjoining regions of Somalia.

Outside Djibouti, the people take their flocks and herds from pasture to arid pasture. The soil and the climate prevent cultivation of all except dates and small amounts of fruit and vegetables.

History

Before the French arrived Djibouti was grazing land for a number of nomadic tribes, chief amongst whom were the Afars and the Issas. The French first moved into the area to counteract the British trading presence and they established themselves in Obock in March 1862 when a treaty with Afar leaders legitimised the acquisition of the coastal region north of Djibouti. Later treaties in 1884, 1885 and 1896 with the Afars, the Issas and Emperor Menelik of Ethiopia, progressively added to the French territory.

Under a treaty of March 1897 the French made an agreement with Emperor Menelik to build a railway from Djibouti to the highlands of Addis Ababa, which was finally completed in 1915. Ethiopian trade using the railway has been a mainstay of the Djibouti economy.

In September 1958 the de Gaulle referendum approved continued association with France. In the sixties, however, the French switched their support from the Issas to the Afars in order to buoy up Emperor Haile

Area: 21,783 sq km
Population: 380,000 (1989 estimate)
Capital: Djibouti

Selassie in Addis Ababa and to counter Somali government claims to the territory. In the 1967 independence referendum, electoral manipulation condoned by France, reduced the Somali vote resulting in an Afar majority who voted in favour of continuing as a French overseas territory.

After reaffirming its links with France, the Afar party won all 40 seats in the enlarged Chamber of Deputies in November 1973. Issa opposition to Afar rule grew progressively in the early seventies and an attempt was made on the life of the Afar leader, Ali Aref, in December 1975. Under international pressure and faced with an increasingly turbulent situation in the Horn of Africa, the French decided finally to withdraw from the territory. A conference in June 1976 finalised decolonisation arrangements and dismantled the Afar-weighted electoral apparatus. The number of enfranchised tribesmen of Somali origin jumped from 19,000 in 1973 to 49,105 in 1977 and a predominantly Issa assembly was elected in the independence referendum in May 1977.

The Republic of Djibouti gained independence on 27 June 1977 with Hassan Gouled, leader of the Issa party, Ligue Populaire Africaine pour l'Indépendance (LPAI), as President.

The main influence on politics in Djibouti during its first year of independence was the course of the war in the neighbouring Ogaden region of Ethiopia. Issa sympathies lay with related tribesmen on the Ethiopian side of the border who, supported by Somalia, were in open rebellion against the new Dergue government in Addis Ababa. Inter-ethnic tensions between Issa and Afar came close to boiling point while the closure of the Ethiopian rail link reduced port activity and increased the country's economic fragility. The ethnic balance was further tilted in favour of the Issa, with the influx of some 10,000 refugees from the Ogaden after Ethiopia's recapture of the region.

In the first six months of independence, Afars were increasingly removed from key government posts and there were massive arrests of young Afars who openly supported the Dergue. However, the success of the Ethiopian counter-offensive in the Ogaden apparently convinced President Gouled of the necessity of a compromise. The majority of Afar prisoners were released and it was agreed to re-integrate Afars into the civil service and security forces, and to concentrate on the development of the northern Afar region. A new party. 'Le Rassemblement Populaire pour le Progrès' was set up in 1978 with the aim of generating wider popular support.

Special efforts have been made with regard to refugees from the conflicts in Eritrea and the Ogaden, now numbering up to 30,000. International aid has been obtained to improve refugee camps and to develop the cultivation of irrigated land. With only ten per cent of its own population fully employed, the influx of refugees remains one of Djibouti's major problems.

Djibouti's national sovereignty remains very much subject to the evolution of the situation in the Horn of Africa – although the country's territorial integrity is guaranteed by the presence of over 3,500 French troops.

General Information

Government

Hassan Gouled Aptidon, president of the ruling party, le Rassemblement Populaire pour le Progrès, is executive president. Elections to the National Assembly are on a single list.

Languages

French and Arabic are official languages, Afar and Somali are spoken locally, while English is spoken by taxi-drivers, shop-keepers and in hotels.

Religion

Largely Muslim with a small number of Christians.

How to Get There

By air: Djibouti airport, 5 km south of the town, is served by Air Djibouti from Ethiopia, Somalia and both Yemen republics. There are flights from Europe, Africa and the Middle East by Air France, Air Maddagascar, Yemen Airways, Al Yemda, Ethiopian Airlines and Somali Airways. There are daily flights between Paris and Djibouti. There is no bus service available from the airport to the city but there are taxis for hire. No left luggage facilities at the airport.

By rail: The Djibouti-Ethiopian railway provides regular services from Addis Ababa and Dire Dawa. It is a long slow journey, but comfortable sleeping accommodation is available in first-class carriages.

By road: There are good roads from Assab and Dire Dawa in Ethiopia, but it may be impossible to enter from Ethiopia and Somalia in view of political conditions in both countries. A tar road now links Djibouti to Addis Ababa; some stretches of road are only useable during the dry season.

Entry Regulations

There are no restrictions with regard to entry visas for visitors in possession of valid passports. Visas are valid for ten days but are easily renewable at the airport or from Djibouti embassies in Paris, New York, Cairo, Djedda, Addis Ababa and Mogadishu. French subjects in possession of valid passports do not need visas for a stay of less than three months.

International certificates of vaccination against yellow fever and cholera arc required.

Customs Regulations

Personal effects are admitted free of duty. Any amount of local or foreign currency may be taken into or out of the territory. US dollars and French francs are welcomed.

Climate

It is extremely hot in Djibouti, and particularly parched between June and August when the temperature can reach 45°C and the dusty Khamsin blows from the desert. Between October and April it is slightly cooler, with occasional light rain. Best time to visit is from November until april.

Clothing should be very light. Avoid synthetic fabrics.

Health Precautions

An anti-malaria prophylactic should be taken before, during and after one's visit. Water should be boiled or filtered before drinking. Precautions should be taken against prickly heat.

Banks and Currency

Banque de Djibouti et de Moyen Orient, BP 2471
Banque Indosuez, Place Lagarde, PO Box 88, tel: 353016
Banque pour le Commerce et l'Industrie, Place Lagarde, tel: 350857
British Bank of The Middle East, Place Lagarde, tel: 353291
Bank of Credit and Commerce International (BCCI), 10 Avenue Pierre Pacal, tel: 351741
Several 'bureaux de change' in the Place Ménélik.

Currency: Djibouti franc (Fr Dj) divided into 100 centimes. (See currency table, page 9).

Banks are open Monday-Saturday from 0700-1200.

Public Holidays

New Year, 2 February 1990
Lailat al-Miraji*, 22 February 1990
Labour Day, 1 May
Eid al-Fitr*, 26/28 April 1990
National Day, 27 June
Eid al-Adha*, 3/6 July 1990
Assumption Day, 15 August
Muslim New Year*, 23 July 1990
Al-Ashura*, 2 August 1990
All Saints Day, 1 November
Prophet's Birthday*, 2 October 1987
Christmas Day, 25 December
The dates of the Muslim holidays marked with an asterisk are only approximate as they depend on sightings of the moon.

Embassies in Djibouti

China: tel: 35 22 46
Ethiopia: tel: 35 07 18
France: tel: 35 25 03/35 09 66
Iraq: tel: 35 34 69
Libya: tel: 35 33 39
Oman: tel: 35 08 52
Saudi Arabia: tel: 35 16 45
Somalia: tel: 35 35 21
Sudan: tel: 35 14 83
USSR: tel: 35 20 51

Yemen Arab Republic: tel: 35 29 75
People's Democratic Republic of Yemen: tel: 35 37 04
USA: tel: 35 39 95/35 38 49

Consulates in Djibouti

Belgium: tel: 35 09 60
Germany FR: tel: 35 05 07
India: tel: 35 02 19
Italy: tel: 35 11 62
Netherlands: tel: 35 20 22
Norway: tel: 35 23 51
Sweden: tel: 35 20 22

Transport

By air: International services are operated daily to Tadjoura and Obock by Air Djibouti (tel: 35 26 51). It is also possible to charter small private aircraft from the Aéro-Club.

By road: The best roads are from Djibouti to Arta and the coast road from Djibouti towards Assab in Ethiopia. The road is also good going west into Ethiopia via Dikhil. Most other roads are rough but passable throughout the year. There are taxis in Djibouti.

Car hire: It is possible to hire a car in Djibouti from Red Sea Cars (Hertz) tel: 35 26 51 or from the Airport, tel: 35 25 13. Four-wheel-drive vehicles for trips into the interior of the country are available from Stophi, tel: 35 24 94. It is advisable to carry plenty of extra water and petrol on any expedition off the main routes.

Taxis: Available in Djibouti and also from the airport to town. Night tariffs increase by 50%. Taxis are also available in Ali-Sabieh, Dikhil, Dorale and Arta.

By rail: Under normal circumstances the train which runs between Djibouti and Addis Ababa three times per week, stops at Ali-Sabieh before the Ethiopian border, and at Dire Dawa and Aouache in Ethiopia. There are three rail classes and overnight sleepers are available.

By sea: There is a ferry which runs from the north of the country to Djibouti and

Tadjoura five days a week, and to Obock once a week. The ferry journey takes approximately three hours and is a practical and economical way of transporting a vehicle.

Accommodation and Food

The air-conditioned hotels in Djibouti are expensive, but the service is generally good. There are restaurants to suit all tastes, serving French, Vietnamese, Chinese, Arab and local specialities. Hotel and restaurant staff are normally tipped 10% of the bill.

Djibouti

The capital of Djibouti, constructed between 1886 and 1900 has an Arab flavour to it; it lies on a peninsula separating the Gulf of Tadjoura from the Gulf of Aden and is the centre for all economic activity and administration in

Hotels

NAME	ADDRESS	TELEPHONE	TELEX
DJIBOUTI			
La Siesta*	POB 508, Plateau du Serpent	35 14 92	–
Djibouti-Palace Hotel*	POB 166, Boulevard de Gaulle	35 09 82	–
Djibouti Sheraton*	POB 1924 Fax: 253 35 58 92	35 04 05	5912
Plein Ciel*	POB 1869, Boulevard Bonhoure	35 38 41	–
Bienvenue	Boulevard du Bender	–	–
Continental*	POB 675 Place Ménélik	35 01 46	–
L'Europe*	POB 83 Place Ménélik	35 04 76	–
Hotel de France	Boulevard de Gaulle	35 18 43	–
Doraleh (bungalows)	10 km from Djibouti	–	–

*These are first class hotels; they are all air-conditioned and have restaurants

the country. The town centre contains a lively and colourful market near the mosque, and retains elements of African, European and Middle Eastern culture.

5 km from Djibouti there are pleasant walks in the Ambouli palm grove and gardens. There are beaches at Dorale (12 kms) and Khor Ambado (15 kms). A 4 wheel-drive vehicle is necessary to reach the latter.

Restaurants: There are expensive restaurants serving European food in most of the larger hotels and also many local restaurants where it is possible to eat well and cheaply. French food is served at the **Restaurant Le Kintz** and **Restaurant Palmier en Zinc,** while Italian food can be found at **Chez Mamma Elena** and **Mickey Restaurant.** Local Ethiopian dishes are served at **Chez Thérese** and the **Hotel Bien Venue**; Chinese food is also available, at the **Vietnam** and **Hanoi** restaurants.

Tourist Information: L'Office de Développement du Tourism, Place Ménélik, BP 1938, tel: 353790; Ambouli Airport, tel: 351641; railway information, Plateau-du-Serpent, tel: 350353; Djibouti Tours, Boulevard de Gaulle, tel: 353022; information on ferries to Obock and Tadjoura, Société du Bac le Goubet, tel: 352351.

Outside Djibouti

The summer resort of **Arta,** situated in the mountains overlooking the Gulf of Tadjoura, lies about 40 km by tarred road from Djibouti. There is a good restaurant there which is part of a hotel school.

100 km south-west of Djibouti is the eerie **Lake Assal,** 153 km below sea level and encircled by mountains. However, the road to the lake is only passable with a four-wheel-drive vehicle. The cold, dead waters of the lake are surrounded by a crystal bank of salt and startling white gypsum. There are hot springs nearby.

On the Ethiopian frontier is **Lake Abbe,** which has an unearthly appearance with jagged needles of rock creating a moon-like landscape. The lake is the home of flocks of flamingoes, ibis and pelicans. En route to the lake one passes through **Dikhil,** an attractive small town perched on a rocky outcrop in the environs of which gazelle, antelope, hyenas, jackals, and camels can be seen. Hunting is forbidden throughout the country.

An interesting excursion for those who have a four-wheel-drive vehicle, is to the Issa town of **Ali-Sabieh** which is situated in the mountains and where there is a large market. It is a major stop-over point for the train between Addis Ababa and Djibouti.

One can reach the opposite side of the Tadjoura Gulf, the settlements at **Obock** and **Tadjoura** itself, by the coast road from Djibouti, by air, or by ferry (see above). For those interested in skin diving, spear-fishing or underwater photography the gulf of Tadjoura (especially Obock) offers a wide variety of flora and fauna as well as many species of fish and different types of coral. The best time for these activities is from September-May when the waters of the Red Sea are clear. Tadjoura itself, town of seven mosques, is situated in a beautiful mountain setting. In the **Goda Mountains** behind the town, there is a fossilized forest and a wealth of rare plants. The forest is now a national park.

ETHIOPIA

Ethiopia has all the ingredients of a fascinating country to visit, with its long history as a centre of a powerful but isolated civilisation, with its own cultural, social and political traditions, and with its mountainous terrain almost defying access from the outside world.

But for more than a decade, Ethiopia has been experiencing significant changes which have ruled out extensive travel to the historic sites of the north. The possibilities of travelling freely around the country remain limited. A social revolution has been underway since the feudal regime of Emperor Haile Selassie was swept away in 1974 and intense political and military conflicts have occurred as a result. The present military rulers have waged campaigns against the independence movements of the Eritreans in the north and the Somalis in the south-east. So far the regime has kept the country in one piece, but at a great cost in lives, suffering and social disruption.

The parts of the country not affected by military conflicts are still well worth visiting for an all-round experience of cultural variety and scenic magnificence. The establishment of the Ethiopian Tourism and Hotel Commission in May 1979, was the first step in the extensive development and promotion of tourism that the Government would eventually like to see.

Please check with Ethiopian Airways or your local Ethiopian embassy that those parts of the country you are interested in are safe to visit.

The Land and the People

The central core of Ethiopia is a vast highland region of faulted volcanic rocks thrown up when the Great Rift started to open and extend from Palestine down the Red Sea, through the Rift Valleys of Ethiopia and Kenya and on to Malawi. The highland areas alone cover an area roughly the size of France and form a watered, temperate world of their own, surrounded by hot, inhospitable deserts which only the most determined have crossed.

The escarpments on either side of Ethiopia are steepest in the north, and the highland terrain there is exceedingly rugged. To the south the countours are generally softer and agricultural potential is much richer.

Along the Eritrean coast and in the northernmost highlands are people who speak Tigre, a Semitic language closest to the ancient Ge'ez which otherwise only survives in church literature. In Tigray Administrative Region, in which Axum lies, another Semitic language, Tigrigna, is spoken. The centre of the country is the home of the official language, Amharic. Further south Guragigna, a Semitic language, is spoken by people of a

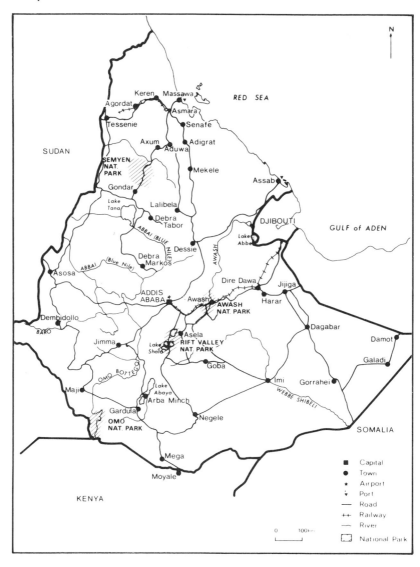

Area: 1,221,900 sq km
Population: 47.6 million (1989 estimate)
Capital: Addis Ababa

Semitic origin.

To the east and south are people who speak Cushitic languages: Oromigna, Denakil and Somali and what is called the Sidama group of languages. These languages form the so-called Eastern Cushitic group of the central Southern Highlands – between the Rift Valley lakes and Lake Turkana/Rudolf on the Kenya border.

The Oromos, by far the most populous of the various nationalities of Ethiopia, dwell on the central highlands and the south eastern lowlands. Although the various Oromo groups and peoples have remained socially distinct, their culture is a fascinating one, adding much to the richness of the Ethiopian cultural scene.

The Adere people who live in the walled city of Harar also have a vivid cultural life; they speak a Semitic language, Aderigna, and are well known for their architecture, distinctive costume and skill in grass weaving and silver smithing.

To the north, the far west and south west are the Nilotic peoples: the Nuer and Anuak near Gambela, and the Geleb and other tribes in the south, each with their own languages.

Within this broad outline there are to be found numerous variations and non-conforming communities whose language and culture reflects some individual quirk of history. Once such group is the Falashas, now living near Gondar, whose culture reflects Ethiopia's early links with Judaic culture.

Among the most prominent of the nationalities known to have nurtured the so-called Axumite civilisation are the Amharas and Tigreans, who in the main occupy the central and northern portion of the central highlands.

The country still retains the Julian calendar (named after the Roman emperor who acquired it from the mathematicians of Alexandria, whence Ethiopia got it direct) which is divided into twelve months of thirty days each, and a thirteenth month of five or six days at the end of the year. The Ethiopian calendar is seven years and eight months behind that of the West. Several church festivals are of considerable interest.

Culture

Ethiopia shares with Egypt the visible remnants of a rich ancient culture; but whereas Egypt's golden age was most closely associated with the Pharaohs, Ethiopia's earliest art sprang from its early Christian heritage with which much of it remained closely involved until recent times. In a land of 15,000 churches religious art permeated much of the culture, especially of the highlands, and priests share with warriors a love of richly embroidered costumes. Places of worship are often living museums of lovely vestments.

The modern dress is often quite different from any other costumes to be found in the world. The *qemis* and the *shemma* are the traditional garments. Handwoven of a tough local cotton fibre bleached snow-white, with a coloured woven border called a *t'ibeb the qemis* (dress) is sometimes embroidered at the neck, the sleeves and the hem, usually in a geometric design, but can include crosses, wheatsheaves or the national Mesqel flower.

The Ethiopian love of design and beauty is reflected not only in dress but in ornaments and in everyday objects. The country is a treasure-house of jewellery, especially in the monasteries and churches. Formal jewel-studded crowns and diadems, daggers and shields set with rubies and emeralds find their more mundane equivalent in the rich artistry of the silver biriles for drinking *t'ej* and in beautifully designed goblets and tableware. Jewellery and ornaments are an important part of Ethiopian dress, so keeping alive the old traditional crafts of the goldsmiths and silversmiths, as well as the humbler but no less impressive skills of the rural weavers of grass, leather, hair, glass and shells.

The monsateries of Ethiopia produced the earliest illuminated parchments, which have reached high standards in book illustration and contributed to establishing a traditional style of painting on parchment.

Ethiopia's music and dances have their own distinctive characteristics and are tremendously varied according to the region and the event.

History

Ethiopia is one of the oldest states in the world. The ancient empire of Axum flourished on the northern plateau during the classical period. Dominated by a Christian culture from the fourth century AD, it was later cut off for a thousand years by the rise of Islam.

In the 14th and 15th centuries there were sporadic clashes with the Muslim Somalis in the south, though by this time relations between the two peoples were generally characterised by peaceful commerce.

Hostilities increased during the 16th century, however, and it was only with the support of the Portuguese, bent on establishing control of the Indian Ocean trade routes, that the Ethiopians were able to repulse an invasion by the powerful Muslim ruler of Harar, Muhammed Gragne. The Portuguese were driven out in the 17th century, having failed in their attempt to substitute Catholicism for the Ethiopian Coptic orthodoxy.

From the mid-18th to the mid-19th centuries, Ethiopia's complex feudal hierarchy was weakened by internal strife. Then, in the process of being strengthened by the Emperor Tewodros (1855-68), it suffered its first imperialist invasion – by the British – in 1867.

During the last quarter of the 19th century the Ethiopian empire was consolidated and expanded to include the vast, arid Ogaden region in the south-east, inhabited by Somali nomads and farmers. The Ethiopians also blocked the advance of European colonialism in the north at the famous battle of Adowa in 1896. Here they defeated the Italians, who nevertheless retained Ethiopia's northernmost region as their colony, Eritrea.

The Ethiopian annexation of southern land continued well into the 20th century. The consolidation of this empire, begun by the Emperor Menilik

(1889-1913) and further developed by Haile Selassie (regent from 1916 and emperor 1932-74) was interrupted by the Italian invasion of 1935. When the Italians were defeated in 1941 the British retained control of Eritrea and the Ogaden until the early 1950s.

The imperial Ethiopian regime set up a system based on religious, ethnic and class divisions, on feudal privilege and corruption. The dominant northern groups imposed their religion, Christianity, and their language, Amharic, on all others. Muslims, a majority in the south and in parts of the north, lacked both religious and political recognition, since nearly all important public posts went to Christians.

The expropriation of southern lands by the crown and feudal aristocracy created among the subsistence farmers a class of landless tenants paying up to half their annual product in rent. As their numbers gradually outstripped their productive capacity under this inhuman system, they grew increasingly restive.

Haile Selassie's 'modernisation' process required the creation of a competent bureaucracy to take over from the creaking feudal apparatus and the centralisation of power under the crown. But since this administrative stratum was largely impotent except in reinforcing the privileges of the feudal elite, it developed into a disaffected and (latterly) radicalised intelligentsia.

From the 1950's, a sluggish peasant economy and lack of domestic capital forced the regime to attempt development through the introduction of foreign capital – a policy which, while failing to create a national bourgeoisie, engendered a proletariat antagonistic both to its foreign exploiters and to a government whose repressive measures made that exploitation possible.

At the same time, the failure of the imperial regime to meet the aspirations of the peoples of Eritrea and the Ogaden sparked the development of liberation movements in those regions from the early 1960's onwards.

By the early 1970's the old regime was sagging under the weight of its own contradictions. Its downfall was hastened by its attempt first to ignore and then to cover up the disastrous drought which killed an estimated 300,000 peasants in 1972-74.

By early 1974 in the towns, under the combined effects of unemployment and inflation, workers, intellectuals and students mounted a massive campaign against employers and the government, while in the countryside many southern peasants rose up against their landlords. The Eritrean liberation movement was gaining support and containing the imperial army, while the army itself was shaken by a series of mutinies.

A Co-Ordinating Committee of the Armed Forces (known as the 'Dergue') took command and deposed the emperor in September 1974. Radicalised by the popular mass movement, whose class base it reflected, the Dergue seized the leadership of the Ethiopian revolution, and proclaimed a socialist state to be guided on the basis of 'Ethiopia Tikdem' – a political philosophy 'which provides for a nationwide socialist reconstruction and ensures equality and freedom among the broad masses of the country'. All major industrial, financial and commercial companies were nationalised, including land and extra houses, throughout the country. Church and state have been separated and 'Crash Programmes' were initiated by the Provisional Military Government in a number of fields. These included, a) the eradication of illiteracy, b) a mass politicisation campaign, c) the National Economic and Cultural Development Campaign, to combat starvation and provide food for all; this in a situation in which several millions of Ethiopians were dependent on international food aid following years of crippling drought.

The most serious threats to the Dergue have come from the liberation fronts in Eritrea and from Somalia's claim to the Ogaden in the south-east. In the Ogaden the Dergue called in Russian and Cuban military support to crush the uprising backed by Somalia in 1977-78, and in 1978 the Dergue then switched its military effort, with Russian support, to containing the Eritrean rebellion. The Eritreans were forced to retreat and to abandon all the towns they had captured, but in January 1980 they struck back and regained much of their lost territory. In March 1980, renewed fighting broke out in the Ogaden. Armed struggles have erupted in three further provinces in Ethiopia, most notably in Tigray. These conflicts remain far from a solution.

Within the Dergue there have been successive purges. A number of prominent men have been executed. Lt Col. Mengistu has been head of government since February 1977. The Dergue has also faced concerted opposition from political organisations dedicated to removing the military's control of the country. In the hope of defusing this pressure the Dergue announced the formation of the Workers Party of Ethiopia, on the tenth anniversary of the revolution, in September 1984. In July 1989 the government began peace talks with the rebels in Eritrea and Tigre to try to restore peace to the troubled land.

Economy

The vast majority of the Ethiopian population are peasants living off a subsistence economy. Coffee accounts for two third of exports.

Industry accounts for 12% of GDP, and the nationalisation of major companies in 1975 was accompanied by a 'Declaration of the Economic Policy of Socialist Ethiopia', proposing state control of industry, raw materials and utilities. Joint public/private enterprise was envisaged in tourism, mining and large-scale construction, leaving a private sector in small-scale manufacturing, commerce, transport and services. This sector has since been further whittled away.

Subsistence farming was a sector under intolerable pressure during the last decade. Given the concentration of landless peasants in the south, the nationalisation of land in March 1975 was a vital political as well as economic step, and was accompanied by the establishment of Peasant Associations throughout the country. These associations (*mehabers*) work in cooperation with government representatives and development agencies such as Oxfam. There is a lot of development activity around the *mehabers* – health clinics, irrigation schemes, construction, and courses for craftsmen in pottery, carpentry, spinning, weaving and tanning.

Repeated drought and famine, plagues of locusts, war, neglect and the displacement of hundreds of thousands of peasants had reduced agricultural production by 30% by 1978, and there were indications that in the turmoil a 'kulak' class of rich peasants was beginning to emerge.

Faced with this potentially disastrous situation, the Provisional Military Administrative Council launched a 'national revolutionary economic development campaign and national planning' in October 1978.

The objectives of the campaign are wide-ranging, and its economic and political components closely linked: it is designed to meet the immediate consumer demands of the population, and to eliminate illiteracy, disease and unemployment. Since 1978, industrial production has begun to recover and the high earnings from coffee have relieved Ethiopia's financial position. The drought and famine in northern Ethiopia in 1984/85 led to about a million deaths. Ethiopia then began an enforced resettlement programme of the most affected peoples.

Wildlife

Ethiopia's geographical location and remarkable physical features have endowed it with a rich and varied natural heritage of vegetation and wildlife. There are a number of animals found nowhere else in the world – the Walia ibex, the Simyen fox, the mountain Nyala (found in the Bale mountains in the south) and the gelada (bleeding-heart baboon) – and twenty three species of birds unique to Ethiopia.

The Nubian ibex is found in the Red Sea hills of northern Eritrea and further north along the Sudan coast. The rare and shy Somali wild ass ranges the Denakil country to the north and the north east.

The Rift Valley, which cuts diagonally through the highlands of Ethiopia and connects the Denakil Desert in the north east to Lake Turkana/Rudolf in the south west, has its own distinctive features.

Commendably, conservation of wildlife is a prominent part of government policy.

National Parks

Lakes Abyata and Shala are being formed into the **Rift Valley National Park** in which the emphasis is upon the abundant bird-life of the alkaline lakes – and import migration route for birds of the northern hemisphere providing a temporary home for many varieties of geese, duck and water-fowl, which are to be seen by the thousand in the winter months of January and February.

The Walia ibex and the gelada baboon are found only in the mountain massif. It is here that the **Simyen National Park** has recently been established.

The **Awash National Park** and the surrounding reserves abound in game. The Beisa oryx is the most common species, while Soemmering's gazelle, Grevy's zebra, greater and lesser kudu, gerenuk, waterbuck, klipspringer, Chandler's reedbuck and the elegant dikdik occur in considerable number.

The remote **Omo National Park,** on the Omo River which flows into Lake Turkana/Rudolf is one of the richest (and least visited) wildlife areas in eastern Africa. Eland may be seen in herds of several hundred, and oryx, Burchell's zebra, Lelwel hartebeest, as well as buffalo, giraffe and elephant, and common species such as waterbuck, kudu, lion, leopard and cheetah.

The old town of Harar

KAY MULDOON

General Information

Government

The Head of State is Lt. Col. Mengistu Haile Mariam. The Provisional Military Administrative Council (PMAC) of Socialist Ethiopia, or Dergue, governs an administrative hierarchy. The Worker's Party of Ethiopia (WPE), established 1984, is the single recognised party.

Languages

The official language, Amharic, is spoken throughout Ethiopia and has its own script. English is the second official language and is understood in the main towns. French, Italian and Arabic are also widely understood, and in all over 100 languages are spoken.

Religions

About 80% of the Ethiopian people adhere to the two main religions of the country, namely Christianity in the form of the Ethiopian Orthodox Church, and Islam. The remainder follow animist or other local beliefs. There are also some Falasha Jews. In accordance with the provision made in the National Democratic Revolution programme, Ethiopians enjoy freedom of worship.

How to Get There

By air: Ethiopian Airlines: flights to and from Accra, Athens, Abu Dhabi, Bahrain, Bombay, Cairo, Dar es Salaam, Djibouti, Douala, Entebbe, Frankfurt, Jeddah, Kigali, Kinshasa, Khartoum, Lagos, London, Nairobi, Paris, Rome, Shanghai, Sanaa and Seychelles.

Ethiopia is also served by Air Djibouti, Air France, Air India, Alitalia, British Airways, Egypt Air, Lufthansa, Aeroflot, Interflug, Cameroon Airlines, Kenya Airways and Alyemda.

Bole airport is about 8 km from Addis Ababa. Airline transport and taxis are available to the city centre.

By road: The all-weather road from Kenya, via Moyale, Yabellow and Dilla is open. Some major roads are surfaced, but most are unreliable. The road network is now undergoing rapid expansion.

A temporary Ethiopian driving licence will be granted on production of a valid licence from your home country – although this is only necessary for visitors staying more than one month: for visits of less than this, the home licence is accepted. Vehicles may be imported duty free for a period of six months. Ownership certificate of vehicle and valid driving licence are all that are required.

By rail: There is a railway to Addis Ababa from Djibouti (accessible by sea) which used to be almost the only means of access for travellers in the early part of this century.

By sea: Ethiopian Shipping Lines and other companies operate regular sailings between several European ports and Massawa and Assab. Djibouti is also an international port of call, but its only connection with Ethiopia is by the railway (see above).

Entry Regulations

Visitors holding valid passports can obtain a 30-day tourist visa on arrival at either of the international airports, Addis Ababa or Asmara. The visa fee in Britain is £7.00. Alternatively tourist and business visas, valid for three months, can be had from any Ethiopian mission abroad.

Visitors who stay more than 30 days must register with the Immigration Office and secure an identity card (10 Birr and 2 photos), also extending their visas if necessary. Exit visas are issued automatically and free of charge for visitors who stay in Ethiopia less than 30 days. For visitors who stay more than 30 days the exit visa is issued free of charge upon surrender of the ID card to the Immigration Office.

Visitors entering and leaving Ethiopia must have valid certificates of vaccination against yellow fever and cholera if coming from an infected area.

Visitors should also have tickets to a point beyond Ethiopia and the requisite health certificates and visas for that country.

Concerning issuance of visas and travel formalities please contact Ethiopian diplomatic missions abroad and/or the Ethiopian Tourism and Hotel Commission.

Customs Regulations

Foreign currency must be declared on arrival. The amount taken out must not exceed that taken in. Foreign currency in notes or coins can only be changed at the National Bank of Ethiopia, but travellers' cheques can be changed at any bank, main hotel or large shop.

The maximum amount of local currency which may be taken into or out of Ethiopia is 50 Birr.

Travellers' personal effects are not subject to duty, but a declaration form must be filled in for cameras and other valuables which may not be sold in Ethiopia unless duty has been paid. One litre of alcoholic liquor and 100 cigarettes are also allowed in free of duty.

There is a duty-free shop at Bole International Airport for departing passengers, payable in foreign currency.

Climate

In Ethiopia the climate depends entirely upon where you are, the main determining factor being, of course, the altitude. The coastal regions and the Denakil plains are among the hottest places in the world. But on the plateau, including Addis Ababa, and the highland historic sites, the climate is a pleasant 10°C to 23°C throughout the year. Some time between February and April the 'small rains' are due – a scattering of showers, in no way off-putting. The 'big rains', which account for about 80% of the country's rainfall, occur from mid-June to September. During these months moderate to heavy showers should be expected for part of most days.

What to wear: In the lowland areas the lightest possible clothing, with a hat and sunglasses is all that is required. In Addis Ababa and throughout the highlands, where the climate is more like that of the Mediterranean in the spring or London, say, in early summer, light to medium weight clothing is appropriate. During the 'big rains' an umbrella or raincoat is more or less essential, and a sweater, as the evenings may be quite chilly.

Health Precautions

Vaccination against typhus, typhoid and tetanus is advisable. Prophylactics against malaria should be taken (this is now recommended even in Addis Ababa which was once considered to be above the malaria line – it is even more important elsewhere); it is wiser to drink only boiled water or bottled mineral waters; swimming in country lakes or rivers should be resisted as there is always a danger of contracting bilharzia, although efforts are currently underway to eradicate this. The various hot-water springs and the alkaline lakes Debre Zeyt (Bishoftu) and Langano are quite safe to swim in.

The high altitude of most of Ethiopia puts strain on the heart and nervous system until one is acclimatised. So avoid any physical exertion for the first few

days. Sufferers from heart ailments or high blood pressure should consult a doctor before going to Ethiopia.

Avoid contact with stray dogs or cats as a precaution against rabies.

Banks and Currency

National Bank of Ethiopia, PO Box 5550, Addis Ababa. (Central Bank)
Commercial Bank of Ethiopia, PO Box 255, Addis Ababa. Tel: 155000
Currency: Ethiopian birr divided into 100. (See Currency table, page 9).

Business Hours

Offices: Monday-Friday 0900-1300 and 1500-1800; Saturday 0900-1300
Banks: Monday-Friday 0830-1230 and 1430-1630; Saturday 0830-1230
Shops: Monday-Saturday 0900-1300 and 1500-2000

Public Holidays

Christmas Day, 7 January
Feast of the Epiphany (Timqet), 19 January
Commemoration of the Battle of Adowa, 2 March
Good Friday, 13 April 1990
Easter Sunday, 15 April 1990
Liberation Day, 6 April
May Day, 1 May
New Year's Day, Eritrean reunion with her Motherland, Feast of St John the Baptist, 11 September
Popular Revolution Commemoration Day, 12 September
Mesqel (Feast of the Finding of the True Cross), 27 September
Id al-Adha, 3/6 July 1990
Mawlid, 2 October 1990

Embassies in Addis Ababa

Austria: PO Box 137
Belgium: PO Box 1239, Fikre Mariam St
Burundi: PO Box 3641
Cameroon: PO Box 1026
Canada: PO Box 1130, Churchill Rd

China People's Republic: PO Box 5643
Cuba: PO Box 5123, Old Airport
Egypt: PO Box 1611
Equatorial Guinea: PO Box 246
Finland: PO Box 1017, Old Airport
France: PO Box 1464, Omedla Rd
Germany DR: PO Box 5507, Tel: 153738
Germany FR: PO Box 660, Qebena St, tel: 120433
Ghana: PO Box 3173
Guinea: PO Box 1190
Italy: PO Box 1105, Qebena District, tel: 113040
Ivory Coast: PO Box 3668
Kenya: PO Box 3301, Fikre Mariam St
Liberia: PO Box 3116
Malawi: PO Box 2316
Netherlands: PO Box 1241
Nigeria: PO Box 1019
Rwanda: PO Box 5618
Senegal: PO Box 2581
Sierra Leone: PO Box 5619, tel: 203210
Spain: PO Box 2312
Sudan: PO Box 1110; Mexico Sq
Sweden: PO Box 1029, Ras Tesemma Sefer
Switzerland: PO Box 1106, Near Old Airport, tel: 201107
Tanzania: PO Box 1077
Uganda: PO Box 5644
UK: PO Box 858, Fikre Mariam St, tel: 182354
USA: PO Box 1014, Int'ot'o
USSR: PO Box 1500
Zaire: PO Box 2723, tel: 204385
Zambia: PO Box 1909

Transport

By air: Probably the most convenient, and sometimes the only, way of travelling is by air. Ethiopian Airlines operates regular flights to and from over 40 towns throughout the country.

By road: There are now all-weather roads to all the provincial capitals and to most of the business and tourist centres. Drive on the right in Ethiopia, and abide by normal 'Continental' rules of the road (except that traffic on a roundabout has the right of way).

From Addis Ababa one can go as far as Lake Lagano by car with a driver and guide, without a permit. But elsewhere a permit is required. This often takes three or four days to obtain. In addition there are, of course, a number of straightforward package tours by which the principal tourist centres may be visited in luxury coaches and, usually, with the services of a guide.

With the help and promotion of the Ethiopian Tourism and Hotels Commission, there are several travel agencies and tour operators offering a variety of tours. **Car hire and tour operators:** Eastern Travel and Tourist Agency (AVIS), PO Box 1136, tel: 448655, cable 'ETTA', Addis Ababa; Forship Travel Agency, PO Box 30754, tel: 112159/115861/111493, cable 'FORSHIP', Addis Ababa; Host Ethiopia, PO Box 5944, tel: 157878/150025/151414, cable 'HOST ETHIOPIA', Addis Ababa; Tourist and Travel Agency (ITCO), PO Box 1048, tel: 444464/444334, cable 'INTRA', telex 21131, Addis Ababa; Wonderland Tours, PO Box 2895, tel: 158015, Addis Ababa.

Useful Phrases

There is a useful English-Amharic Conversation Manual, prepared by the Ethiopian Tourism and Hotels Commission, widely available and recommended. A few phrases in Amharic will help the visitor feel at home. Perhaps the most useful are:

Hello	*T'ena yist'illign*
How do you do?	*Indemin allu*
How much is this?	*Sint new?*
Alright or yes	*Ishi*
It's expensive	*Wid new*
No!	*Yellem*
Please	*Ibakwon*
Wait a minute	*Tinnish yigoyu*
Please hurray	*Tolo Yibelu*
Thank you	*Ameseghinalehu*

Accommodation and Food

There are international standard hotels in Addis Ababa and good hotels in tourist and business centres. Accommodation can be arranged through the Ethiopian Hotels Commission, PO Box 2183, Addis Ababa, tel: 447470, Cable: Ethio-tourist, telex: 21067.

In the best hotels the menus follow normal international practice. Addis Ababa also has a number of good restaurants serving Chinese, Italian and Indian food.

Ethiopian food centres on dishes, called *we't*, which may be of meat, chicken or vegetables, cooked in a hot Ethiopian pepper sauce to be eaten with, and traditionally upon, a flat, spongy bread called *injera*. While chicken *we't* is probably the single most typical Ethiopian dish, a meal will consist of a number of dishes.

The vegetarian has a wide choice, but shouldn't miss *shirro* and *misir* (chick peas and lentils, Ethiopian style). *Tibs* is a crisply fried steak. A wide variety of fish food exists, such as – sole, Red Sea snapper, lake fish, trout and, of course, prawns.

A traditional setting for a meal is around a gaily-coloured basket-weave table called a *masob*. Before you begin to eat, you will be offered soap, water and a clean towel, as the right hand is used to break off pieces of *injera* with which the *we't* is gathered up. Cutlery is not used. Finish the meal with a cup of Ethiopian coffee from the province of Kaffa. For extra aroma add a little rue – named here the 'health of Adam'.

All internationally known beverages can be found in Ethiopia. The local red wines and dry white wines are worth sampling, also *talla* – Ethiopian beer with a special taste. Don't miss *katikala*, a pure grain alcohol, or *tej*, an alcoholic drink based on the fermentation of honey.

There are restaurants in the larger

cities, where Ethiopian food may be had in the grand manner (and it is a recommended experience). More simple Ethiopian food may, of course, be had very cheaply in all parts of the country that the tourist visits.

Tipping: In most hotels and restaurants a service charge is added to the bill. Tipping is a fairly frequent custom, but the amounts are small – say 5-10% on restaurant bills and 10-15% for small services.

Hotels

NAME	ADDRESS	TELEPHONE	TELEX
ADDIS ABABA			
Addis Ababa Hilton	PO Box 1164	44-84-00	21104
Africa Hotel	PO Box 1120	44-73-85	
Ethiopia Hotel	PO Box 1131	44-74-00	21072
Ghion Hotel	PO Box 1643	44-71-30	21112
Harambee Hotel	PO Box 3340	15-40-00	
Awraris Hotel	PO Box 7	11-32-40	
Ras Hotel	PO Box 1632	44-70-60	
Wabi Shebelle Hotel	PO Box 3154	44-71-87	
ASMARA			
Adulis Hotel	Asmara	–	
Imperial	PO Box 181	11-82-22	
Keren Hotel	Asmara	11-07-40	
Nyala	PO Box 867	11-31-11	2040

Addis Ababa

Located almost in the centre of the country, Addis Ababa (population 1.32 million) is not only the political capital but also the economic and social nerve centre of Ethiopia.

Founded in the 1880's by Emperor Menilik the city is built on the side of the Int'ot'o mountain range, which rises just behind the city to over 3,000 m above sea level. Addis Ababa rambles across a number of gullies and mountain streams, and covers an area of 10 km by 8 km. Most parts of the city lie 2,200 m and 2,500 m above sea level (7,500-8,500 ft).

While there was clearly little prepatory planning for so large a city, it has grown in a very natural way, with no social or economic segregation. Thus the most modern buildings, gleaming in their marble and anodised aluminium, lie adjacent to simple country-style houses with chickens and perhaps a sheep or two. Everywhere there are eucalyptus trees which give the city much of its character and charm.

Places of interest: Africa Hall: birthplace of the Organisation of African Unity, whose charter was signed here on 25 May 1963. The building behind Africa Hall houses the UN Economic Commission for Africa. The OAU's offices are in a new block beyond Mexico Square.

Addis Ababa University: Up beyond Siddist Kilo, the main campus occupies the house and grounds of a palace. The Institute of Ethiopian Studies museum is well worth a visit.

St George Cathedral: Built in 1896 in the traditional octagonal shape in commemoration of St. George, the dragon killer and patron saint of the soldier (because of Ethiopia's success at the battle of Adowa). In 1937 the Italian Fascists tried to burn it down (not very successfully – it is built of stone!) and it was restored after the war. It houses some interesting paintings by Ethiopia's internationally-known artist Afework Tekle and others.

Trinity Church and the Menilik Mausoleum: just behind the Old Ghibbi (Palace) lies the mausoleum built in 1911 in which Emperor Menilik II lies buried with his wife Empress T'aytu. Not far away, on the other side of the parliament building, is Trinity Church built in 1941 to commemorate Ethiopia's liberation from Fascist rule.

The Market (Mercato): Covering a vast area to the west side of the town, it is one of the largest markets in Africa and presents the visitor with a confusing, fascinating kaleidoscope of impressions and experiences. It is divided into areas specialising in all types of goods and produce.

While that of most interest to visitors is probably the section dealing with Ethiopian arts, crafts and antiques (for beautiful crosses, manuscript books, old swords), other parts of the Mercato should also be seen.

Int'ot'o: A visit to the site of Menilik's earlier capital on the top of the mountain range behind the town is well worthwhile. Little remains of the town here except the two churches, Int'ot'o Mariam, where Menilik was crowned in 1882, and Int'ot'o Raguel which may be difficult to enter but which has some fine paintings. The views from here are marvellous.

Restaurants: The restaurants of the following hotels serve European food: Hilton, Ghion, Ethiopia and Africa Hotel. For French food there are also the Buffet de la Gare and La Taverne, which specialises in exotic cocktails and a good pate; for Italian, Castelli's, the Villa Verde, the Lombardia and the Oroscopo; for Austrian, the Cottage and for Middle Eastern, the Omar Khayam. For Chinese food try the Hong Kong, the Chung Hwa and the Chinese Bar and Restaurant. The Sangam is the only notable Indian restaurant.

There are innumerable small restaurants serving the national food of Ethiopia. Those listed below have a large selection, and also provide an authentic setting: the 'Addis Ababa' has traditional costumes, decoration and entertainment; the Maru Dembia, in addition to good food, has traditional music by *azmari* or wandering musicians. Further out of town are the Elfign, on the way to the airport, and the Mintamer Yifat, set high up in the hills.

There are many little snack bars and cake shops in Addis Ababa. Dotted around the city are the Mini serving hamburgers and fresh fruit juices (a papaya shake is a speciality). Enrico and Kariazis (both near the Piazza) serve cakes, home-made ice cream and coffee, as does Mimmo (near the Commercial Bank head office). The Hilton also has a cake and coffee shop.

Entertainments: There are several cinemas showing a wide range of international films, either in English, or with sub-titles in English. There are several night-clubs, the most interesting of which are the Ghion, Ras Night, Wabi Shebelle and Hilton.

Shopping: Addis Ababa must have one of the largest displays of souvenirs in the world. For the traveller in a hurry, most hotels and the airport have shops selling local crafts, but for someone with a little time, wandering around the small shops of the town centre or the Mercato is a really tremendous experience.

The ETTC Gift Shop is a boon for the tourist with little time for shopping. Situated near the Ghion Hotel, it has a wide range of handicrafts from all over the nation, and fixed prices.

The shops are well stocked with a wide range of goods. Especially desirable is the local jewellery, which is sold by the actual weight of gold or silver. It ranges from small hand-made silver crosses to great lumps of natural amber interspersed with silver balls to make a heavy necklace. Wood-carvings are also found in many forms. Various statues, three-legged chairs and stools from Jimma, carved with a single piece of tree trunk, small paintings on wood, and crescent-shaped head-rests are worth looking out for.

There are also illuminated manuscripts and prayer scrolls, heavy processional crosses, leather shields, spears, drums and carpets. If buying animal skins, buy from authorised shops only, and check first that they have the stamp of the Ethiopian Wildlife Conservation Organisation, otherwise export permission will be refused.

The Mercato has a wonderful range of goods and produce, as well as Ethiopian art and curios. In the market places a certain amount of bargaining is expected – so allow time for it. At shops in town, however, prices are fixed, although a small discount is often allowed on large purchases.

The Ethiopian Ceramic Workshop, 3 km from the centre on the Bole International Airport Road, welcomes tourists as its factory.

Tourist Information: Ethiopian Tourism and Hotels Commission, PO Box 2183, telex 21067.

Excursions: Debre Zeyt (Bishoftu): An hour or so away, centring on some interesting volcanic crater lakes with swimming and sailing facilities.

Menagesha National Park: About 35 km from Addis Ababa, a forest sanctuary for birds and wildlife. To go far into the park a four-wheel-drive vehicle is recommended.

Hagere Hiywet (Ambo): About 125 km from Addis Ababa on the same road as the Menagesha National Park, it has a hot-water spring and swimming pool which attracts many people at weekends. Some 30 km beyond is the breathtakingly beautiful crater lake of Wenchi.

Debre Libanos: About 100 km north of Addis Ababa, the revered monastery of Debre Libanos is set on the edge of an immense gorge of one of the Blue Nile tributaries, and well worth visiting.

Please check with the Ethiopian Hotels and Tourism Commission that the following parts of the country can be visited safely:

Asmara

The capital of the 'administrative region' of Eritrea, Asmara lies at an altitude of 2,300 m. Its climate is typical of the Ethiopian highlands. Prior to the Italian occupation in 1889, it had been a small Coptic village and the camp of Ras Alula, the Administrator of Hamasien. Under the Italians it developed into a substantial town with a 'native quarter', now the Market, and a European section, the main part of the present town.

Liberated by British forces in April 1941, Eritrea was administered by a

British Military Administration until 11 September 1952 when, under a United Nations resolution, Eritrea was federated with Ethiopia.

The Asmara Archeological Museum houses an excellent collection of historical objects from the pre-Axumite and Axumite periods (1000BC-AD1000) found at sites in Eritrea and Tigray.

Restaurants: There are several Italian restaurants in Asmara, the most notable being the Esposito, San Giorgio, Rino's, the Capri and the restaurant in Keren Hotel. Local food may be had at the Shoa restaurant and at the Sport restaurant.

Travel agent: Ufficio Viaggi, PO Box 877.

Axum

Capital of the ancient kingdom of the Queen of Sheba, Axum is a town of dramatic contrasts. Over the ancient city sprawls a small country town, apparently unaware and uncaring of the relics all around. The old (probably 15th century, but on a very ancient site) Cathedral of St. Mary of Zion is interesting. The new Cathedral is impressive. Here are kept the crowns of many of Ethiopia's former Emperors. Here, too, according to legend is the original Ark of the Covenant.

But the most astonishing relics of all are the obelisks or stelae, some still standing made of single blocks of granite and carved to represent multi-storey buildings. The tallest, now fallen, was over 33 m in height and represented 13 storeys. The largest still standing is 20 m in height and shows 10 floors. The carving is deep and totally clear, showing the floor-beams for each floor and the windows. The style of construction is similar to that in use in the Hadramoyt (People's Democratic Republic of Yemen) today.

While the origins and purposes of these stelae are still debated, it is probable that the statues were erected by the early Auxmite kings in remembrance of the sort of houses they had before crossing the Red Sea. Along the Sabean coast, where land was scarce, it made sense to build skyscrapers, and it may be supposed that each king built a new one in the same way as, in the 17th and 18th centuries, each of the Ethiopian Emperors built his own castle at Gondar.

Other sites of interest include the grave of King Kaleb and Gebre Mesqel, the so-called Queen of Sheba's Bath, and the ruins of the vast Royal Palace over which the road to Gondar now passes. The market has interesting curios including old coins. It is advisable to make reservations at the Axum Hotel in advance as it is often fully booked.

Historical Sites

South from Asmara to Senafe and Adigrat lies, first at 116km a small site of ancient Axumite buildings. Pillars of Axumite buildings can be seen on the right side of the road. Between the 121 and 122km posts, a track leads off to the left to one of the most famous ancient cities in Ethiopia: Qohayto (or Coloe as the Greeks called it). Extensive remains of buildings, tombs and a beautifully cut reservoir remain, and in the cliffs nearby are some interesting cave-paintings.

Matara near Senafe and 135km from Asmara, is the only undisturbed site of an Axumite city. The ruins include walls and staircases in near-perfect condition, and an obelisk bearing one of the earliest examples of Ge'ez writing. Excavations are continuing. On the road from Adigrat to Axum is the monastery of Debre Damo (from which Judith seized the sons of the last Axumite king late in the 10th century) and the oldest surviving Axumite building at Yeha (fourth or fifth century BC).

The Department of Antiquities imposes fees on visitors to the sites at Axum, Lalibela, Gondar and Bahir Dar.

Lalibela

The best way to get here is by plane, followed by a 45 minute journey by Land Rover or a three hour journey by mule along a beautiful mountain trail. The country here is among the most rugged and mountainous anywhere. It is an astonishing terrain in which to find the ancient town of King Lalibela, who initiated the spate of rock-church buildings, which has left 11 such churches of the 12th and 13th centuries in the town itself. Their incredible execution (one cannot say 'construction' since they were simply carved, inside and out, from the solid rock to look as though they had been constructed), their rich ecclesiastical treasures, and the priests who serve in them, somehow express all that is most fascinating about Ethiopia's Middle Ages. During the 'big rains' (June-September) the town is inaccessible, but a visit at Easter, Timquet or some other church festival is particularly exciting. Hotel reservations can be made at the Severn Olives and Roha Hotel via Ethiopian Airlines.

Massawa

The island of Massawa was occupied by the Turks in the 16th century. Around 1850 control passed from them to Egypt, from whom the Italians took it over by arrangement in 1885. A causeway now connects Massawa to Taulud Island and another causeway runs from Taulud to the mainland. Arkiko, now just a village on the mainland and a mile or so south, was the main port of entry for Ethiopia until the 1850's. While some of the smaller buildings on Massawa Island are several hundred years old, most of the larger ones date from 1870-1890: the Imperial Palace was built around 1871-3 by Werner Munzinger, a Swiss scholar and businessman employed by the Egyptian Khedive as Governor of Massawa. In the bay, a short boat trip from Massawa is Green Island which has

a pleasant beach. Gurgusum Beach, with two small hotels lies just north along the coast.

There are two hotels in Massawa, the Red Sea and the simpler Luna.

Gondar

Capital of Ethiopia from the time of Fasil (1632-1665) until the rise of Tewodros (1855-1868), Gondar's unique Imperial Precinct contains a number of castles, built by various Emperors throughout this period, which seem, in their typical plateau setting, quite astonishing. Although the earliest of these was built by Fasil just after he expelled the Portuguese, it appears at first to reflect Moorish/European influence, but closer study reveals both interesting architectural traits of the Auxumite traditions and also strong connections with the great castles of South Arabia of about the same period. An element of real mystery remains as to the intellectual parentage of the ideas and skills with which these fine castles were erected.

Elsewhere in the town in the palace known as Ras-Beit which was built in the 18th century as the private residence of a Lord of Tigray, Ras Mikael Sehul, and which has been in continuous occupation ever since. A short distance away is the Bath of Fasile, and the so-called House of Chickens.

Within range of the town lies the monastery and ruined palace at Qusqwam and the church of Debre Birhan Selassie with its glorious painted roof and walls. The town has a lively and interesting market and the major hotels are the Tarara, Quara, Fogera and Goha.

Dire Dawa

To the east of Addis Ababa, approximately half way by train to Djibouti, Dire Dawa has a warm, dry climate and a large market frequented by Oromo, Somali and Afar peoples with their camel caravans. There are three hotels, the new air-conditioned Ras Hotel and the old but comfortable Continental and Omedla.

Harar

The 54 km drive up the edge of the Rift Escarpment to Asbe Tafari and Harar is a memorable experience. The warm, desert-like atmosphere of Dire Dawa soon gives way to rolling, rich green farmlands. The road passes Lake Adele and Alemaya. In these mountainous areas some of Ethiopia's best coffee is grown – as well as *ch'at*, a mild stimulant if chewed to extract the juices.

The whole setting of Harar, with its medieval walls tightly holding the ancient city together, its rich and exciting market (for the variety of tourist goods probably the single most exciting market in Ethiopia), the broad sweeping views to the mountains around, and the glorious, cool climate, make it an ideal place to spend a day or two.

From Harar the road to Hargeisa (Somalia) leads to Jijiga, an important market centre for much of the Ogaden, and on to the border at Tug Wujale.

Mekele

Capital of Tigray Administrative Region, Mekele has the old castle of Emperor Yohannes IV. Another castle of the same period at the other end of the town has been turned into an excellent hotel, the Abraha W'atsbaha Hotel, tel: Mekele 62. Booking is advisable.

Expeditions to the 130 rock churches in Tigray can best be arranged from Mekele.

Rift Valley Lakes

The lakes of the Rift Valley, and especially the alkaline Lakes Abyata, Shala and Langano, provide one of the most exciting bird sanctuaries in the world. This region is well provided with hotels. The chain of Bekele Molla Hotels has one in almost every town, large or small, from Mojo to Arba Minch. These are good, if simple, tourist hotels. The one at Lake Langano occupies an especially delightful site on a beach with safe swimming.

Camel caravan in Dire Dawa

CAMERA PRESS

KENYA

Kenya has wildlife in staggering diversity and profusion; endless scenery of majestic proportions, forests, deserts, mountains, lakes and an exquisite tropical coastline; a wealth of lively traditional cultures, and (to make tourism possible) an efficient network of roads, air services to resorts with hotels and restaurants to suit all tastes. With so many attractive assets it is hardly surprising that Kenya is by far the most-visited country in Black Africa.

Every type of holiday is possible in Kenya. The very simplest is a week or two on the coastal beaches, swimming, sunbathing, fishing and goggling on the reefs. It is more usual to take in at least one game park, with short excursions from Nairobi or Mombasa. A large number of tour operators and travel agents organise a variety of game park, coastal and other scenic combinations But it is also quite possible to be your own tour operator, by hiring a vehicle or by taking local transport. The more adventurous trips to Lake Turkana and the far north have to be tackled this way (unless you cheat and fly there).

The game park trips require proper organisation, whether by a tour operator or in private groups. You need to learn something about the animals' habits in each park from wardens and other experts, or else you waste considerable energy. Accommodation has to be booked, sometimes even in the camp sites. The preparation is always rewarding, for Kenya has almost the entire range of East African animals, birds, reptiles, fish and insects.

Big game hunting was banned in 1977 after a long campaign by conservation groups, but may be reintroduced in the future. There is now a total ban on the sale or purchase of game trophies and wildlife products, and it is strictly prohibited to pick up bones, skulls or horns in national parks.

Kenya uniquely combines the utterly ancient with the utterly modern. In most areas in Kenya there are stark contrasts between the primeval world, where man has his earliest origins (and the same wildlife roamed free), and the impact of subsequent societies, whether in the subtle ways of nomadic herders, village agriculturalists and Arab traders, or the more obvious recent invasions of European planters, Asian shopkeepers, modern globe-trotting businessmen, and of tourists themselves. All these interacting elements have shaped and are shaping the direction in which Kenya is developing as a kind of microcosm world history.

While the visitor is unlikely to notice all the shades of cultural complexity during a short stay in Kenya, he will become aware of how much has happened so fast in recent years.

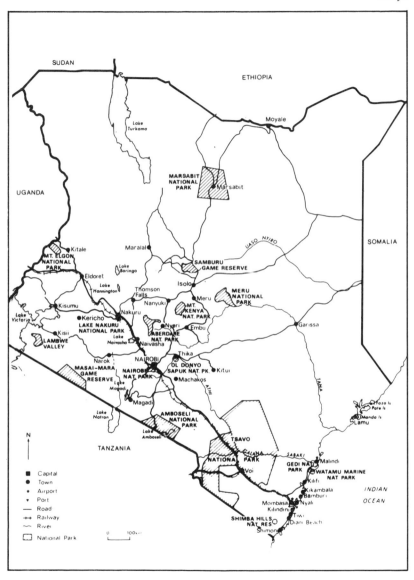

Area: 582,644 sq km
Population: 23.85 million (1989 estimate)
Capital: Nairobi

The Land and The People

Kenya has a wide range of geographic and climatic conditions. It combines arid deserts in the north and the rolling savannah country of the southern plains; ocean shores in the east and those of Africa's largest lake, Victoria, in the west. The highlands in the centre of the country, where Nairobi is situated, and of the west have a temperate climate, warm by day and cool, or even cold, by night.

The Great Rift Valley slices through the country from north to south, while right on the equator stands Mount Kenya with its snow-capped peaks. The semi-deserts of the north are populated by nomadic peoples like the Turkana, the Samburu and the Somali, with their herds of cattle, goats and camels. This area, occupying more than one-third of the country, has two major lakes, Turkana and Baringo, and contains only small towns and villages. Apart from the new Nairobi-Addis Ababa highway, the region has few good roads.

The highlands are among the most productive areas of Africa. In addition to food grown for local consumption, the main crops – tea, coffee, sisal and pyrethrum – are largely for export. The inhabitants are mainly Bantu-speaking, such as the Kikuyu, Kenya's largest tribe, who are well represented in the business community.

Farther west, in the Rift Valley Province, are Kalenjin-speaking tribes such as the Kipsigi and the Nandi. Traditionally their economy was based upon cattle, but they are increasingly turning to agriculture. Also around the Rift Valley are the Masai. Although numerically not significant, their splendid physique, colourful dress and their attachment to their traditional way of life makes them one of the country's best-known tribes.

One of the largest groups in Kenya are the Nilotic Luo who live mainly on the shores of Lake Victoria. The Luo travel widely in search of paid employment and play a prominent role in the political and trade union life of the country. Also in the west are the Kisii the Abaluhya who farm the rich but densely populated higher land near Lake Victoria.

Over to the east, between the highlands and the coast, the Kamba herd their cattle on the open plains and farm in the hills. They are famous for their carvings and their acrobatic dancing. Traditionally they are great travellers and fighters. Early foreign explorers and traders – Arabs and Europeans – made use of the Kamba as guides, porters and soldiers.

The coastal region differs from the rest of Kenya in having been cosmopolitan for centuries. The dominant element is Islam, of which the most immediately visible aspects apparent to the visitor are the mosques and the black veils (bui-bui) of the women. Over the centuries Islamic traditions have fused with other African elements to produce a Swahili culture with its own distinctive language – Ki-Swahili, the lingua franca of East Africa.

On the northern coast are the seafaring Islamic Bajun of Lamu and the other islands. Close to Malindi are the Giriama, who have largely resisted alien cultures.

READERS WHO ARE LEADERS

Marketing capital equipment, technology and luxury goods and services in the primary markets of Africa and the Middle East means reaching the decision-makers. People with affluence and influence.

But where do you find them?

You find them reading the magazines which are specifically tailored to *their* needs. Magazines which give them the *truly* independent view of crucial matters.

The Middle East, New African and **African Business** – all of them proven market leaders; all of them written for – and read by – people at the top.

Contact: **Chris Irwin,** Int. Advertisement Director

IC Publications Ltd
P.O. Box 261, Carlton House,
69 Great Queen Street,
London WC2B 5BN, England

Tel: 071-404 4333 Telex: 8811757
Fax: 071-404 5336

Apart from these well-defined regions, much of Kenya is savannah country, with vast, rolling, tree-dotted plains and tall grasses. This is many people's idea of the real Africa, and it is in these regions that one finds the large game parks, such as Tsavo, Amboseli and Meru.

There are three main African language groups: Bantu, Nilotic and Hamitic (from the Horn of Africa). Swahili is the lingua franca, readily understood by most people in addition to their mother tongues of Kikuyu, Embu, Meru, Luhya, Kamba, Kisii and Mijikenda. The Nilotic peoples are divided into the highland groups on the Uganda border who speak Nandi and Kipsigi, and the river-lake group around the Winam Gulf (or Nyanza Gulf) who speak Luo. The nomadic Nilo-Hamitic groups of the central Kenya plains speak Masai, Samburu and Turkana. Their languages have borrowed widely from the Hamitic. The Hamitic peoples living in the north-west are mostly nomadic Somali.

Culture

Like many other African nations, Kenya has an ambivalent attitude towards its traditional culture, especially its external manifestations. It is difficult to maintain the obligations of, say, the extended family in a money-based economy where advancement is supposed to be on merit and not according to kinship.

Even more of a problem is how to maintain traditional arts and crafts at a time when modern developments have made them less relevant in everyday life. Most dancing displays still preserve the traditional steps, movement and tunes, but the dress, regalia and often the instruments of the dancers are of foreign origin. A further complication is that Kenya's modernising elite wants visitors to see their country as a modern and progressive society: some feel that traditional dancing preserves the stereotype of 'primitive Africa'.

Visitors wishing to judge for themselves should make sure they are taken to a display in a coastal village or in one of the remoter areas, as well as seeing one of the more refined performances given in the hotels. Bomas of Kenya is an amphitheatre in Langata (just outside Nairobi) with permanent displays by traditional dance troupes. One of the best known is the Harambee Dancers. For good measure travellers would be advised to visit one of the nightclubs where the ordinary people congregate and dance, to listen to the music and see the dancing of modern, urban Africa.

Other traditional art forms are woodcarving, particularly by the Kamba, and the shaping of soapstone by Kisii artists. At the coast more elaborate works – stools, chests and doors – are carved and inlaid with ivory and metals. In many parts of the country beads and sisal are strung and woven into decorations and ornaments.

While the literary traditions, especially of the KiSwahili, flourish in a modern form, Kenyans are also making an important contribution to poetry, drama, novels and academic writing, especially history.

History

The Stone Age: The Rift Valley which runs between Tanzania, Kenya and Ethiopia to the west of Nairobi was probably the cradle of all mankind. In 1972 Richard Leakey found a skull with large brain capacity, dated at 2.6 million years, at a site east of Lake Turkana.

The Growth of the Swahili Towns: (to AD 1600): From Mogadishu (Somalia) to Sofala (Mozambique) a series of rival city-States grew up between the 10th and 15th centuries as an integral part of the Indian Ocean trading network, visited by ships from Arabia, Persia, India and even China.

By the 2nd century AD, when merchants from the Roman Empire frequented the coast, there were already trading villages where some Arabs had settled and inter-married with the local Africans, but it was not until the 9th and 10th centuries that major towns were built. All the towns have Chronicles, mostly written is KiSwahili (the Arabic word for coast) in Arabic script several hundreds of years ago. They record traditional stories about the foundation of the town by Arabs and Persians who then mixed with the coastal Africans to form the Swahili ruling class.

They built houses of stone and mud and, of course, mosques for they brought Islam with them and lived in comparative luxury with silks and porcelain from the east. The towns were usually sited on islands like Mombasa, Lamu, Manda and Pate. Lamu's narrow streets still retain something of the atmosphere the town must then have had, and the vast acres of ruins at Gedi show the extent of its founders' wealth.

Meanwhile, on the mainland Bantu speaking peoples were entering Kenya from the south and Nilotic peoples came in from Sudan in the north. A unique group was the so-called 'Nilo-Hamites' (Masai, Samburu, Turkanas and Kalenjin), who arrived in successive waves from the north. The coastal traders did not travel far inland but depended upon the people of the interior to bring them ivory, the main export item.

During the 15th century, Mombasa took over from Kilwa (Tanzania) and Mogadishu as the most powerful city, so it was here that Vasco da Gama, the Portuguese explorer, came to find a pilot to guide him to India in 1498. The arrival of the Portuguese in the Indian Ocean disrupted established trade patterns and some of the Swahili towns were reduced to subsistence agriculture. Mombasa, however, did not finally succumb to Portuguese rule until 1589 when a Portuguese attack coincided with turmoil inland caused by the fierce Zimba who had stormed up from the Zambezi region to face their final defeat by the Segeju near Mombasa. The Portuguese took Mombasa and to defend their garrison they built Fort Jesus. Today the Fort is a comprehensive museum where relics of their rule are preserved.

The Middle Era (1600-1900): In addition to Portuguese threats from the sea, Kenya's coastal cities in the 16th and 17th centuries faced danger from the formidable Galla who overran southern Ethiopia and large areas of Somalia and north-east Kenya. The people of the northern towns like Malindi abandoned their homes and fled to Tanzania or congregated in the safety of

Mombasa. Others from the Shungwaya region (probably in southern Somalia) fled to the inhospitable Nyika territory behind Mombasa and established the Mijikenda ('nine tribes') community. The repercussions were also felt inland – here lived the Kamba and, beyond them, the Kikuyu cultivated the fertile slopes of Mount Kenya.

In the highlands of the far west the Kalenjin were being hard-pressed from the west by the Luo coming in to the Lakeshore region from Uganda, and from the east by the fast-expanding Masai who were spreading during the 17th century from the lands of the related Turkana and Samburu far south into Tanzania. These were pastoral rather than agricultural people, moving their dwellings to follow the pasture. The Masai believed that at the Creation God had given all cattle to them and the *moran* (youth) had to prove their worth by capturing cattle belonging to anyone else.

The Portuguese were driven out of Mombasa in 1698 after a three-year siege by Arabs from Oman. For the next century the town enjoyed a resurgence of power under the Mazrui dynasty, ruling the coast from Malindi to Pemba Island. In 1837 it was taken over by the famous Seyyid Said, Sultan of Oman and Zanzibar, and became an outpost of the flourishing Zanzibari trading system. The inland people were suspicious of traders' motives. The Kikuyu, for example, would only allow them to wait on their borders to buy \ivory. The general indifference to the temptations of trade kept Kenya largely free of the slave trade.

Colonialism and Independence (1895 to the present): Kenya did not at first attract foreign powers but was declared a British protectorate because it straddled the proposed railway route to Uganda. Only a few hundred of the Indian labourers brought in to work on the railway remained after their contracts expired but many traders followed the line inland and secured a monopoly of trade there.

In the early 20th century Europeans were attracted by Kenya's healthy climate and came either under their own steam or on Government-sponsored schemes. The main political struggle was for a time between the Indian and European residents, but the Europeans managed to get the upper hand by having 16,700 sq miles of the highlands reserved by the White Highlands Ordinance for whites, where they became successful farmers producing most of the exports.

Kenyan Africans, in marked contrast with Ugandans, were not encouraged to grow cash crops and the colonial Government actively helped white settlers in the unpopular recruitment of contract workers who were paid only in kind.

Kenyans served against the Germans in Tanzania during the First World War and against the Italians in Somalia and the Japanese in Burma during the Second World War. The soldiers, returning with wider horizons, faced unemployment, rocketing prices and a shortage of land for the growing population in eroded African 'reserves'.

In 1946 Jomo Kenyatta, a highly-educated man who in London had been first President of the Pan-African Federation, returned after 15 years abroad and became leader of the already active Kenya African Union. Eventually Kikuyu land-hunger on the edge of the 'white' highlands erupted in the Mau Mau revolt (1952), in which atrocities were commited on both sides. Jomo Kenyatta was arrested on 20 October 1952. This is now a major national holiday known as Kenyatta Day. The revolt broke the power and nerve of those settlers who might have favoured Rhodesian-style white rule and persuaded the British Government that Africans must be given more legitimate means of expression.

After brief experiments with multi-racial constitutions, Kenya became African-ruled in January 1963, led by Jomo Kenyatta who had been released by the authorities in 1961 and was respected as *Mzee* (the Elder) by all Africans. By his statements he soon allayed European and Asian fears and, from independence in December 1963, he led his country along a deliberately moderate path, encouraging foreign investment and links with the West.

Kenya has effectively been a one-party state since 1965 when the Kenya African Democratic Union was disbanded and its members joined the ruling Kenya African National Union. On 22 August 1978 President Kenyatta died, and was succeeded in an orderly fashion by his Vice President Daniel arap Moi. President Moi has continued in the footsteps of his predecessor (*nyayo* – footsteps – is his national slogan), and few changes have been brought about.

The closure of the border with Tanzania in February 1977 undoubtedly had adverse effects on Kenya's trade and communications with central and southern Africa. Until the beginning of 1984, when air links were resumed, the major airlines were not able to fly between Nairobi and Dar es Salaam and all road and rail links between the two countries were cut. The land borders were re-opened in December 1983 and air links shortly afterwards.

Kenya was shaken by the first serious attempted coup since independence on 1 August 1982, in which rebels captured the radio station and students came onto the streets to demonstrate support. The government rapidly regained control, but rioting had been severe and there were hundreds of deaths.

Since then Kenya has returned to its peaceful and democratic ways. President Moi has consolidated his position and has rid himself of many potential rivals.

Economy

Kenya's economy is based on agriculture and a great proportion of the population live and work on the land. Agricultural production is carried out on both large estates and small-holder farms. Since independence there has been considerable change in the form of land ownership in the country and more land in Kenya is now owned by African citizens. A number of African businessmen have moved into large-scale farming, although some major foreign firms still have extensive plantations leased to them by the government. The government is encouraging smallholder cultivation in line with its 'Africanisation' programme.

Coffee, tea and sisal have constituted the major agricultural exports since the 1920s. Over the past few years coffee and tea production has expanded rapidly (especially since the price increases on the world market). Sugar is a small-holder crop grown mainly in the west. Cotton production is being further developed to fulfill the growing demand from Kenya's textile industry.

Despite the agricultural bias of the economy, Kenya has one of the most important industrial sectors of any black African country. Although the government guarantees the protection of foreign investment, it is committed to promoting the 'Africanisation' of the economy in both trade and industry. Since 1975 the government will only permit foreign investment if there is a form of government participation in the ownership of enterprises, and in considering new projects stress is laid on the training of local personnel and the utilisation of local raw materials. Industrial production in Kenya is dominated by food processing, manufacturing and oil refining. Kenya contains no primary raw materials such as coal or oil. Important industrial investment was made in motor car assembly, and Kenya now produces Volkswagens, Land-Rovers, other commercial vehicles and some small passenger cars.

Tourism continues as a major source of revenue for the country, with West Germany remaining the most significant market. However, the tourist market is expanding and Kenya is fast becoming a new holiday destination for travellers from many other Western countries.

Wildlife

East Africa is the part of the world where the largest number of big mammals still roam over vast areas, and Kenya has a long experience of arranging for the game to be viewed in reasonable comfort with the least interference to the natural habitat.

Although lions have been killed in many areas because of their threat to livestock, they are still fairly common in the parks, and there is a good chance of seeing lions hunting their prey – usually antelope – even in the Nairobi National Park. Elephants are extremely common in suitable habitats both on the plains and in the hills. They are so numerous that there is a continuing debate as to whether or not they should be culled. You can sometimes see numbers of them if you drive along the main road from Nairobi to Mombasa.

Great herds of buffalo, considered by many to be the most dangerous of the large animals in Kenya, roam over the plains, and are also seen in the mountains. There are about a dozen common species of antelope as well as many of the rarer breeds, from the tiny and graceful dikdik to the massive eland. Other animals one can expect to see include zebra, wild dog, jackal, giraffe, hyenas, monkeys and baboons. Cheetah and leopard are less common, but a safari to the areas they are known to inhabit will normally prove rewarding, particularly to Mount Kenya and the Meru National Park.

Kenya also has a huge variety of birdlife. Lake Nakuru, where millions of flamingoes assemble, is one of the world's wonders.

National Parks

Kenya has set aside certain areas for wildlife conservation. The present system of twenty main sanctuaries, totalling over 34,000 sq km, covers the entire geographic range of Africa and contains nearly all species of life native to Africa.

At the coast are three Marine Parks, protecting ancient coral gardens off the beaches at Malindi, Watamu and Shimoni, and acting as aquaria for the wealth of reef fish and underwater life-forms.

The inland National Parks and Reserves are areas set aside for exclusive, or, occasionally, quasi-exclusive use by wild animals to roam at will and to lead a natural life unmolested by man. They often adjoin large areas where wild animals wander just as freely in places only sparsely populated by human beings. Most parks can be visited in your own vehicle and normally you can drive where you wish along a network of murram and dirt tracks during daylight hours. In most cases you may only get out of your car at appointed viewing places or at lodges. In certain parks, for example when visiting Treetops or The Ark in the Aberdare National Park, you must use the special transport provided. Most parks have a reasonable entrance fee.

Booking for all lodges should be made through a travel agent in Nairobi.

Nairobi National Park: Only 8 km from the city centre Nairobi National Park is a mere 115 sq km in area, yet you can see more game there within two or three hours than in many of the larger parks. Behind it to the south lies the Ngong National Reserve and the animals roam between Park and Reserve at will. Thus the Park itself is a display of a much larger stock of wildlife, with occasional lions, leopards and cheetahs, as well as herds of giraffe and zebra.

All the roads in the park are accessible by ordinary saloon car, although you can hire Land-Rovers from touring companies. Among the advantages of a Land-Rover are that you can see more easily into the long grass and the space is less confined when taking photographs.

Most of the park consists of open grassy plains, where you can see herds of buck, gazelle and zebra. There are wooded ravines and a small forest area where giraffe, monkeys and baboons can be found in large numbers, and where rhino and buffalo can be seen. The elephant is the only large animal not found in Nairobi Park. There are numerous birds, from the large, ungainly ostrich and the unusual secretary bird, to the tiny, brightly coloured sunbird and the African king-fisher. Altogether there are over 100 species of animals and 400 species of birds in the Park.

At the entrance to the Park is the famous Animal Orphanage which cares for abandoned young animals until they can fend for themselves.

Amboseli National Park: Only 40 km north of Mount Kilimanjaro this Park has the most photogenic backdrop of any wildlife sanctuary in Africa. The Park consists mainly of a dried lake-bed, but Mount Kilimanjaro provides a subterranean run-off of fresh water to the springs and swamps at the park's centre.

The Masai used to control this game reserve but alternative water is being provided for their cattle so that the central 'Ol Tukai' water source is free for game viewing. There is an extremely delicate ecological balance in the Amboseli Park and visitors should not drive off the tracks or raise too much dust, which kills the grasses. There are herds of wildebeeste, zebra, buffalo, gazelle, impala and some lion, cheetah and leopard.

Tsavo National Park: Covering an area of 20,000 sq km Tsavo is the biggest national park in the world. It offers many contrasts in scenery and contains the largest variety of game species to be found in Kenya. The park is divided into two parts (west and east) by the Nairobi-Mombasa road. The main entrances are on this road at Voi and Mtito Andei. There are more than 20,000 elephant, and numbers of black rhino, hippo (best seen at Mzima Springs), crocodile (at Lugard's Falls), lion, cheetah, leopard and different species of monkeys.

Meru National Park: Situated to the north east of Mount Kenya some 110 km from Meru, it covers an area of 820 sq km. Animals in this park include lion, buffalo, elephant, leopard and rhino. It is the only national park offering fishing facilities, and the only place where white rhino can be seen.

Masai-Mara Game Reserve: Covering an area of 1,800 sq km it lies on the Kenya-Tanzania border and adjoins the Serengeti National Park in Tanzania. The wide variety of game includes rhino, buffalo, lion, elephant and antelope.

The reserve is famous for the annual migration of thousands of zebra and wildebeeste, who cross from Tanzania in search of food during April and May, returning back again in September and October.

Marsabit National Park and Samburu Game Reserve: Marsabit Park lies in the remote northern part of Kenya and covers an area of 592 sq km – a freak forest in the middle of the desert, with huge numbers of elephant, lion, leopard, kudu, giraffe, hyena and aardvark. The Game Reserves of Samburu, Isiolo and Shaba, north of Mount Kenya and more accessible than Marsabit, have thick riverine forest and dry bush landscapes. There are elephant, hippo, crocodile, Beisa oryz, ostrich, gerenuk and Grevy's zebra.

Aberdare National Park: Situated in the Aberdare Mountains, most of the park is moorland lying above 3,000 m. It has a special floral interest and is a sanctuary for elephant, buffalo, rhino and many other game animals. There are campsites in the park. This park is often closed in the rainy season because of impassable roads.

Mount Kenya National Park: The highest mountain in Kenya is situated about 160 km north east of Nairobi. The mountain slopes are clothed with amazing tropical mountain vegetation, including giant lobelia and giant groundsel, and the rivers provide excellent sport for anglers. The view from the twin snow-capped peaks – Batian (5,199 m) and Nelion (5,188 m) – may extend as far as Kilimanjaro 300 km away. The park comprises the whole of Mount Kenya above 3,200 m and covers an area of 480 sq km. Several tracks enable cars and jeeps to reach a high altitude. Climbing on the two highest peaks should only be attempted by experienced climbers with proper equipment, but vast areas below the peaks are ideal for mountain walking and scrambling. There are well marked campsites within the park.

Lake Nakuru National Park: The Park is situated 160 km from Nairobi, along a good tarmac road which passes Lake Naivasha and Lake Elementeita. Many tour operators organise day-trips, including a picnic lunch, or you can hire a private car and have meals in the town. The whole lake is about 40 sq km in extent, but the Park area has been extended to cover 200 sq km. Known as the 'home of two million flamingoes', lake Nakuru has been described as the world's greatest bird spectacle. The lesser flamingoes gather there in masses, sometimes over 250,000 to a flock, and surround the lake in a shimmering band of pink.

Mount Elgon National Park: Although much smaller than the lowland parks, the slopes of this extinct volcano, which rises to 2,000 m, offer a great range of mountain flora and fauna to the serious student of natural history.

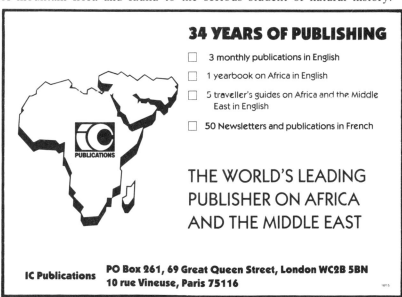

General Information

Government

Republic within the Commonwealth, with the President heading the Executive and a National Assembly forming the Legislature. It is a one party state, the ruling party being the Kenya African National Union (KANU).

Languages

KiSwahili is the national language. English is the official language of communication.

Religion

Christianity, Islam and traditional religions.

How to Get There

By air: Nairobi has a large international airport capable of taking Jumbo jets. There are regular daily services from Europe, Asia, America and other parts of Africa. Mombasa airport has now also been raised to international status and many planes go there directly. Tour operators in many European countries and in America organise all-inclusive tours.

Apart from Kenya Airways, the national airline, the following international airlines operate to and from Kenya: Aeroflot, Air Djibouti, Air France, Air India, Air Madagascar, Air Malawi, Alitalia, British Airways, Cameroon Airlines, EgyptAir, El Al, Ethiopian Airlines, KLM, Lufthansa, Olympic Airways, PIA, Sabena, SAS, Somali Airlines, Sudan Airways, Swissair, TWA, Uganda Airways, Iberia, Pan Am and Zambia Airways.

By road: Roads enter Kenya from Uganda, Tanzania and Ethiopia. A valid driving licence from the visitor's own country is acceptable for up to 90 days but it should be endorsed for Kenya at a local police station. Visitors bringing in vehicles with other than Ugandan or Tanzanian registration must, within seven days of arrival in Kenya, acquire an international circulation permit from the Licensing Officer, Nairobi. This will be issued free of charge on production of (a) an international certificate of motor vehicles; (b) a fiscal permit of customs duty receipt; and (c) a certificate of insurance (third party). For further information, apply to the Registrar of Motor Vehicles, Gill House, Government Road, Nairobi (PO Box 30440), or from any District Commissioner's office.

By sea: Occasional passenger ships come to Mombasa from Europe and America. Short-distance ships ply between Mombasa and Dar es Salaam and Zanzibar.

Entry Regulations

All visitors must have a valid passport and onward air ticket. Visas are required by all visitors except British and Commonwealth citizens and nationals of Australia, Barbados, Botswana, Canada, Ceylon, Cyprus, Denmark, Eire, Ethiopia, Gambia, Germany FR, Ghana, Guyana, India, Italy, Jamaica, Lesotho, Malawi, Malaysia, Maldive Is., Mauritius, New Zealand, Nigeria, Norway, W. Somoa, San Marino, Sierra Leone, Singapore, Spain, Swaziland, Sweden, Tanzania, Trinidad, Turkey, Uganda, Uruguay and Zambia. A visitors pass is issued free on arrival, valid for three months. Yellow fever certificates are necessary for those travelling from infected areas.

Customs Regulations

Duty-free articles are: used personal

effects, cameras, unexposed films, 250 kg of tobacco or the equivalent in cigarettes, and limited quantities of alcohol and perfume. Firearms and ammunition require a police permit before they are released from customs.

There is no restriction on imported foreign currency but it should be declared on arrival. A record must be kept of all foreign currency exchange during a visit; this may be required on departure. No tourist may take out more than the amount of foreign currency brought in. No Kenyan currency may be taken into or out of the country. There have been prosecutions following incidents at the airport, so make sure you are aware of current regulations.

Climate

The coast is tropical and hot (21°C-32°C) but the humidity is relieved by monsoon winds from January to November. The hottest months are February-March and the coolest June-July. The best season for visitors is September-October. Rain can fall at any time but the wettest months are April, May and November. The lowland belt behind the coast is hot but dry.

The highlands, despite being on the equator, enjoy a temperate, invigorating climate. In Nairobi, for example, temperatures vary from 10°C-28°C. There are four seasons: January-March – a warm, sunny dry season; March-June – the long rains; June-September – cool, cloudy, dry season; October-December – the short rains. Near Lake Victoria the temperature is hotter (16°C-30°C) and rainfall can be high.

What to wear: On the coast – beach clothes, cool cottons and linens. Synthetic fabrics should be avoided. A woollen sweater may be useful in the early morning. An umbrella is more convenient than a raincoat.

In the highlands summer clothes are also worn all the year round. A warm jacket and light raincoat are advisable.

Dress is generally informal but some of the larger city hotels may require a jacket and tie for evening wear.

Health Precautions

Kenya has in general a very healthy climate but it is strongly advised to take prophylactic tablets against Malaria two weeks before departure. Tap water may be safely drunk in the main centres. Swimming is, of course, popular in the sea – the reef keeps out the sharks – but should be avoided in rivers and lakes because of bilharzia.

The East African Flying Doctor Services have introduced a special Tourist Membership which guarantees that any member injured or seriously ill while on safari in East Africa can call on the Flying Doctor for free air transport to a medical centre (Flying Doctors' Society headquarters, PO Box 30125, tel: 27281, Nairobi). There are public and private hospitals in Mombasa and Nairobi. Elsewhere health facilities are limited.

Banks and Currency

Central Bank of Kenya, PO Box 30463, Nairobi tel: 26431.
Kenya Commercial Bank, Moi Ave, Nairobi, tel: 339441
National Bank of Kenya Ltd, Harambee Ave, Nairobi, tel: 26471
Bank of Credit and Commerce International, PO Box 44080, Nairobi, tel: 333826
Barclays Bank of Kenya Ltd, Mama Ngina St, Nairobi, tel: 23161
Commercial Bank of Africa Ltd, Standard St, Nairobi, tel: 340200
First National Bank of Chicago, Mama Ngina St, Nairobi
Grindlays Bank International Ltd, Kenyatta Ave, Nairobi, tel 335888
Habib Bank Ltd, PO Box 83055, Nkrumah Rd, Fort Mansion, Mombasa
Standard Bank Ltd, PO Box 30003, Nairobi, tel 331210
Currency: Kenya shilling (Sh) divided

into 100 cents. (See currency table, page 9).

Business Hours

Banks: Monday-Friday 0900-1400, First and last Saturdays each month 0900-1100. The airport banks are open until midnight every day.
Shops: Monday-Saturday 0830-1230 and 1400-1630
Government Offices: Coast Province Monday-Friday 0745-1200 and 1400-1600; Saturdays 0745-1200. Other Areas Monday-Friday 0815-1245 and 1400-1630; Saturday 0815-1215.
Bar-licensing hours: 1100-1400 and 1700-2300

Public Holidays

New Year's Day, 1 January
Good Friday, 13 April 1990
Easter Monday, 16 April 1990
Ramadan Begins, 27 March 1990
Labour Day, 1 May
Eid el-Fitr, 26/28 April 1990
Madaraka (date of self-government), 1 June
Kenyatta Day, 20 October
Republic Day, 12 December
Christmas Day, 25 December
Boxing Day, 26 December

Embassies in Nairobi

Argentina: tel: 335242
Australia: Development House, Moi Ave, tel: 334666
Austria: City House, Wabera St, tel: 28281
Belgium: Silopark House, Mama Ngina St
Burundi: Extelcoms House, Halle Selassie Ave
Canada: Comcraft House, Haile Selassie Ave, tel: 34033
Denmark: Hughes Bldg, Kenyatta Ave, tel: 331088
Egypt: Chai House, Koinange St, tel: 25591
Ethiopia: State House Ave
Finland: Diamond Trust House, Moi Ave, tel: 334777
France: Embassy House, Harambee Ave, tel: 339783
Germany FR: Embassy House, Harambee Ave, tel: 26661
Italy: Prudential Assurance Bldg Wabera St
Japan: Wabera St, tel 332955
Lesotho: International Life House, Mama Ngina St
Liberia: Bruce House, Standard St
Malawi: Gateway House, Moi Ave
Netherlands: Uchumi House, Nkrumah Ave
Nigeria: Kencom House, Moi Ave
Norway: Rehani house, Kenyatta Ave, tel: 337121
Rwanda: International Life House, Mama Ngina St, tel: 334341
Somalia: International Life House, Mama Ngina St
Spain: Bruce House, Standard St
Sudan: ICDC House, Moi Ave, tel: 720853
Swaziland: Silopark House, Moi Ave
Sweden: International Life House, Mama Ngina St, tel: 29042
Switzerland: International Life House, Mama Ngina St
UK: Bruce House, Standard St, tel: 335944
USA: Cotts House, Wabera St, tel: 334141
Zaire: Electricity House, Harambee Ave
Zambia City Hall Annexe, Muindi Mbingu St

Transport

By air: Kenya Airways operates an extensive internal service, including scheduled flights to Mombasa, Malindi and Kisumu. There are private airlines (e.g. Sunbird) operating light aircraft to small airstrips. Planes can also be chartered (Air Kenya, PO Box 30357, Nairobi; Sunbird, PO Box 30103,

Lamu seafront

Nairobi; Africair, PO Box 45646; Ticair, PO Box 146, Malindi).

By rail: Kenya Railways Corporation (PO Box 30121, Nairobi) runs passenger trains between Nairobi and Mombasa and regular connections to Kisumu and to Malaba; and along branch lines to Nyeri, and Nanyuki. Modern first- and second-class rolling stock provide comfortable accommodation convertible for night travel and third-class also exists.

By road: All major roads are now tarred and many of the other murram surfaces have been improved, but vast areas of the north still have little means of communication. Care should be taken when leaving trunk roads as the surfaces of the lesser roads vary in quality, especially in the rainy season. Petrol stations are fairly frequent on the highways. East African Road Services Ltd (PO Box 30475, Nairobi) provide bus services from Nairobi to major towns in Kenya.

Kenya is very well served by long-distance taxis (carrying seven passengers). The most efficient of these services are between Nairobi and Nakuru and Nairobi and Mombasa. Taxis and mini-buses are an easy method of travel on the coast.

Hitch-hiking is possible, but not recommended.

Car hire: Self-drive and chauffeur-driven cars may be hired from a number of travel agents in Nairobi, Mombasa and Malindi.

Tours and safaris: Many tour companies in Nairobi offer package arrangements for visits to the game parks and other attractions. Before booking it is important to know what the all-in prices do *not* cover. Travel to Tanzania from Kenya is not normally permitted and should be checked. Tanzanian tour operators are based in Arusha. Apart from regular photographic safaris the larger operators offer special tours for groups of 15 or more with common interest whether ornithology, mineralogy, trout fishing, archaeology or gambling.

113

Accommodation and Food

A full range of acommodation is available, from small 'up-country' hotels, which offer basic services (you pay when you book in) and which if carefully selected offer clean, friendly and inexpensive accommodation, to international-standard hotels. The popular resorts all have modern luxury hotels mostly with there own swimming pools. There are also smaller beachside hotels. Private houses and chalets (service included) can be rented. All the game parks have comfortable safari lodges as well as permanent tented camps. Privately owned camping sites have been established in some parts of the country. For information about hostels, write to: Kenya Youth Hostels Association, Hon. Gen. Secretary, Mr. N.B. Shah, PO Box 48661, Nairobi, tel: 21789.

We have included a small selection of Kenya's hotels in this book; a full list can be obtained from the Kenyan Tourist Office. Hotels are classified by the Ministry of Tourism according to elaborate guidelines. They are first divided into three different groups: town hotels, vacation hotels, lodges and country hotels. Within each category they are graded according to amenities, variety of facilities, etc. The rating award is subject to the fulfilment of severe requirements covering technical equipment, comfort, services, sanitation and security.

Kenya's national dishes appear on most hotels menus although for modern tastes meat has been added to the traditional grain and milk diet. The country's beef, chicken, lamb and pork are outstandingly good, as are the wide variety of tropical fruits: pawpaws, mangoes, avocados, bananas, oranges and grapefruit. Local trout, Nile perch and, on the coast, lobster, shrimps and Mombasa oysters are delicious.

The larger towns have restaurants serving continental and oriental dishes.

Hotels

NAME	ADDRESS	TELEPHONE	TELEX
NAIROBI			
Ambassadeur*****	Moi Ave, POB 30399	336803	22223
Boulevard***	Harry Thuku Rd, POB 42831	27567/8/9	22086
Devon Hotel	Westlands Rd, POB 41123	74868, 742813, 742600	
Fairview***	Bishops Rd, POB 40842	723211, 722878	25584
Heron Court Hotel***	POB 41848	720740/4	
Hilton International*****	Mama Ngina St, POB 30624	334000	22252
Intercontinental*****	City Hall Way, POB 30353	335550	22631
Jacaranda***	Chiromo Rd, POB 14287	742272/6	23295
Meridian Court Hotel***	POB 54673	330918	22779
Milimani***	Milimani Rd, POB 30715	720760	22613

[Hotels]

Nairobi Safari Club*****	University Way, POB 43564	330621	25391
New Stanley*****	Kimathi St, POB 30680	333233	22223
Norfolk*****	Harry Thuku Rd, POB 40064	335422	22559
Panafric****	Kenyatta Ave, POB 30486	720822	22454
Safari Park Hotel***	Thika Rd, POB 45038	802311, 802611	22114
Serena (Nairobi)*****	Kenyatta Ave, POB 46302	337978	22377
Six-Eighty****	Kenyatta Ave, POB 43436	332680	22513
Utalii Hotel*****	Thika Rd, POB 31067	335597, 802540	22509

[Hotels]

COAST HOTELS

Hotels below sometimes give Nairobi address, where bookings can be made, rather than local address.

MOMBASA TOWN

Castle Hotel**	POB 84231	23403, 21683	
Manor Hotel**	POB 84851	21821/2, 314643	
Mombasa Hilton*****	POB 30624	334000	22252
New Outrigger Hotel**	POB 82345	315810/2	21368

SOUTH COAST

African Sea Lodge*****	POB 84616	01261-2021/5	22591
Diani Reef*****	POB 35, Ukunda	01261-2175/7	21078
Diani Sea Lodge***			
Golden Beach*****	POB 31, Ukunda	01261-2054/9	21226
Jadini Beach****	POB 84616, Mombasa	01261-2021/5	22591
Leisure Lodge	POB 84383, Mombasa	01261-2011/4	21184
Leopard Beach*****	POB 34, Ukunda	01261-2110/3	21169
Robinson Baobab****	POB 32, Ukunda	01261-2026/8	21132
Safari Beach****	POB 90690	01261-2726	22591
Trade Winds***	POB 90604, Mombasa	25509, 20627/8	21018

[Hotels]

Two Fishes****	POB 90604, Mombasa	25509, 20627/8	21018

NORTH COAST

Nyali

Mombasa Beach*****	POB 90414, Mombasa	471861	21186
Nyali Beach Hotel*****	POB 90581, Mombasa	471551, 471567	
Reef Hotel*****	POB 82234, Mombasa	471771/6	21199

Bamburi

Bamburi Beach***	POB 83966, Mombasa	485611/12/13	21181
Neptune*** Ocean View*** Severin Plaza*****	POB 83125	485701/5	21386
Severin Sea Lodge****	POB 82169, Mombasa	485721	
Whitesands****	POB 90173, Mombasa	485926/69	21175

Shanzu

Serena Beach*****	POB 90352, Mombasa	485721/4	21220
Intercontinental*****	POB 83492, Mombasa	485811/5	21153

Kikambala

Whispering Palms***	POB 90604, Mombasa	22509, 20627/8	21018
Sun 'N Sand***	POB 2	Kikambala 8	21423

Malindi

Blue Marlin***	POB 54, Malindi	4	
Driftwood**	POB 63, Malindi	20155	21065
Eden Roc***	POB 350, Malindi	8 or 91	21225

[Hotels]

Lawfords***			
Sea Horse***			
Seafarers***			
Sinbad****	POB 30, Malindi	20880	21175
Suli Suli***			

Watamu

Ocean Sports**	POB 340, Malindi	Watamu 8	
Turtle Bay Beach Hotel***	POB 457	Watamu 3/80	21074

Lamu

Peponi Hotel***	POB 24, Lamu	29	
Pctlcys Inn***	POB 24, Lamu	48	

GAME LODGES AND COUNTRY HOTELS

Mount Kenya/Aberdares

Aberdeen County Club***			
Green Hills Hotel***			
Outspan***	POB 47557, Nairobi	335807	22146
Mountain Lodge*****	POB 30471, Nairobi	336858	22033
Naro Moru River Lodge***	POB 18, Naro Moru	23	22591
Mount Kenya Safari Club*****	POB 54546, Nairobi	333232	22016
Treetops*****	POB 47557, Nairobi	335807	22146
The Ark*****	POB 59749, Nairobi	335900/887	

Samburu/Buffalo Springs/Shaba National Reserve/Meru National Park

Samburu Lodge*****	POB 47557, Nairobi	335807	22146

[Hotels]

Samburu Serena Lodge	POB 48690	338656	22878
Buffalo Springs Tented	POB 30471, Nairobi	336858	22033
Maralal Safari Lodge*****	POB 42475	25641, 25941	
Meru Mulika Lodge***	POB 42013, Nairobi	29751, 330820	22033
River Lodge Samburu***			

Lake Baringo

Lake Baringo Club***	POB 47557, Nairobi	335807	22146
Thomsons Falls Lodge***			

Lake Naivasha/Nakuru

Lake Naivasha Hotel***	POB 15, Naivasha	11	
	POB 47557, Nairobi	335807	22146
Safariland Lodge***	POB 41178, Nairobi	27930/39	22228
Lake Nakuru Lodge***	POB 70559, Nairobi	220225, 26778	22658
Sarova Lion Hill	POB 30680, Nairobi	333233	22223

Masai Mara National Reserve

Keekorok Lodge*****	POB 47557, Nairobi	335807	22146
Mara Serena Lodge*****	POB 48690, Nairobi	338656/57	22878
Governor's Camp (Class A)	POB 48217, Nairobi		
Fig Tree Camp (Class A)	POB 40683, Nairobi	21439, 20592	22401
Kichwa Tembo Camp (Class A)			
Mara Buffalo Camp (Class A)			
Mara Intrepid Camp (Class A)			
Cottar's Camp (Class B)	POB 41178, Nairobi	27930/39	22228
Sarova Mara	POB 30680, Nairobi	333233	22223

[Hotels]

Lake Turkana/Sibioli National Park/Marsabit National Reserve

Lake Turkana Lodge	POB 41078, Nairobi	226623, 26808	22120
Marsabit Lodge	POB 42013, Nairobi	29751, 23488	22033

Amboseli National Park

Amboseli New Lodge***	POB 30139 Nairobi	337510	22371
Amboseli Serena Lodge*****	POB 48690, Nairobi	338656/57	22878
Kilimanjaro Buffalo*****	POB 72630, Nairobi	336088, 336724	22479
Kilimanjaro Safari Lodge***	POB 30139, Nairobi	337510, 332334	22371

Tsavo National Park

Kilaguni Lodge*****	POB 30471, Nairobi	336858	22033
Ngulia Camp (Class A)	POB 30471	336858	
Ngulia Lodge*****	POB 30471, Nairobi	336858	22033
Salt Lick Lodge*****	POB 30624	334000	
Tsavo Inn (Class B)	POB Mtito Andei	1Y1	
Tsavo Safari Camp***	POB 30139, Nairobi	337510	22371
Taita Hills Lodge*****	POB 30624, Nairobi	334000	22252
Voi Safari Lodge*****	POB 30471, Nairobi	336858	22033

Some of the more enterprising game park lodges serve gazelle, impala, eland, kudu and buffalo steaks marinaded in local liqueurs and berries and garnished with wild honey and cream. Of the local spirits, try Mount Kenya Liqueur, made to a secret formula from the country's finest coffee.

Tipping: Usually about 10% except when there is already a service charge; then an additional small tip can be made at the visitor's discretion.

Nairobi

Nairobi – a Masai word meaning 'place of

119

cool waters' – is the largest city in East and Central Africa and one of the most beautiful 'international' cities in the world. Rightly called the 'City of Flowers', its high altitude, healthy climate, fertile soil and sunshine all favour the growth of tropical and temperate flowers and plants. Graceful jacaranda trees and bright bougainvillea line with main streets.

An international commercial and communications centre, it is the only city in the world which can boast of a National Park, teeming with its original wildlife, just 8 km from the city centre. It is the headquarters of the United Nations Environment Programme secretariat. With its hotels and new conference centre and numerous direct, daily flights to and from all parts of the world, Nairobi is a popular venue for major international meetings. It is a place to combine business with pleasure; the exhilarating climate is suitable for both.

Large areas of Nairobi are taken up by spacious parks and gardens. The city area covers 700 sq km, most of it beautiful stretches of open countryside, forest areas and small cultivated farms. A drive through the outer suburbs like Langata, Karen and Limuru will show you fine houses set among exotic trees in large gardens with sweeping lawns and colourful flowerbeds. The main thoroughfares are crowded only for brief rush-hour periods. The traffic is orderly, the main shopping streets and places of interest are within walking distance of the central hotels and it is easy to find your way around. You can sit in open-air cafes and watch the city's unhurried cosmopolitan life.

The most favoured spot is The Thorn Tree at the New Stanley Hotel. At night you can wine, dine and dance, if you choose, in luxurious surroundings.

The visitor rarely sees the 'other side' of Nairobi, where there is poor housing, overcrowding, massive unemployment and occasional violence, but a short trip down River Road in daylight gives a flavour of the area where most of Nairobi's people live – in a constant struggle for survival.

Restaurants: The best hotels offer a high standard of food and service, while the country hotels around Nairobi specialise in excellent food in beautiful surroundings. There are numerous retaurants and snack bars in and around the city, although some close early in the evening and other are not open on Saturday afternoons or Sundays.

The Coffee House, run by the Coffee Board of Kenya, offers the best cup of coffee in Kenya. There are a number of Chinese and Oriental restaurants as well as Italian and French-style restaurants. Some are expensive, while others are very reasonably priced for excellent food.

Entertainments: Nairobi offers a wide choice of entertainment for the visitor. The National Museum and Snake Park, situated together on Museum Hill, are well worth visiting. The Museum has a fascinating pre-history section and fine wildlife pictures. The Snake Park has 200 species of snake.

Other day-time activities include visits to local villages, where you can see displays of Kenyan culture and traditional dancing. The best displays are those given by the Bomas of Kenya at their theatre near Nairobi National Park.

Most of the major hotels have dancing with live bands or discotheques each evening. The Casino has a restaurant, bars, floor shows, dancing and gaming rooms. There are a few nightclubs which an African flavour – but unfortunately some of the best from a few years back have degenerated, with not even good music to recommend them. Kenyan popular music has not flourished – the best bands still come from Zaire.

Nairobi has a large selection of cinemas including: Kenya Cinema, 20th Century, Globe, Thika, Drive-in, Belle View (drive-in), Metropole, Cameo, Odeon, Embassy, Liberty, The Nairobi, Casino,

TAKE A GUIDE ROUND AFRICA

You can explore Africa with IC's four regional travel guides. Each pocket-sized paperback guide contains over 200 pages of comprehensive, up-to-date information on the travel and tourist facilities, handicrafts, customs regulations, hotels, currencies, climate, health, economy, culture, people and political history of the countries of each region. Each guide is fully illustrated with maps and photographs.

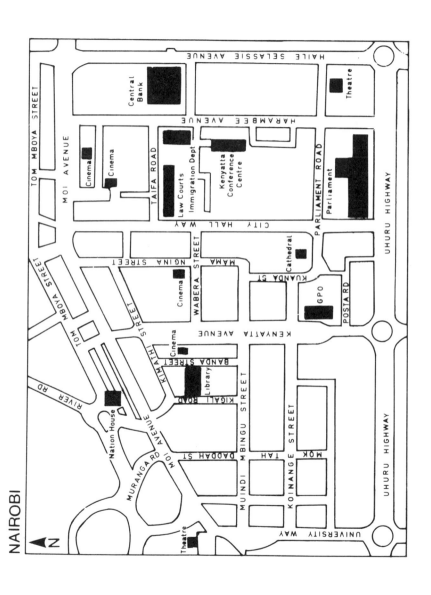

Shan and Sun City. A good selection of American, British and European films are shown. Some cinemas specialise in Indian films.

The Donovan Maule Theatre (Parliament Road) has a resident professional repertory company, consisting mainly of expatriates performing popular London hits. The Kenya National Theatre is used by a variety of groups for plays, dancing, music and other cultural activities.

The French Cultural Centre has a daily programme of theatre and films.

Sport: Kenya has splendid sports facilities. The country has produced more Olympic medallists than any other African State. The Kenya Golf Union has 30 affiliated clubs. The Muthaiga Golf Club and the Royal Nairobi have resident professionals. Others include Karen Golf Club, Limuru Country Club, Railway Golf Club and Sigona Golf Club. A municipal golf range on the Langata Road hires clubs and balls as well as providing tuition.

Ngong, Langata and Karura forests provide outstanding horse rides through tea and coffee plantations or across open country, often close to giraffe and other game. Polo is played in Nairobi and elsewhere. Racing at Ngong Road provides an enjoyable day's outing, and should not be missed. Both car and motor bike racing can be seen regularly at tracks in Nairobi and Nakuru. The Safari Rally, one of the world's toughest races, takes place during Easter.

Trout-fishing in mountain streams and angling for black bass and tilapia on the lakes can all be arranged from a Nairobi base. Sailing and water-skiing are available on Nairobi dam, although the visitor might prefer the more open and warmer waters of the Indian Ocean. There are a number of swimming pools in Nairobi.

Most sports clubs accept visitors on a reciprocal or temporary membership basis.

Shopping: Foreign goods are expensive, but local produce and services are reasonably priced. Tailors make up suits and clothing items quickly. The popular *kanga* and other brightly coloured local cottons can be bought and made up into day or evening dresses, or shirts at reasonable prices.

Near to Biashara Street, originally the Indian Bazaar area, is the Municipal Market in Market Street. The ground floor has fruit, vegetables and flowers, while the upper gallery has stalls selling African curios. Buying everything in one place usually means a better discount. Always bargain. Goods can be made to order, and most shops will pack and despatch items to overseas addresses.

Three distinctive types of carvings are worth shopping for: those made locally are the work of the Kamba who live between Nairobi and Tsavo Park; more expensive and original is the work of the Makonde from Mozambique; stone carving is a Kisii craft, usual items being vases and bowls with engraved flower and animal motifs. There are useful bowls and utensils carved in wood as well as traditional three-legged and four-legged stools, often inlaid with beadwork.

Glass beads, originally imported as a form of currency, are incorporated in jewellery and trinkets to make cheap but attractive, easy-to-carry gifts from Kenya. More difficult to carry is the decorated gourd, sometimes cut in half to form a ladle. Traditional pottery follows the shape of gourds and the genuine items are rough, but rather attractive. They are shaped by hand without the use of a wheel. Bark cloth, made from tree bark, was a traditional form of dress but is mainly used now for decorative purposes such as table mats, often with a raffia design.

The many shapes and sizes and designs of baskets make them a popular and cheap item for visitors. There are also well-made handbags, coats, jackets and rugs made from animal and reptile skins.

Gold, silver and other jewellery,

mostly from India or the Middle East, are other suitable souvenirs. Two traditional imports are rugs from Persia or India, and superb carved Arab chests from Zanzibar.

Tourist Information: The Visitors' Information Bureau in the city centre (tel: 23285) is open Monday to Friday 0830-1245 and 1400-1700. Saturday 0830-1230. The bureau has a wide range of guide books, including their Nairobi Handbook, pamphlets and maps, hotel lists and brochures.

Naivasha

Just an hour's drive from Nairobi on a scenically beautiful road, with particularly magnificent views from the top of the Limuru Escarpment, Lake Naivasha is rapidly becoming a recreational centre, with sailing, fishing, water-skiing, boats for hire, and bird-watching. More than 300 varieties of birds have been noted on the islands of this beautiful freshwater lake, including egrets, spoonbills, herons, fish eagles, crested grebes and cormorants. For those who like walking, Mount Longonot, at 3,000 m, stands overlooking the lake. The hike to the edge of the crater is a day-long trip and should only

Masai child

MIRELLA RICCIARDI

be attempted by seasoned walkers. Less arduous is the walk through the magnificent Hell's Gate. Rockclimbing and horseback-riding are also recommended in this area.

Accommodation is available at the **Lake Naivasha Hotel** and the **Safariland Lodge** (both Class B) in simple lodge-type style. Camping sites are at the Naivasha Marina, reached by taking the left turn towards the Lake Hotel on the Nairobi-Naivasha road – the Marina is a further two miles along this road. Club membership for visitors is available at the Marina for sporting facilities.

Nyeri

At an altitude of 2,000 m Nyeri is the capital of the rich agricultural Central Province. The town lies in the trough between Mount Kenya and the Aberdares, and provides an ideal centre for a holiday. A few kilometres from Nyeri are the famous game-viewing hotels, Treetops and the Ark. Trips to Mount Kenya National Park and Aberdare National Park can be arranged from the Outspan Hotel.

Nanyuki

Nanyuki is a busy farming centre at the foot of Mount Kenya and the starting-off point for excursions to the North Eastern Province. Nearby are the famous Mount Kenya Safari Club and Game Ranch, Mountain Lodge (similar to Treetops) and Secret Valley where black rhino, buffalo, sometimes leopard, elephant, and forest birds can be glimpsed from observation posts among the trees.

The Rift Valley

Nakuru is in the Rift Valley, about 230 km west of Nairobi, with which it is connected by a first-class highway, and the main railway line. Lying in the heart of the old White Highlands, it still has the air of a frontier town. Many of the buildings along the main street are single-storeyed, with a covered walkway, and the side streets often peter out very suddenly into the open grasslands of the Rift Valley. Lake Nakuru National Park just outside the town is renowned for its flamingoes (see National Park).

Above the town is the Menengai Crater, a fine example of an extinct volcano. The 'caldera' or cone is 11 km across and although the road is steep you can drive to the top in a car. The wooded crater is 400 m deep and descent is only for the adventurous. There are magnificent views of the Solai Valley, the town and the lake, and within the crater you can see steam jets and some wildlife, including giraffe and several kinds of buck.

Kisumu

Kisumu is the commercial centre of the expanding Nyanza province, an important grain-producing area. It is linked with Nairobi by a tarmac highway, passing through Kericho, the important tea centre. The section of the road through the lovely rolling Kipsigi hills is being resurfaced and is rough in places, but still provides one of the most scenically beautiful drives in the country. The **Tea Hotel** at Kericho is a good place to break your journey. The road from Kericho passes through the highly cultivated Kipsigi countryside and then drops down into the Luo country.

Kisumu stands on Lake Victoria, the second largest freshwater lake in the world. The lake steamers are running again from Kisumu to Mwanza since the Tanzania links were renewed in 1984. From Kisumu you can also visit the Olambwe Valley and Mount Elgon Game Parks. Olambwe Valley has been made into a national park and there is a lodge there.

Restaurants: There is one good restaurant specialising in Indian dishes. The local dish of lake fish (tilapia) and *ugali* can be had in any local eating-house.

Mombasa

Mombasa is Kenya's second biggest city and chief port. Combining ancient and modern, this colourful island contains two harbours and two towns. The old harbour is still used by Arab dhows from the Persian Gulf, while the commercial harbour at Kilindini is one of the most highly mechanised in Africa. The Old Town has many reminders of its stormy history, when Mombasa was named by the Arabs the 'Island of War'. But the Old Town is now an oasis of calm in an otherwise noisy and hectic city. Its labyrinth of tiny streets evokes some of the mystery and magic of the Orient. This is the original Mombasa with its numerous mosques and village atmosphere, where children play freely without danger from traffic. Modern Mombasa town is a bustling, thriving community of many different peoples and a popular resort with good hotels, splendid beaches and coral reefs nearby.

Many people regard Mombasa, rather than Nairobi, as the most interesting and exciting town in East Africa. It has everything from the luxury hotels to hordes of beggars and lepers. The sleazy nightlife reflects the city's long history as an important seaport.

To the north and south of the island-town stretch the beaches which are the basis of Kenya's sunshine holiday business. Going north from Mombasa the resorts are Nyalo, Bamburi, Shanzu, Kikambala, Kilifi, Turtle Bay-Watamu, Malindi and Lamu; to the south are Likoni, Tiwi, Diani Beach and Shimoni.

Mombasa's most prominent monument is Fort Jesus (at the end of Nkrumah Road). Built in 1593 by the Portuguese to protect the coast against Arab and Turkish raids it was attacked and besieged and changed hands many times in the 17th and 18th centuries, until the Portuguese finally abandoned it to the Arabs in 1729. It was used as a fort until 1875 when the British Navy bombarded it to repress a rebellion. Thereafter it became a prison. Fort Jesus is now a national monument and houses an excellent museum.

The Old Harbour down Mbarak Hinawy Road has been used for thousands of years by the dhows plying between East Africa and Arabia, Persia and India. Other sights include: the Hindu Temple at Mwagogo Road with its dome surfaced in pure gold and the one in Haile Selassie Road which has a brilliantly painted door showing two soldiers dressed in Indian fashion; the Ivory Room off Treasury Square, the enormous elephant tusks spanning Kilindini Road and the nearby Uhuru Fountain built in the shape of Africa and adorned with the Mombasa Coat of Arms; the fascinating industry of Wakamba woodcarvers; and numerous bazaars and markets.

Restaurants: Seafood is the speciality and is inexpensive. Reflecting its cosmopolitan history, Mombasa is well served by restaurants specialising in seafood, Arab, Indian and Middle Eastern dishes. There are places to suit most tastes from Continental and Chinese to fish-and-chips. Recommended for seafood are the **Tamarind** and the **Red Lobster.** Worth trying are the **Kenya Coffee House** and **Copper Kettle** for snacks, the **Shanghai** in Hotel Splendid and the **Hong Kong** for Chinese dishes, the **Metropolitan Hotel** for Indian curries and the **New Carlton Hotel** for seafood.

Entertainments: A short distance from town are the northern beaches. A bus from the central Bus Station can drop you outside one of the hotels along the coast road. These hotels often have facilities for sailing, fishing, water-skiing, goggling or just swimming and sunbathing.

The dhow harbour, Fort Jesus and the Old Town make fascinating visits – the latter for shopping as well as sightseeing.

The four cinemas tend to concentrate on westerns and other adventure movies when they are not showing Indian films.

The nightlife is mainly centred on the

Kilindini Road, leading from the port. Apart from the numerous bars there are half a dozen lively nightclubs.

Shopping and markets: For craft goods and tailoring the Old Town is best. Silver and goldsmiths, tailors, carvers, cabinet-makers and many others have their shop-cum-workshops here. There is a covered municipal food market and an open-air market for general merchandise. Parallel to Jomo Kenyatta Avenue is Biashara Street, the best shopping area for *kikoi, kanga, kitenge* and other cloth, basketwork and local crafts – at prices lower than the craft stalls outside hotels.

Carvings and other curios can be bought in many of the shops or from pavement vendors. To quench your thirst there are itinerant sellers of coffee and of fresh coconut milk (*madafu*).

Tourist information: The Information Centre is in Kilindini Road, close to the archway of tusks which span the road. Many of the tour operators, travel companies, airways and car-hire firms have their offices in the vicinity.

Malindi and the North Coast

Malindi is the site of one of the most ancient towns on the coast, 125 km north of Mombasa, to which it is linked by a good tarmac road. There is, however, a ferry crossing at Kilifi which can mean long delays. The resort area consists of a string of hotels spread along a sandy beach, adjacent to the old town which has interesting bazaar and market areas.

The Malindi and Watamu Marine National Parks are a unique form of environmental protection, offering the visitor a wonderful chance to see, by glass-bottomed boat, snorkeling or skin-diving, the colours of an undisturbed reef. Just outside Mombasa there are two aquaria containing shallow-water fish and deep seafish.

Driving along the road from Mombasa to Malindi the coastal scenery ranges through palm groves, citrus orchards, sisal and cotton plantations, sheep and cattle farms. All kinds of tropical fruits grow by the roadside such as pineapples and bananas.

Beyond the Kilifi creek is the Arabuko-Sokoki forest where valuable timbers like ebony grow under natural conditions and birdlife flourishes.

The picturesque beach resorts north of Mombasa are **Nyali, Kenyatta Beach** (Bamburi), **Shanzu, Kikambala, Kilifi, Turtle Bay-Watamu.** The coral barrier makes the Turtle Bay-Watamu beaches safe for swimming and encloses some of the finest fishing areas in the Indian Ocean. Nearly all the hotels listed below have facilities for fishing and other watersports.

Restaurants: All the hotels have à la carte restaurants and open air bars. Beach barbecues and dances are frequently held. Seafood is the speciality and the lobsters, prawns and fish you eat will certainly have been bought absolutely fresh only a few hours before. There is an abundance of fresh fruit and pineapples, pawpaws, bananas and mangoes will tempt you at every meal. Sunday lunch at **Ocean Sports** in Turtle Bay should not be missed.

Entertainments: The beach and the Indian ocean dominate Malindi's amusement attractions. There is excellent surfing, goggling, sailing, water-skiing and fishing. These and deep sea fishing can be arranged through the hotels and the modern boats are fully equipped with the necessary tackle and trained crews. Although there is fishing all the year round, the best game fishing is from November to March when catches of marlin, sailfish, tuna, barracuda and kingfish abound.

Temporary membership is also available at the Malindi Golf Club which in addition to a nine-hold course offers tennis, squash, bowls, obstacle golf, water-skiing, sailing and horse riding. At night the hotels have dancing and beach barbecues in a friendly and informal atmosphere.

There are many interesting places to visit in an around Malindi. Near to Watamu is the Gedi National Park and an extremely well preserved ruined city, believed to have been founded in the 13th century. The first archaeological excavation was started in 1948 but the mystery of its desertion is unsolved. The excavated buildings include the Jamaa mosque, the palace pillar tombs and a number of large private residences.

A few miles north of Malindi is the little coastal village of Mambrui where a huge ornate mosque towers above the little thatched houses.

Lamu

Away to the north is another ancient city, Lamu, which can only be reached by ferry. It is the island of the legendary Sindbad the Sailor. Normally the traveller arrives at the adjacent island of Manda by air from Mombasa, Malindi or

Nairobi. At most times of the year it is accessible by road from Malindi via Garsen and Witu; there are taxis and minibuses. Lamu is unique. By its very remoteness this island town has preserved both physically and socially the Swahili culture that flowered in the 18th century. But it also quietly prospers now, in its functions as port, district capital and tourist resort. These functions have not yet required the motor car or disfigured the town's alleyways and impressive old mansions. Traditional crafts of building, wood carving, and boat construction persist, as does the only means of transport, the small local *ngalawa*.

Lamu is also a centre of Islamic learning, with its twenty-two mosques (each with its own calls to prayer at regular intervals of the day and night) and with the continued festivals of *medrassa* music.

A look around Lamu Museum is an essential part of any visit. There are displays of Swahili costumes, furniture and some beautiful model dhows. The long contact with Arabia is very evident, and there is ancient pottery from India,

the Persian Gulf and China.

The surrounding islands of Pate and Faza are accessible for those who have a few days to spare. Nearby, and taking only a few hours there and back, are the 16th century Takwa ruins on Manda island. These ruins are contemporary with Gedi and feature a mosque and a pillar tomb. To reach the islands dhow transport can be negotiated on the Lamu seafront. You can walk to the beaches beyond Shela, a distance of 2 km, or else walk through the cultivated area behind Lamu town for a view of the local vegetation and coconut palms.

The South Coast

South from Mombasa, across the Likoni ferry and accessible by an excellent new road, are some of the most beautiful beaches of East Africa. A coral reef extends all the way down the coast, creating clear blue lagoons with safe bathing. Most of the beaches are fringed with trees. The resorts on the south coast from Mombasa are at Likoni, Tiwi, Diani Beach and Shimoni.

Zebra

MARION KAPLAN

MADAGASCAR

A country with a unique culture dating from Malayo-Polynesians perhaps 2,000 years ago, Madagascar is a combination of Africa and Indonesia. As an island it has developed independently with its own traditions, customs and religion, although it came under French influence in the colonial period. Now Madagascar is reasserting its own social and political traditions, while the Government is also attempting to forge a modern socialist state.

With its beautiful coasts, interesting wildlife and mountain scenery Madagascar is well adapted for tourism of an adventurous kind, and it is just beginning to open up. It offers many of the scenic and climatic attractions of Mauritius or the Seychelles, with greater historical interest, and without the surfeit of South African and other tourists. You will find the palatial, white-washed, French colonial, resort hotels practically deserted.

Some airlines offer cheap excursion flights from the African mainland (especially from Malawi).

Diversity and Unity

Madagascar's five major ecological regions have their own climate, vegetation and scenery. The capital Antananarivo, is set among the twelve sacred hills near the centre of the mountain massif called the Hauts Plateaux – a landscape of bare rounded hills between 1,500 and 2,000 m high.

The east coast, a narrow strip between the central mountains and the Indian Ocean, is partly covered with tropical rainforests, despite the ravages of a shifting cultivation. The west coast has large areas of dry deciduous forest but much of this has been destroyed leaving great expanses of grassland savannah dotted with Borassus palms and other secondary vegetation where huge herds of zebu cattle graze.

The southern region, south of a line drawn from Toleara to Farafangana, has the most striking vegetation. Cactus-like plants that have adapted to the semi-arid climate form great expanses of forest. Nearly all of them are indigenous to Madagascar.

The northern tip of the island forms the fifth ecological region, with its high rainfall, but abundant sunshine. This is where the popular holiday island of Nossi-be is situated, and where exotic perfume plants such as ylang-ylang are grown.

Madagascar has many great rivers, the longest being the Ikopa which runs north from Antananarivo to Mahajanga. Many of those running east have spectacular falls: Namorona and Sakaleona. There are a number of lakes: Itasy lies in a recent volcanic zone about 120 km west of Antananarivo;

Madagascar

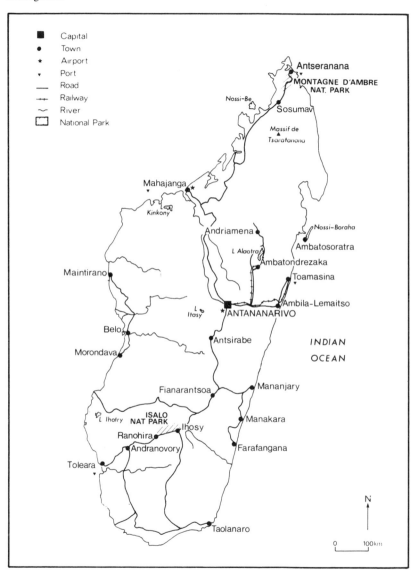

Key:
- ■ Capital
- ● Town
- ★ Airport
- ▼ Port
- — Road
- ┼┼┼ Railway
- ～ River
- ▭ National Park

Antseranana
MONTAGNE D'AMBRE
NAT. PARK
Nossi-Be
Sosumav
Massif de
Tsarafanona
Mahajanga
Kinkony
Andriamena
Nossi-Boraha
L Alaotra
Ambatosoratra
Ambatondrezaka
Maintirano
Toamasina
L Itasy
Ambila-Lemaitso
ANTANANARIVO
Belo
Antsirabe
INDIAN
OCEAN
Morondava
Fianarantsoa
Mananjary
L Ihotry
ISALO NAT PARK
Manakara
Ranohira
Ihosy
Andranovory
Farafangana
Toleara
N
Taolanaro
0   100km

Area: 587,041 sq km
Population: 11.5 million (1989 estimate)
Capital: Antananarivo

Alaotra, the largest lake, lies in a 'rift valley' parallel to the east coast; Kinkony and Ihotry are on the west coast. They are the breeding grounds of water-fowl and wild duck, and teem with many species of fish.

The Malagasy are basically of the same stock as the Malayo-Polynesians, with possible Melanesian elements. The African element in part derived from slaves imported from the mainland, and in part from early settlers.

The 'proto-Malagasy' sailed from somewhere in Indonesia, using the type of large double canoe known to have been used by the Maoris in their migrations. The immigrants came equipped with useful plants – taro, sugar-cane, bananas, coconuts – which retain their Malay-based names. Some may have sailed directly across the Indian Ocean, but most took the long route around the northern and western Indian Ocean.

There were many migrations over several centuries; resulting in a number of physical types among the people. There is, however, only one language – Malagasy – spoken in different dialects. There is also unity of custom and way of life among the 18 ethnic groups.

Of the 18 groups, the Sakalava are the most widespread and occupy the western part of the island from Mahajanga to Morandava. The Antankarana inhabit the northern part and along the east coast are the Betsimisaraka and the Antaimoro. In the south-east are the Antaisaka and the Antanosy. The Antandroy live in the south and the Bara inland. The Mahafaly live in the south-west. Along the west coast are Vezo fishermen, who travel great distances up and down the coast and into the Mozambique channel. In the central region are the Tanala, Betsileo, Merina (around Antananarivo), the Bezanozano, Sihanaka and Tsimihety.

Madagascar is an agricultural country. Rice is grown all over the island except in the arid south. Coffee, vanilla, pepper, cloves and perfume products are grown for export. Sisal, sugar-cane, maize, groundnuts and tobacco are grown for home consumption.

Culture

The Malagasy language was first written in Arabic script. Early books, called the *sora be*, were inscribed on ox-hide and contain mainly magical formulae. Some of them, dating probably from the 18th century, can be seen in the library of the *Académie Malgache*. In 1836 missionaries translated the Bible and wrote the Malagasy language in Latin Script, which is still used today.

The Malagasy are a musically gifted people. Each ethnic group has its characteristic style in dances and songs. A large number of instruments are found in the different regions, many of them closely related to similar instruments in Indonesia, others showing an African origin.

Death and ancestral spirits play a significant role in Madagascar and the funerary theme is reflected in many of the handicrafts, such as the Vezo erotic statues which are placed on tombs in the Morondava region, and the remarkable *bibi-olona* (animal-man) of the west, or the *aloalo*, the tall carved posts surmounted by figures of zebu cattle which are placed on tombs in the south.

Among the interesting souvenirs to be found are turtle shells, large mounted butterflies in frames, detailed model boats (Mahajanga, Morondava and Toleara), coral objects and along the west coast large and beautiful sea shells. The Antaimoro hand-made paper – incorporating real flowers and grasses – is obtainable in Ambalavao or in Antananarivo. Fine marquetry furniture is made in Ambositra. Weaving of raffia, baskets and straw hats is widespread. Many Malagasy work in silver, minerals and semi-precious stones. The visitor will find ornaments made of rock crystal, obsidian, petrified wood and jewels.

History

Although Madagascar has only one language and basically one culture, the physical diversity points to a fascinating mixture of origins.

The Indonesian element is assumed to stem from parties of adventurers crossing the sea between 200 BC and AD 800 in huge outrigger canoes, each capable of holding 200 people.

They brought their language (an archaic form of Malayo-Polynesian), crops and customs such as the building of the large square family tombs still found all round Antananarivo.

The northern tip of Madagascar was always an extreme limb of the Arab-dominated Indian Ocean trade, where alluvial gold and mined silver from the interior was bought and a small-scale two-way traffic in slaves grew up with East Africa.

Arabs and Swahili built towns, such as Vohemar, dating back to the 11th century, where Chinese porcelain and Persian glass have been found.

Some settled along the east coast, notably the Antaimoro who have preserved what are called 'the great writings' in Arabic-script Malagasy.

After the first Europeans rounded the Cape of Good Hope and discovered Madagascar at the beginning of the 16th century, a number of areas of the island became important as victualling posts for the ships of various European nations, led by the Portuguese, on their way to the East. The French made several attempts to form commercial centres, though without trying to take possession of the whole island by force.

Of the Malagasy 'kingdoms' those of the Betsimisaraka on the east coast and of the Sakalava on the west attained considerable power over wide areas. But both were eventually supplanted by the unified Merina kingdom which was first formed around Antananarivo by Andrianampoinimerina (1787-1810). He claimed that 'the sea is the limit of my rice-field' and took a first step towards making a reality of that idea of Madagascar being a single political unit by conquering the powerful Betsileo to the south. The Merina were a 'caste' society which used slaves to till the fields for the freemen and nobility. The latter were the craftsmen and monopolised trade with the coast.

The next king, Radama (1810-1828) had three great ambitions – to have a European-style army; to bring the rest of the island under his control with the help of that army; and to be regarded by the world as the King of Madagascar, a title which seems to have been first conferred on him by the British. He succeeded in greatly extending his control and the process was continued by his chief wife who became Queen Ranavalona (1828-1861). Radama had forwarded the work of the London Missionary Society which promoted literacy and introduced various skills. But Ranavalona and her advisers led a nationalist campaign against Europeans, driving most of them out and persecuting and killing the Malagasy Christians, in the interest of Malagasy culture and sovereignty. She did, however, encourage one specially interesting attempt at Mantasoa to make European goods with the help of an enterprising shipwrecked Frenchman, Laborde.

The island was opened up to the world again under succeeding rulers from the 1860's onwards, chiefly through the influence of the Prime Minister Rainilaiarivony. France and Britain, both of which had interests in the island, were played off against each other. Treaties were made with Britain, France and other powers. But there were special difficulties with France. After the first Franco-Malagasy War of 1883-1885 Madagascar became a French Protectorate. In 1890 Britain, to the disgust of the Malagasy who regarded the action as a betrayal, traded its main interest for French recognition of its own Protectorate in Zanzibar. After a military expedition, Madagascar became a French colony in 1896, being extensively settled by French planters.

Even before World War I there was considerable nationalist fervour among a number of intellectuals and the Merina nobility, who resented the fact that an independent Madagascar had been demoted to a 'colony'; and resented too the day-to-day effects of that subject status. The French suppressed a society generally known as VVS which they regarded as subversive, especially in war-time. After the Popular Front in France, World War II and the Atlantic Charter conditions had changed. When constitutional development was proposed the MDRM party won the 1946 elections by a large majority, with ultimate self-government as its main objective. Progress, however, was too slow for some and what was officially described as a 'rebellion' broke out in 1947 on the east side of the island (a plan proposed for the capital was aborted). In many ways this is still a sensitive area of Malagasy history, but there is an annual Remembrance Day for those who died violently at the hands of the French or through illness and malnutrition when they fled to the forest. The number lies somewhere between 12,000 and 80,000.

In the 1950's an attempt was made to stabilise and develop the damaged economy and also to extend political opportunities (*Loi Cadre*). In 1958 the former French colony and overseas territory became the Malagasy Republic within the French Community. On 26 June 1960 Madagascar was declared an independent State. The dominant political party, the PSD, was led by its founder President Tsiranana. A high proportion of key posts went to persons from areas far from the centre. The new freedom led to a proliferation of parties, the most important being the AKFM. Tsiranana adopted a conservative policy of political, economic and military co-operation with France.

Despite French planning and considerable aid, economic growth was not as great as had been expected. The dominating attitude of the PSD and some administrative methods, as well as foreign policy, were resented. A warning sign was given by a restrained 'rising' in the extreme south in 1971 which was, however, harshly suppressed. In May 1972 student and worker unrest broke out in Antananarivo and other towns, forcing Tsiranana to hand over power to the military, which radically changed the direction of Malagasy policy. Agreements with France were revised or abrogated, links with South Africa severed, and approaches made to Eastern countries.

A political and economic crisis in the first half of 1975 produced a new government headed by a naval officer, Didier Ratsiraka. Following Ratsiraka's Revolutionary Charter, several political parties are allowed to exist, but policy is formulated and applied by the Supreme Revolutionary Council. Land reform is being extended and an extensive range of State companies control the key sectors of the economy. The government's aim is to create a socialist society by the year 2000.

Economy

Over 85 out of every 100 Malagasy live in rural conditions, with their main interests lying in agriculture and stock-raising. The most important crop is rice, which forms the staple diet. A high rate of increase in population still requires that some rice must be imported; though special high grades are exported to obtain foreign currency. On the east coast, coffee and vanilla are the main crops; on the west, cotton, beans and sugar.

There is a wide variety of minerals, but often in small, scattered, uneconomic quantities. Graphite and mica are important and there are large

Madagascar country scene

CAMERA PRESS

bauxite deposits. In January 1980 President Ratsiraka announced the discovery of oil and gas off the south-east coast in Morondava Basin. Four major oil companies are now involved in prospection.

There is some light industry and an attempt is being made to produce many goods locally to save imports; for example, cloth, paper and cement. A number of major companies have been nationalised; the use of State-run organisation is being extended. An unfavourable balance of payments has been reduced by strict controls, causing shortages of some goods. The IMF has been heavily involved in an economic adjustment programme since May 1982.

Wildlife

Madagascar's mammals and birds evolved before the separation of the island from the mainland of Africa some 20 million years ago, but there are many species unique to the island. The best-known animals are the lemurs with their fox-like heads. They climb trees and leap among the tree-tops.

The fosa is related to the civet, it is the size of a large dog. It inhabits the forests and feeds on poultry. There are a number of small mammals of interest to zoologists. The 'African' animals found on the island are crocodile, bush-pig, and guinea-fowl.

The prehistoric fish, the coelacanth, is found in the Mozambique Channel. Madagascar is poor in freshwater fish but carp, tilapia and black bass have been used to stock the lakes and rivers, and good line-fishing is available.

The birds of Madagascar are distinctive. Out of about 300 species, 67 are indigenous. About 1,200 years ago the biggest bird in the world lumbered through the tropical forests. *Aepyornis maximus* was three metres tall and weighed half a ton. The Académie Malgache has a museum of fossils.

Many of the island's strange flora and fauna can be seen in the park and zoo at Tsimbazaza in Antananarivo.

National Parks

Isalo: Lying to the north of the road from Antananarivo to Toleara, just after Ranohira (about 800 km), Isalo is situated in a spectacular chain of sandstone mountains. Camping is possible, but access should be by four-wheel-drive or on foot, with a guide from Ranohira. Official permission may be required.

The park contains some extensive caves, including the Grottes des Portugais where shipwrecked Portuguese sailors apparently lived in the 16th century.

Montagne d'Ambre: This is a rainforest park around the summit of the 1,475 m tertiary volcano in the region of Antseranana (Diego Suarez). The peak receives about 5,000 mm of rain per annum. The forest contains many orchids and lemurs. Access is by forest paths or on foot from Joffreville, 32 km west of Antseranana.

General Information

Government

Military-backed Supreme Revolutionary Council (CSR) with executive power. A People's National Assembly acts as adviser to the CSR.

Languages

Malagasy (with different dialects) and French.

Religions

Christianity, traditional beliefs and Islam.

How to Get There

By air: Direct and regular flights from Europe. From Paris by Air France and Air Madagascar; from Rome by Alitalia and Air Madagascar. Regional flights from Nairobi, Dar es Salaam, Djibouti, Lilongwe, Maputo, Reunion and Mauritius.

By sea: There are 18 ports, including four for long-distance calls: Toamasina, Antseranana, Mahajanga and Toleara.

Entry Regulations

Visitors require a valid passport and visa except nationals of Lesotho, Malawi and Tanzania. Visas can be obtained from the consular section of the Malagasy Embassy, 7 Boulevard Suchet, Paris 16, France, tel: 504.18.16. Early application is advised.

Visitors require international certificates of vaccination against cholera and yellow fever if coming from endemic areas. Enquiries as to current regulations should be made before travelling.

Customs Regulations

Any amount of foreign currency may be taken into the country, but visitors are advised not to cash more travellers' cheques than they need, as reconversion of Malagasy currency into sterling or dollars is impossible. You can take 500 cigarettes, 25 cigars or 50 grms of tobacco into the country as well as one bottle of alcohol. However there is no free import of perfume.

Climate

A hot and rainy season from November to March and a cooler dry season from April to October. On the west coast the dry season lasts for about seven months; the south-west is hot, dry and semi-arid. The monsoon is between December and March.

What to wear: Clothing depends very much on the area. On the high central tableland in summer lightweight clothing, with something warmer for the evenings, is recommended. The weather can turn quite chilly, so a warm overcoat is useful. Dress is normally informal, although one may be expected to look reasonably smart in the evening in the bigger hotels.

On the coast and in the north and south light clothing is required all the year round. Because of the climatic variations, raincoats and umbrellas should not be forgotten.

Health Precautions

On the central highlands there are very few mosquitoes, but they exist elsewhere in the island so it is wise to take a prophylactic. Mosquito nets are usually provided in the big hotels along the coast but if camping, bring your own.

Care should be taken to sterilise

drinking water, except in the main town where it is treated. Many lakes and paddy fields are infected with bilharzia.

Banks and Currency

Banque Centrale de Madagascar: ave. de la Revolution, BP 550, Antananarivo
Bankin'ny Indostria (BNI) 74 Rue du 26 Juin, Antananarivo
Bankin'ny Tantsaha Mpamokatra (BTM): Place de l'Indépendence, BP 183, Antananarivo.

It is worth noting that these banks will change 'Euro-cheques'.
Currency: Malagasy franc (FMG)
(See currency table, page 9).

Business Hours

Banks: Monday-Friday 0800-1100 and 1400-1600
Offices: Monday-Friday 0800-1130 and 1400-1730; Saturday 0800-1200
Shops: Monday-Saturday 0800-1200 and 1400-1800.
Many local grocers are open on Sunday morning.

Public Holidays

New Year's Day, 1 January
Memorial Day, 29 March
Good Friday, 13 April 1990
Easter Monday, 16 April 1990
Labour Day, 1 May
Ascension Day, 24 May 1990
Whit Monday, 4 June 1990
Independence Day, 26 June
Assumption Day, 15 August
All Saints' Day, 1 November
Christmas Day, 25 December
Anniversary of the Republic,
   30 December

Embassies in Antananarivo

Egypt: 47 Avenue Lenin, tel: 25233
France: 3 rue Jean Jaures, BP 204
Germany FR: 101 route circulaire, Ambodirotra, tel: 23802
UK: Immeuble Ny Havana, BP 167, tel 27749
USA: 14 Lalana Rainitovo, Antsahavola

Transport

By road: In Antananarivo transport is fairly plentiful. Taxis will go anywhere in town – they have no meters and prices are fixed below a certain mileage, and above that you will have to haggle with the driver. After 8pm double tariff is charged. It is not customary to tip taxi drivers. There are also bus services in Antananarivo, but these can sometimes be confusing, Air Route Services ATO operates buses between Avato airport and Antananarivo.

In Toamasina, Mahajanga, Antserana-na and other towns the *pousse-pousse* – a kind of rickshaw – is common. These are very cheap and the driver usually expects

Street market

JAN KOPEC

137

a tip.

Road transport between towns exists in a number of forms. The most common are the *taxi-brousse* and the *taxibe*. These travel the main roads between Antananarivo and the provinces and link main towns. Fares are usually reasonable, but do not expect great comfort.

Car hire: Hertz, 31 Avenue de l'Indépendence, BP 4152, Antananarivo, tel: 233-36. Avis, Madagascar Hilton.

By rail: The railway system is not extensive but does provide services between Antanarivo and Toamasina, stopping at the towns along the line.

There are also rail links between Antananarivo and Ambatosoratra and Antsirabe, and Fianarantsoa and Manakara. These journeys are slow, but are usually through picturesque country, particularly so between Manakara and Fianarantsoa.

Trains do not always manage to leave at the advertised time, so be prepared for long waits at the station.

By air: Internal flights by Air Madagascar cover the whole country, serving over 35 airfields, including all the main towns. All flights are heavily booked and it is important to get to the airport on time.

Good day, how are you?	*Akory hianao, tompoko; manao ahoana hianao?*
Well, thank you	*Tsara fa misaotra*
Goodbye	*Veloma, tompoko*
Yes	*eny*
No	*tsia*
Which road goes to . . .?	*aiza ny lalana mankany . . .?*
I/We are going to . . .	*mandeha ho any . . . aho/izahay*
how much?	*hoatrinona?*
one franc	*iraimbilanja*
five francs (dollar)	*ariary*
ten francs (two dollars)	*ariary roa*
water	*rano*
food, meal	*sakafo*
rice	*vary*
coffee	*kafe*
tea	*dite*

Accommodation and Food

In most towns you will find hotels and restaurants of varying degress of quality serving French, Italian, Indian, Indonesian, Chinese, Vietnamese or Arab food.

It is practially impossible to sample good Malagasy cooking unless invited to a private house. Malagasy will invite a foreigner if they are quite sure their food will be appreciated but such a degree of acquaintance takes time.

Hotely Gasy – which means both hotel and restaurant – are to be found almost everywhere. They are usually small and cheap, providing a rice and meat dish. These establishments are essentially Malagasy and are not tourist-orientated, although the proprietor will be happy to welcome foreigners. But don't be fooled by the name – very often there is no sleeping accommodation.

Tipping: In the European-style hotels and restaurants the French custom of tipping is followed. One should also tip in Chinese and Vietnamese establishments, but in the *Hotely Gasy* tips are not usually expected.

Hotels

NAME	ADDRESS	TELEPHONE	TELEX
ANTANANARIVO			
Acropole	–	233.80	–
Colbert	BP 341, 29 rue Prinsty-Ratsimananga	202.02	22248
de France	BP 607, 34 Ave de l'Independence	202.93	22322
Madagascar Hilton	BP 959	260.60	22261
Mélisse	central	–	–
Motel Agip	BP 3850, Anosy	250.40	–
Select	BP 1741, Ave du 18 juin	210.01	–
Terminus	central	–	–
ANTSERANANA (DIEGO-SUAREZ)			
Nouvel	–	162	–
de la Poste	BP 121	44	–
Tropical	–	323	–
ANTSIRABE			
Truchet	BP 47	480.36	–
FIANARANTSOA			
Chez Papillon	–	–	–
MAHAJANGA (MAJUNGA)			
de France	BP 45	26.07	–
les Roches Rouges	Blvd Marcoz, BP 481	21.61	--

NOSSI-BE			
Holiday Inn	Nossi-Be	61176	87206
Palm Beach	Nossi-Be	–	–
TAOLANARO (FORT DAUPHIN)			
le Dauphin	BP 54	138	–
de France	BP 8	–	–
Motel Libanoana	Libanoana	136	–
TOAMASINA (TAMATAVE)			
les Flamboyants	ave de la Libération	323.50	–
Joffre	–	323.90	–
TOLEARA (TULEAR)			
le Capricorne	ave de Belemboka, BP 158	295	–
le Coquillage	–	125	–
le Tropical	–	69	

Antananarivo

Antananarivo means the 'town of a thousand men' but if it were named for the number of steps and stairways it would be more apt – there are certainly more than a thousand of them. The tall, balconied brick houses closely pack the steep sides of a horseshoe-shaped hill, and most are only approachable by narrow stone staircases and a maze of footpaths.

The capital is built on three levels. At the highest point is the sacred hill, graced by the Queen's Palace which commands a view over the city and dominates the scenery for miles around. On the lowest level, between the two arms of the horseshoe, lies Lake Anosy and the great market of Analakely. The *Zoma*, the main market, is held every day, but on Fridays the stalls multiply and spill over most of the town centre. *Zoma* means Friday and has become synonymous with the market. Everything is sold here from poultry, fruit and vegetables to a great variety of handicrafts. Beware of pick-pockets and handbag snatchers in the market.

Other parts of the town have their markets too – Andravoahangy on Wednesdays, Mahamasina on Thursdays and Isotry on Saturdays.

Places of Interest: The Queen's Palace is now a national monument and well worth a visit. Centuries before the French colonised Madagascar, Merina monarchs created the Rova, the royal village, on the sacred peak. The Palace is a fantastic network of wood and stone with beautiful panelling inside. Other palaces in the Rova closely resemble Indonesian architecture. Near the Queen's Palace is an Italian-style church, designed by William Pool, an English architect, for Queen Ranavalona II. Madagascar Airtours offer tours of the *Zoma*, the Queen's Palace, Botanical gardens and Antananarivo by night.

The countryside for 200 km around Antananarivo is varied and beautiful. Accessible by moderately good roads, there are several places worth a visit, such as the former royal residence of Ambohimanga (20 km) and Lake Itasy (120 km), the falls of Tsinjoarivo (120 km), and Lake Mantasoa (40 km). In the sub-tropical climate, walking is pleasant and the surrounding hills and villages are easily reached on foot.

Entertainments: There are a few nightclubs.

Tourist information: Office National du Tourisme de Madagascar, BP 610, Place d'Ambohij-Atovo, Antananarivo; Madagascar Airtours, Galerie Marchande Hilton, tel: 265.15; Transcontinents, 10 Avenue de l'Indépendance, tel: 233.98.

Antsirabe

Developed by the French after 1923 when the railway was extended south from Antananarivo (167 km), Antsirabe is a four-hour train journey from the capital. At about 1,600 m above sea level Antsirabe is a cooling spot, getting the occasional frost in June and July. It is situated near to Tsiafajavona, the second highest mountain in Madagascar (2,600 km), and has a distinctly European appearance, with many villas on the outskirts which might be in Normandy or a Paris suburb.

Antsirabe is especially famed for its thermal springs, earning it the name of the 'Malagasy Vichy'. Not far from the centre of town is the Swiss-like Lake Andraikiba. In the region is the strange volcanic lake of Tritriva.

Fianarantsoa

South on the tarred road to Tulear, Fianarantsoa is 407 km from Antananarivo and 1,370 km above sea level. The hill on which the town was built gave it is original name: Vognea, but Queen Ranavalona I ordered a new city to be built and gave it the name it has borne ever since. Fianarantsoa means 'the city where one learns the good life', or just 'happiness'. It is the centre of a rich agricultural region in which rice and coffee are important.

Toamasina (Tamatave)

This well laid out town is Madagascar's chief port. The straight, broad streets are shaded with royal palms and flame trees and the sea-front is lined with casuarinas. It is an eight-hour drive from Antananarivo (or 14-hour train journey) through beautiful mountainous country of forests and coffee plantations. Toamasina is the centre for the export of cloves, vanilla, raffia, coffee, groundnuts, graphite and mica.

The town has a large well-stocked market with many handicrafts. The sea around Toamasina is shark-infested and it is not advisable to bathe off any of the beaches. A beautiful island with excellent swimming lies up the coast from Toamasina. Known as Nossi Boraha or Ile St. Marie, it has hotel accommodation and is served by flights from Antananarivo.

Mahajanga (Majunga)

On the west coast, Mahajanga is the second largest port of Madagascar but it is rapidly silting up with red soil brought down from the deforested Hauts Plateaux by the Ikopa. Ships have to lie offshore and unload into lighters. Japanese and Lebanese shrimp-fishing fleets operate from the port.

The weather is hot for most of the year, especially from November to May when temperatures of 35°C are common. A pleasant breeze blows in from the sea after sunset, when much of the population frequents the palm-shaded sea front. About 10 km north of the town, near the airport, is La Grande Plage – a fine beach with clean white sand and quite safe from sharks.

Antseranana (Diego-Suarez)

Situated in the extreme north, Antseranana has one of the most beautiful harbours in the world. This cosmopolitan town has Malagasy, Arabs, Indians, Reunionnais and French.

By road, Antseranana is about 1,200 km from Antananarivo. Only 700 km has been tarred and much of the road is impassable from November to June. The best way to reach it is by air or sea.

The province is rich in legends, folklore and ceremonial rituals such as the sacrifices in the sacred lake of Anivorano North. Much of the tradition is reflected in the local handicrafts. The province also produces most of Madagascar's vanilla.

Nossi-Be

'Nossi' means Island and 'Be' is Great. The largest of Madagascar's satellite islands, it is sometimes called Perfume island because of the numerous plants such as ylang-ylang (from which is extracted macassar oil which is essential to the perfume industry), patchouli, vetiver and lemon grass, and the scent of vanilla pods drying in the sun.

Situated about 150 km south-west of Antseranana, the island can be reached by boat at the port of Hell-Ville, or, more easily, by air. Air Madagascar operates daily flights from Antananarivo (two hours), Mahajanga and Antseranana.

The hills are of volcanic origin, and contain deep crater lakes, the largest being that of Amparihibe, inhabited by crocodiles renowned for the quality of the

skins. Of the beaches, the finest is the palm-fringed Andilana. At Palm Beach (Ambondro) there is a hotel with a casino and nightclub, water-skiing, skin-diving and goggle fishing. The beaches are safe for bathing.

Other interesting sights are the Scientific Research Aquarium, the Indian cemetery of Ambanoro; and Dzamandzar, a small village of balloon-shaped houses.

Taolanaro (Fort Dauphin)

A beautiful town but difficult to reach by road. The visitor with little time would be advised to fly. However, the two roads to Taolanaro (from Ihosy and Toleara) pass through magnificent scenery.

The old city was the site of the first French settlement in the 17th century and remains of the fort may be seen in the Malagasy army barracks. Set along semi-circular beaches under high forest-clad mountains, Taolanaro is famous for its excellent lobsters and oysters.

Toleara (Tulear)

The sun shines for most of the year at this seaside town. The esplanade is planted with palms and the broad streets are shaded with *kily* or tamarind trees.

The inhabitants, mainly of Vezo descent, are fishermen and sailors who have preserved the Polynesian outrigger canoe of their ancestors. They live in villages along the shore or sleep under sails rigged as tents on their boats when travelling up and down the coast.

Toleara has white sandy beaches, safe for swimming and water sports. There are no sharks on the landward side of a large coral reef 10 km offshore where there is sailing, skin-diving and fishing.

Many local jewellers work in silver, making the characteristic bracelets for men, and smaller bracelets and necklaces for women. There is a colourful market held in the town centre near a large tamarind tree.

MAURITIUS

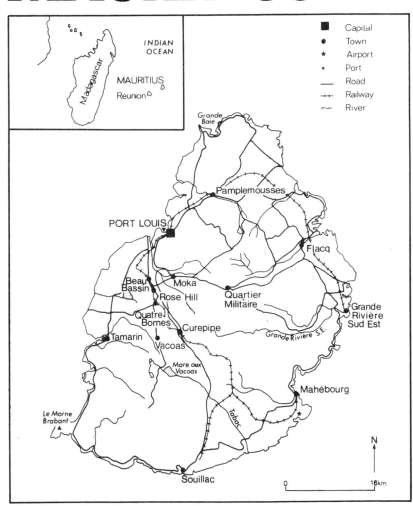

Capital ■
Town ●
Airport ★
Port ▼
Road —
Railway +—+
River ～

INDIAN OCEAN

MAURITIUS
Reunion

Madagascar

Grande Baie

Pamplemousses

PORT LOUIS

Flacq

Beau Bassin

Moka

Rose Hill

Quartier Militaire

Grande Rivière Sud Est

Quatre Bornes

Curepipe

Grande Rivière S.E.

Tamarin

Vacoas

Mare aux Vacoas

Mahébourg

Le Morne Brabant

Tabac

N

0   16km

Souillac

Area: 2,040 sq km
Population: 1.04 million (1989 estimate)
Capital: Port Louis

Lying 2,000 km from the south-eastern coast of Africa, Mauritius is a small, independent island-state whose predominantly Asian population lives largely off the proceeds of sugar-cane.

Tourism has been expanding fast in recent years. The lure of Mauritius' beautiful tropical beaches attracted over 140,000 visitors in 1984.

The Land and The People

Mauritius stands on what was once a land bridge between Asia and Africa – the Mascarene archipelago. From the coast the land rises to form a broad, fertile plateau on which flourish rows and rows of sugar-cane, broken only by a few towns and a large number of shanty villages.

Some 500 km to the east is Rodrigues Island which is subject to intense heat and frequent hurricanes. The 25,000 Rodrigues farmers and villagers are Creoles of African, Malagasy and French stock. To the north-east of Mauritius is the lonely Cargados Carajos Shoals (Saint Brandon), and 900 km to the north is solitary Agalega, all inhabited by small crews of fishermen, copra plantation workers and guano diggers, birds, turtles and marine life.

An awareness of 'being Mauritian' has only recently begun to spread among the separate communities of Mauritius. The majority of the people are Hindu, descended from indentured field labour transported from India after the liberation of African, Malagasy and Creole slaves in 1835. The emancipated bondsmen gravitated towards towns and coastal villages, where many of the 250,000 Creoles now occupy professional positions. Muslims from the Indian sub-continent number 150,000 many of them artisans and tradesmen. There is a middle-class Chinese community of less than 30,000, and a 'European' (Franco-Mauritian) plutocracy of 10,000.

There has been great political activity in Mauritius in recent years, with a strong attack from the left on the island's established interests.

Culture

It is now 200 years since Bernardin de Saint Pierre evoked images of a tropical paradise when he used the island as an idyllic setting for *Paul et Virginie*. Since then Mauritius has produced artists of its own, some of whom have gained world-wide recognition.

The British presence would appear to have exerted very little influence on the cultural life of the various communities. Creole (a French-Bantu-Malagasy mixture) is the most widely spoken language, while English is taught in schools and used (with French) in the Mauritian Parliament.

The festivals which take place throughout the year are as diverse as the communities which make up the population of Mauritius. The Hindus celebrate Divalee in October or November and Maha Shivaratree in February or March. The Chinese maintain their own traditions while the Muslims celebrate New Year (Muharram) with great ceremony and colour.

MARION KAPLAN

Indian traders in the market place

History

Lying south of the monsoon belt, Mauritius was little known in Europe until it became a station between the Cape of Good Hope and the East Indies in the 16th century. Dutch merchantmen occupied it for a few years, but left in 1710. From 1721, France developed a colonial society there of planters, traders, naval forces and corsairs, using slaves from southern Africa and Madagascar. Governor Mahe de Labourdonnais (1735-47) was responsible for Mauritius' prosperity, in conjunction with nearby Réunion (then called Bourbon) and other tiny islands in a sea that was disputed by all major European powers.

The British took control of Mauritius in 1810. After the emancipation of slaves in 1835, intensive sugar cane cultivation required new sources of labour, and several waves of indentured workers came from India, many of them remaining after the expiration of their contracts. By 1860 the Indian population had reached two-thirds of the total population.

By 1910 the educated Creoles and poor whites had become politically active, while the Indian labourers had begun to protest against their work conditions. The Labour Party was founded in 1936 and the political struggle for independence was launched during 1950's under the leadership of Dr Seewoosagur Ramgoolam.

High birth rates, advances in public health and limited opportunities for emigration have combined to produce serious overpopulation on the island. Declining living standards, rising unemployment and stagnating investment during the 1950's heightened tensions between the communities.

Sir Seewoosagur Ramgoolam became Prime Minister at independence in 1968. A left-wing opposition party, *Mouvement Militant Mauricien* (MMM), became the largest single party in the 1976 general elections, Sir Seewoosagur then formed a coalition to maintain his majority. But in the elections of June 1982 the MMM swept the polls, gaining all 60 directly elected seats. Aneerood Jugnauth became Prime Minister. His party split in 1983, after which he led a coalition government.

Economy

Mauritius is a classic example of a one crop economy with sugar being the mainstay since the 18th century. Sugar covers 90% of the cultivable land, provides 88% of total exports, employs 28% of the labour force and accounts for nearly 30% of the Gross Domestic Product. Since 1975 both production of sugar and prices have been low, with unfortunate effects on the economy.

The Government is keen on diversification. It has successfully encouraged production of tea, which is now a valuable export, and some industry has started up. But food production remains inadequate for the needs of the population. Thus one of the aims of the current development plan is to make the island self-sufficient in food crops. Over two-thirds of the vegetables are home grown but the shortage of irrigated land means that the vast majority of rice requirements are still imported. Fortunately Mauritius has its own sources of power from hydro-electric plants and sugar by-products. by-products.

Economic power still belongs to the Franco-Mauritians (the plantation owners). Their dominance has been reinforced by the rise of tourism in which they play a major role. Tourism is the second largest foreign exchange earner, and has been expanding fast, rising from 15,000 tourists in 1968 to 140,000 in 1984. But the tourism infrastructure – new hotels, extra power, water, foodstuffs, roads and transport equipment – had to be paid for, and the net benefit to Mauritius is scarcely half of the gross revenue total. The impact on unemployment has also been marginal, providing only 5,000 new jobs directly.

The severity of the recent economic crisis can be attributed to the surplus production of sugar throughout the world, mounting pressure from the European beet sugar producers, and to the failure of the development strategy adopted by the government since independence. The economic and social manifestations of the crisis are obvious: an increasing balance of payments deficit, the deterioration of housing and public transport and rising unemployment and inflation.

Wildlife

Mauritius' mountain slopes retain a small herd of deer, carefully protected but open to hunting in the June-August season. The indigenous dodo and giant land tortoise can now only be seen in natural history museums, but there are still many monkeys, rabbits and fish on and around the island.

General Information

Government

Independent member of the Commonwealth. Parliamentary government with a coalition government in power under Prime Minister Aneerood Jugnauth.

Languages

English, French, Hindustani and Creole.

Religion

Hinduism, Islam and Christianity (Roman Catholic and Protestant).

How to Get There

By air: There are several flights a week to and from Plaisance Airport by British Airways, Air France, Qantas, South African Airways, Air India, Air Mauritius, Alitalia, Lufthansa, Air Malawi, Zambia Airways, Royal Swazi National Airways.
By sea: Messageries Maritimes monthly from Marseilles via Cape Town, Madagascar, Reunion and occasionally the Comoro Islands. British, French, American and many other lines connect Mauritius with all continents.

Entry Regulations

All visitors require valid passports, return tickets and international certificates of vaccination against smallpox (vaccination against yellow fever and cholera if arriving after travel through an infected area).

Visas are not required by citizens of the UK and Commonwealth countries. South Africa and most West European countries except for visits exceeding six months (three months for West Germans and Israelis). British consulates issue visas wherever Mauritius is not represented diplomatically. Airport tax on departure, 100 rupees.

Customs Regulations

Foreign currencies and travellers cheques may be taken into and out of Mauritius at liberty. A maximum of Rs700 can be imported and any unused balance of the Rupees is virtually worthless outside the island, so sterling or travellers' cheques should be used as often as possible. The major international and sterling credit cards are acceptable.

Personal baggage and 250 grammes of tobacco (including cigars and cigarettes); 75 centilitres of spirits; and 2 litres of wine may be taken in free of duty.

Climate

Mauritius' coasts are warm the year round, averaging 25°C between January and April, around 19°C at other times: they are coolest and driest from June to October. Humidity and rainfall increase with altitude: temperatures drop about 5°C from the coast to the residential plateau around Curepipe. January to March is cyclone season: there may be a succession of tropical storms during this period, but with a bit of luck the island offers abundant sunshine and maritime breezes all year (the south coast is the breeziest). Good off-season periods for visiting are May-June and October-December. Deep-sea fishing is best in the period from October to March.
What to wear: On the coast, cool casual wear is best; one can usually buy cotton shirts and 'wrap arounds' on the beaches. It is advisable to take a cardigan or shawl for the evenings. During the winter months you will need some woollens. A jacket and a raincoat are often useful, especially in the Curepipe plateau area.

Health Precautions

Normal prudence satisfies most needs on Mauritius.

Malaria and other endemic tropical diseases are virtually non-existent, water and foodstuffs generally safe, the sun benign, although insects are sometimes troublesome. Take an antiseptic cream to soothe any bites.

Banks and Currencies

Bank of Mauritius: POB 29, Sir William Newton St, Port Louis
Bank of Credit and Commerce International SA: Desforges St, Port Louis
Mauritius Co-operative Central Bank: Dumat St, Port Louis
Indian Ocean International Bank: Sir William Newton St
Mauritius Commercial Bank: Sir William Newton St
State Commercial Bank: Treasury bldg. Intendance St
Currency: Mauritian rupee divided into 100 cents.
(See currency table, page 9).

Business Hours

Offices: 0900-1600 Monday-Friday and 0900-1200 Saturday
Banks: 1000-1400 Monday-Friday and 0930-1130 Saturday
Shops (Port Louis): 0800-1700 Monday-Friday and 0800-1200 Saturday.
Shops (Curepipe and Rose Hill): 0800-1900 Monday-Friday; 0800-1300 Thursday and Sunday

Public Holidays

New Year's Day, 1 and 2 January
Yaum-un-Nabi, 30 January
Cavadee, 31 January
Maha Shivaratree, 14 February
Chinese New Year, 16 February
Holi, 2 March
Independence Day, 12 March
Ougadi, 17 March
Varusha Piruppu, 13 April
Easter Monday, 16 April 1990
Labour Day, 1 May
Eid el-Fitr, 26/28 April 1990
Assumption Day, 15 August
Ganesh Chaturthi, 14 September
Chinese Autumn Festival, 23 September
Eid el-Adha, 3/6 July 1990
United Nations Day, 24 October
All Saints Day, 1 November
Divali, 7 November
Ganga Asnan, 22 November
Christmas Day, 25 December
Boxing Day, 26 December

Embassies in Mauritius

Australia: Port Louis
China PR: Royal Road, tel: 43073
Egypt: King Georges Ave, tel: 65012
France: St Georges St, Port Louis
Madagascar: Sir William Newton St, Port Louis
UK: Cerne House, La Chaussée, Port Louis, tel: 20201
USSR: Queen Mary Ave, tel: 61545
USA: Anglo-Mauritius House, Port Louis, tel: 23218

Transport

By air: The island's airport is situated in the south-east about 30 miles from Port Louis, about 15 miles from Curepipe and 18 miles from Vacoas. Air Mauritius connects Plaisance Airport and Rodrigues Island about four times a week.
By road: There is a good network of asphalted roads, including a dual highway between Port Louis and Curepipe. Bus services link all parts of the island. There are taxi services in urban areas and larger villages (shared). There are numerous self-drive car-hire firms. Traffic is driven on the left.
Car hire: Mauritius Touring Co (Hertz), Caltex Filling Station, Royal Road, Curepipe, tel: 86-1453/54/55, telex TRAVCO IW 4227. Avis, Brabant Street, Port Louis, tel: 081621. ERC, Pailles, tel: 2-1946. Europcars, Evenor

Mament Street, Rose Hill, tel: 4-3078 or 4-3447. Concorde, Chaussée, Port Louis, tel: 2-6001.

Accommodation and Food

As hotels increase, the number of family pensions and modest beach bungalows diminishes, but those that exist provide reasonable accommodation for families. The Mauritius Youth House in Port Louis and Port Louis Diocese (for Roman Catholics) have camping and other accommodation for young people.

Reservations should be made for all hotels during the June-September high season, although one seldom has difficulty finding adequate lodgings somewhere on the island.

A few restaurants offer authentic French, Chinese or Indian cuisine, and many try to combine all three styles. Fruit, meat, vegetables and even fresh seafood are often in short supply, and depend on imports. Venison in season, *camarons* (fresh-water crayfish) in hot sauces, creole fish, rice and curry are among the island's specialities. While motoring around the villages, travellers can depend on the refrigerator stocks at Chinese groceries. Rum and beer are staple beverages for Mauritians, but there is good local milk, imported wine and mineral water as well.

Tipping: A tip of 10% is usual in most hotels and restaurants. Taxi drivers do not expect a tip.

Hotels

NAME	ADDRESS	TELEPHONE	TELEX
BEACH HOTELS			
Royal Palm	Grand Bay	038 353	4653
Merville Hotel	Grand Bay	038 531	
Isle de France Hotel	Isle de France	038 543/5	
Trou aux Biches Village Hotel	Trou aux Biches	036 562/4	
Arc en Ciel	Tombeau Bay	37 616/7	
Capri Hotel	Tombeau Bay	37 533	
Villas Caroline	Flic en Flac	538 411	
La Pirogue Hotel (Sun)	Flic en Flac	538 441/3	4255
Pearle Beach Hotel	Wolmar	538 428	
Tamarin Hotel	Tamarin	536 581	
Le Meridien Brabant	Le Morne Brabant	613 22/3	4444
Le Meridien Paradis	Le Morne Brabant	613 22/3	4444

[Hotels]

Beachcomber Club	Blue Bay	873 511	
Blue Lagoon Hotel	Point d'Esny	71 529	
Touessrok Hotel (Sun)	Trou d'Eau Douce	532 451	4229
La Fayette	La Fayette	039 336	4227
St Geran Hotel (Sun)	Belle Mare	532 825/6	4320
Maritim Hotel	Belle Mare	532 518	
Belle Mare Plage	Belle Mare	6 5685	
Charleroi Hotel	Pereybere	038 641/2	

BUNGALOWS

Merville Bungalows	Grand Bay	038 531
Isle de France Bungalows	Grand Bay	038 543
Casuarina Village Hotel	Grand Bay	036 552
Etoile de Mer Bungalows	Grand Bay	036 561
Villas Caroline Bungalows	Flic en Flac	538 411
Tamarin Hotel	Tamarin	536 581
Mocambo Bungalows	Tamarin	536 538
Le Morne Bungalows	Le Morne Brabant	536 531
Villas Pointe aux Rochas	Souillac	76 538
Maritim Hotel	Belle Mere Plage	532 518
Charleroi Hotel	Pereybere	038 641
Pereybere Guest House	Pereybere	038 676
Palm Beach Hotel	Pereybere	2 4590

PORT LOUIS

Ambassador Hotel	Desforges Street	080320/2

[Hotels]

Bourbon Tourist Hotel	Jummah Mosque Street	2 4407	
Flore Oriental Hotel	Desforges Street	2 3017	
France Tourist Hotel	Joseph Riviere Street	2 2087	
National Hotel	Pope Hennessy Street	2 0453	
Palais D'Or	Jummah Mosque Street	2 5231	
President Tourist Hotel	Remy Ollier Street	080380/1	
Rossignol Hotel	33 Pope Hennessy Street	2 1983	

COROMANDEL

Sunray Hotel	Coromandel	088156

ROSE HILL

Oasis Hotel	Vandermeersch St	4 2058

BELLE ROSE

Riverside Hotel	Belle Rose	4 4957

QUATRE BORNES

Gavnor Hotel	Quatre Bornes	4 1884
El Monaco Hotel	St Jean Road	4 2282

CUREPIPE

Continental Hotel	Currimjee Arcades	6 2036/7	4389

FLOREAL

Mandarin Hotel	Floreal	6 5031/2

PLAINE MAGNIEN

Tourist Rendez-Vous Hotel	Plaine Magnien	73 516

Port Louis

Most of the activity of Port Louis is concentrated around the bustling port and the neighbouring commercial area. On Pope Hennessy and other streets there are pretty wooden Creole houses with iron balustrades and louvre shutters. The Indian and Chinese bourgeoisie live on the slopes of Signal Hill.

Government House, built by the illustrious 18th-century Governor Mahe de Labourdonnais, presides over an esplanade (Place d'Armes) leading between tall palm trees to the port. The avenues behind it contain banks and major office buildings. Nearby is the handsome Mauritius Institute building, housing the excellent National Archives and Natural History Museum, both dedicated to Indian Ocean history, flora and fauna.

The Hippodrome at the Champ de Mars (built in 1812) has horse racing on weekends between May and October. Other places of interest include the Anglican and Roman Catholic cathedrals, the Jummah Mosque, the Chinese Pagoda (on the outskirts of town near the Hippodrome), the Old Theatre, the Town Hall, and various statues and monuments.

Most visitors stay at the beach hotels or on the residential plateau, but Port Louis itself has a number of adequate hotels, the majority having air-conditioning.

Restaurants: La Flore Mauricienne, Intendance Street; Carri Poulé, Place d'Armes (very good for lunch); Lai Min, Royal Street (Chinese, excellent); Arc en Ciel, Farquar Street (Chinese); La Flore Orientale, Ramgoolam Street; La Bonne Marmite, Sir William Newton Street.

Entertainments and Sports: It is worth paying a visit to the Chinese Casinos in the Chinese quartier, and for those who prefer to dance there are discos and clubs. For the racegoers, there is the picturesque racecourse at Champ de Mars situated at the base of the

mountains, open from May to October. At Reduit, just south of Port Louis, is the French colonial residence of the Governors of Mauritius, set in 325 acres of beautiful gardens. Signal Mountain overlooks the whole of Port Louis.

Shopping: Every visitor to Port Louis must try to visit the Central Market, packed with beautifully displayed goods – fruit and vegetables, spices, handicrafts, fish and meat. While wandering through the hustle and bustle of people you can stop for a snack of fresh pineapple coated with chili sauce or a drink of *alouda* (almond drink) or fresh coconut water. There are a few large stores and many specialist shops where you can buy almost anything.

Tourist information: Mauritius Government Tourist Office, Registrar General Building, Jules Koenig Street, tel: 011703; Mauritius Travel and Tourist Bureau Ltd (semi-official), Sir William Newton Street; Alliance Touristique de l'Océan Indien (ATOI), Galerie Remy Ollier, Place Foch.

Curepipe and The Plateau

Private gardens, monumental schools and other public buildings, shopping arcades and theatres, down-at-heel business districts and busy traffic mark the island's central residential zone. In spite of frequent afternoon rains Curepipe, 600 m in altitude, is a good base for operations. Other central towns – Beau Bassin, Rose Hill, Vacoas – serve mainly as dormitories for the sugar industry and Port Louis.

Places of interest include the Curepipe botanical gardens, the French colonial-style City Hall, and a scenic drive along the rim of the Trou aux Cerfs crater above the town.

At Moka there are waterfalls, and opportunities for mountain climbing. The Reduit, near Moka, the Governor General's residence has splendid lawns and a fine view of cliffs and the sea. Saint

Pierre and other sugar mills near Moka are worth a visit during October and November.

Restaurants: Continental Hotel, Sir Winston Churchill Street; Tropicana, Royal Road (excellent Chinese); Nobby's Steak House, Curepipe Road (very good steak and seafood); Mandarin Hotel, St Paul Avenue, Floreal (superb Chinese food, worth booking table and food in advance for large parties).

Shopping: Jewellery, Chinese and Indian ivory work, jade, teak and silks, tortoise shells, basketry, pottery and sea shells are available at numerous shops in Curepipe, including Handicrafts Ltd and Corinne, and at Commercial Centre in Rose Hill.

The Coasts

Villages, beaches, lagoons and inlets, cliffs, bamboo and banana palm forests, canefields and fishing grounds all form part of the Mauritian coast. Every visitor should undertake at least one day-long circuit along the island's roadways. Starting from Plaisance Airport in the south-east, visit Mahebourg, the beautifully situated old colonial capital with mementoes of the Napoleonic Wars and an interesting historical museum nearby; then proceed along the coast, coming first to Blue Bay, then to Souillac with the Rochester Falls and a little museum in the coral house of the poet, the late Robert Edward Hart.

The rugged cliffs of Morne Brabant overlook an exceedingly fine beach. Grande Case and Le Chamarel are below the wild forests and ravines of the Riviere Noire mountains, with strange rock configurations, waterfalls and wildlife. Chamarel (coloured earths) is a mound of undulating land made up of contrasting layers of coloured earths; the patches of blue, green, red and yellow earth are thought to be the result of weathering. The nearby Chamarel waterfall emerges from the moors and primeval vegetation and is startlingly beautiful. Grand Bassin,

one of the island's two natural lakes, lies in the crater of an extinct volcano. It is a place of pilgrimage for many Indo-Mauritians of the Hindu faith.

Riviere Noire is a Creole fishermen's district, where *sega* dancing is especially lively on Saturday nights. Trou aux Biches in the north-west, just south of the new Club Mediterrannée vacation village at Pointe aux Canonniers, is excellent for surfing.

The Pamplemousses Gardens are known to naturalists throughout the world for their large collection of indigenous and exotic plants, including the Giant Victoria Regia lillies and many species of palm trees. There is one, the talipot palm, which is said to flower once after 100 years and then die. Grand Baie, north of Pamplemousses Gardens, is a favourite beach area for Mauritian residents, with excellent fishing and skin-diving at Pointe aux Piments and swimming in the Cove of Péyrebere. The yacht club stages sailing regattas from July to October.

Grande Baie

KEN LAMBERT

REUNION

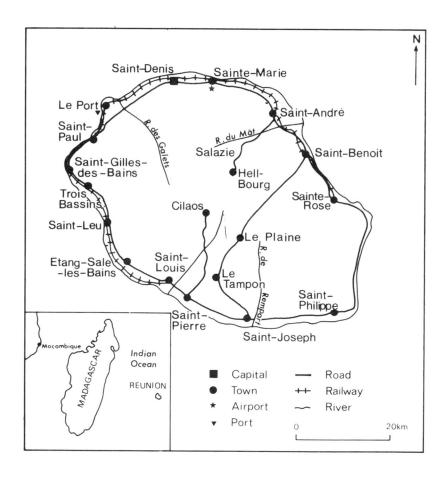

Area: 2,510 sq km
Population: 583,000 (1989 estimate)
Capital: Saint Denis

A spectacular, far-flung French possession, Réunion lies between Madagascar and Mauritius. Its landscape is volcanic, its climate tropical, its *lingua franca* is Creole, and most of its people are of mixed race. The island has fine beaches, good fishing and very beautiful hill country traversed by trout streams. However, the visitor will also observe much 'picturesque poverty'.

The Land and the People

Running diagonally across Réunion is a chain of volcanic peaks, separating it into a green, humid eastern zone (called Le Vent) and a dry, sheltered south and west (Sous le Vent).

Most of the population lives along the coast. The majority are Roman Catholics but there is also a large community of Hindus, descendants of indentured workers brought here from India after the emancipation of slaves in 1848, as well as a smaller minority of Muslims from Pakistan and the Comoro Islands, and some 20,000 Chinese. The unassimilated Asians and the Europeans comprise a quarter of the otherwise *metis* (mixed race) population.

Culture

Traditional Creole *sega* dancing is popular. Hindus and Muslims have preserved some of their rituals, including the so-called Malabar dancing and ordeals of fire-walking. Craftmanship on the island includes some fine lace and embroidery from the hills around Cilaos.

History

Governed until 1767 by the French East India Company, Réunion produced spices and Arabic coffee and served as a station for French shipping around the Cape of Good Hope. Occupied by British forces from 1810 to 1815 – with an increasing slave population – the island was returned to France at the Congress of Vienna, although its twin Mascarene, Ile de France, was retained by England, as Mauritius.

Réunion is now governed as an Overseas Department of France and administered by a Prefect delegated from Paris, 11,000 km away. This status entitles it to a share of French national taxes, budget allocations and parliamentary seats.

However, the last 15 years have seen an increasing struggle to change the island's status, led mainly by the Réunion federation of the French Communist Party, the Réunion Communist Party (PCR). A Liberation Committee report on Réunion was adopted at the Ministerial Council of the OAU in February 1978, although France is doing all it can to avoid the question of decolonisation. Réunion has been integrated into the Common

Market. A left coalition won victory in a newly created regional council in February 1983.

Economy

Réunion has been a colony with an essentially agricultural economy for 300 years. Sugar-cane – the mono-crop which takes up 70% of cultivated land – constitutes a large source of profit for the metropolitan power. Food crops which might compete with French producers are not developed and vegetables, fruit and meat are imported when they could be produced locally.

Although cane and its derivatives represent 88% of the value of the island's exports, there has been a stagnation in production. Small and medium-scale planters find it difficult to hold their own against the large landowners and the regular increase in production costs and stagnation of sugar prices have forced thousands of small-scale planters to leave the land. Furthermore the mechanisation of cane cutting is likely to constitute a fatal blow for agricultural day-labourers who are already joining the ranks of unemployed.

Réunion exports almost everything it produces and imports almost everything it consumes. Moreover, France supplies 65% of imports and purchases 75% of exports. The goods that Réunion purchases from France, which holds a trade monopoly, could be bought more cheaply elsewhere. Added problems include a fall in export crops such as geranium and vetyver oil, and in vanilla production.

With employment falling in agriculture and industry there has been a very sharp increase in unemployment – this combined with a large population growth rate has forced many young people to emigrate to France.

Salazie village church.

156

General Information

Government

Réunion is an Overseas Department of France, administered by an appointed Prefect, with an elected Regional council. It sends three deputies to the French National Assembly.

Languages

French and Creole.

Religion

Mainly Roman Catholic with Hindu, Muslim and Buddhist minorities.

How to Get There

By air: Air France, in conjunction with Air Madagascar, call seven times a week en route Paris-Athens-Cairo-Djibouti-Nairobi-Dar es Salaam-Antananarivo-Reunion-Mauritius. From Mauritius: Air France and Air Mauritius (daily) connecting in Mauritius with flights from UK, Western Europe, East Africa, India, South Africa and Australia.

By sea: From Europe: Messageries Maritimes passenger liners call fortnightly, and passenger-freighters of the Nouvelle Compagnie Havraise Péninsulaire and other French lines from Marseilles via South Africa and Madagascar call at regular intervals, as do British, Scandinavian and South African lines.

Entry Regulations

Basic regulations conform to those of France. Visas are not required for visits of up to three months by holders of most West European, American or African passports.

An international certificate of vaccination against smallpox is required, as are yellow fever and cholera vaccinations for travellers arriving from infected areas.

Customs Regulations

Personal effects and limited amounts of alcohol and tobacco may be taken into Réunion. The importation of sugar cane is prohibted and other live plants are subject to strict controls.

Climate

The island is at its best from May to October when temperatures average from 18°C to 30°C on the coasts, while the hills are considerably cooler (dropping to freezing on certain nights in the highlands). It turns hot and wet during the cyclone season (January to March). The eastern half of the island (Le Vent) and the mountain slopes are subject to substantial rainfall most of the year.

What to wear: Dress is informal. Be prepared for considerable temperature contrast between coasts and mountains, and for wet weather, especially in the east. A mountain hike requires sturdy shoes and a hat.

Health Precautions

Réunion's climate is relatively benign, particularly in the bracing air of the hills. Water is safe to drink and sanitation facilities normal. There is malaria on the coasts and anti-malarial drugs should be taken 14 days before, during, and 14 days after the visit. The sun can be deceptively vicious and sunbathing should be done in moderation.

Banks and Currency

Institut d'Emission des Départemers d'Outremer: 6 rue de la Compagnie,

97487 Saint-Denis
Banque Francaise Commerciale, 60 rue Alexis de Villeneuve
Banque Nationale de Paris, 49 rue Juliette Dodu
Banque de la Réunion: 27 rue Jean-Chatel, Saint-Denis, tel: 21 32 20
Currency: French franc divided into 100 centimes
(See currency table, page 9).

Business Hours

Normal hours of business are 0800-1200 and 1400-1800.

Public Holidays

New Year's Day, 1 January
Easter Monday, 16 April 1990
Labour Day, 1 May
Ascension Day, 24 May 1990
Whit Monday, 4 June 1990
National Day, 14 August
Assumption Day, 15 August
All Saints' Day, 1 November
Armistice Day, 11 November
Christmas Day, 25 December

Consulates in Saint-Denis

Belgium and the Netherlands: BP 785, Saint-Denis, tel: 21.10.85-21.38.01
Germany FR: rue Rontaunay, Saint-Denis, tel: 21.33.04
Madagascar: 13 rue Labourdonnais, Saint-Denis
Norway: 2 rue Renaudiere de Vaux, Le Port, tel: 22.00.85
South Africa: rue la Caussade
UK: rue de Paris, BP 99, Saint-Denis, tel: 21.06.19
The nearest European and US diplomatic missions are at Port Louis, Mauritius and Antananarivo, Madagascar

Transport

By air: Two aero-clubs at Gillot Airport hire planes for flights over the craters and contours of the island – an experience worth the price.

By road: There are paved highways around the island, and two zig-zag roads across the centre. These can be covered on public buses, by taxi or hired vehicle.
Car hire: Hertz rentals are located at the Meridian Hotel; you can also hire cars at Transcontinents, 5 rue du Mat de Pavillion in the capital.
By sea: Private boats can be hired in the fishing ports and at Saint-Gilles.

Energetic travellers should come prepared to hike, climb, and even to hitch-hike.

Accommodation and Food

There is a good network of small hotels, provincial inns, family lodges and pensions. The prices are high but the food is often excellent, even when plumbing and other conveniences leave something to be desired. There are shelters (called *gites*) for hikers at La Roche Ecrite, Cilaos and Pas de Bellecombe.

A variety of restaurants caters for French and exotic tastes fairly well. Réunion's Creole specialities include seafood with sauces (often called *rougail*), curries, rice and dried fish, a good rum and Arabic coffee (*Café Bourbon*).

Hotel tariffs usually include bed and breakfast, taxes and service charges. Tipping is sporadic but is all the more welcome when service has proved its merit.

Saint-Denis

A fast-growing city of 100,000 people, Saint-Denis stands on the north coast between Gillot Airport and the island's seaport, Pointe des Galets. The capital possesses a number of dignified old French buildings (especially the Prefecture, former residence of the great 18th century Governor Mahe de La Bourdonnais) several white-verandahed Creole houses (particularly on rue de Paris), a Hippodrome, a handsome

Museum of Natural History in the Botanical Gardens, the Dierx Museum of Art, and abundant statues and fountains. Its markets are lively just after sunrise, and the sea promenade (Le Barachois), once a functioning port, is popular in the evening. You can drive part of the way up La Roche Ecrite and clamber the rest of the way (2,000 m) without great difficulty; the view is superb.

Hotels

St François, three star, Rampes de St François, B.P. 1197, tel: 21.27.14, 75 rooms.
Labourdonnais, two star, Pl de la Prefecture, tel: 21.37.10, 40 rooms.
Meridien Hotel – Four star.
Touring Hotel, 6 rue Juliette Dodu, tel: 21.22.48, 17 rooms.
Les Mascareignes, 3 rue Lafferiere, tel: 21.15.28.

Restaurants: Le Bosquet (out of town), Le Rallye for Creole and Malagasy food. The hotel restaurants serve excellent French cuisine.

Tourist Information: Syndicat d'Initiative – Office du Tourisme, rue Rontaunay, Saint-Denis.

The Coasts

To the south-west is the old East India Company capital of Saint-Paul, full of literary and historical reminiscences and set against a fine natural hinterland of lakes and woods. South of Saint-Paul, along the Sous le Vent coasts, lie the largest and most popular of Réunion's beaches, Saint-Gilles-des-Bains, with a reef-protected lagoon, fine coral sand edged by filao trees, several lively bars and restaurants, and sailing at the Club Nautique.

Further along the coast are Saint-Leu, a small fishing village with a good beach, and Etang-Sales-les-Bains, with black lava sand. For more solitary beachcombing and water-sports (but be careful to inquire about sharks) try Saint-Philippe.

Hotels
Saint-Benoit: La Confiance, 3 rooms.
Saint-Gilles-des-Bains: Loulou, 20 rooms, Creole and Indian food.
Saint-Philippe: Le Baril, 8 rooms, extensive sporting facilities and good food.
Saint-Pierre: Les Horizons, 23 rooms.

Restaurants: Apart from the hotels, the good restaurants along the coast are La Taverne, at Saint Pierre and L'Arche de Noé, Etang Sale les Hauts.

The Mountains

Réunion's Plaines, peaks and Cirques (high volcanic basins) offer rest cures and mountaineering. There is excellent trout fishing at the Takamaka Falls on the Rivière des Marsouins in the north-east. The Cirque de Cilaos can be reached from St. Louis. The town of Cilaos itself is a mountain spa with curative waters, set in the midst of rocky volcanic scenery.

In the Cirque de Salazie on the other side of the 3,000 m Piton des Neiges stands Hell-Bourg, a pretty town with a bracing climate. One can walk between Hell-Bourg and Cilaos in as little as six hours.

Crossing the island in the south-east permits a two- or three-day trek from the arid, bracing Plaine des Cafres east to the Pas de Bellecombe (an overnight shelter, farthest point of the traversable road) into the Piton de la Fournaise, a broad, smoking crater 8 km in diameter, 2,336 m at its highest point. The volcano is in steady activity; it last erupted in 1961.

Hotels
Cilaos: grand Hotel, 21 rooms.
Hell-Bourg: Hotel des Salazes, 11 rooms. Good French provincial cooking.
Plaine des Cafres: Hotel Lalemand, 23rd km., 17 rooms. Auberge du Volcan, 27th km., 5 rooms.
Tampon: La Paille en Queue, 10 rooms. Metro Hotel, 20 rooms.

SEYCHELLES

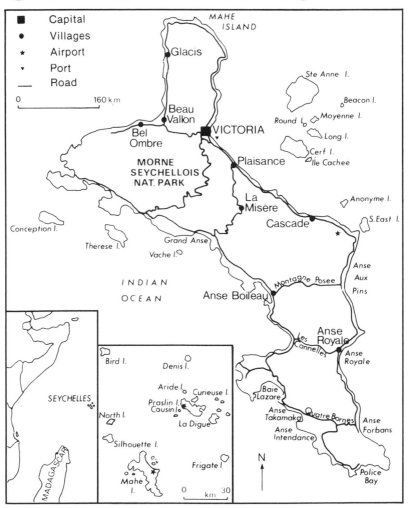

Map legend:
- ■ Capital
- ● Villages
- ★ Airport
- ▼ Port
- — Road

0 ————— 160 km

MAHE ISLAND

Glacis

Ste Anne I.

Beacon I.

Round I. Moyenne I.

Beau Vallon

Long I.

Bel Ombre

VICTORIA

Cerf I.
Ile Cachee

Plaisance

MORNE SEYCHELLOIS NAT. PARK

Anonyme I.

La Misère

S. East I.

Cascade

Conception I.

Grand Anse

Therese I.

Vache I.

Anse Aux Pins

INDIAN OCEAN

Montagne Posee

Anse Boileau

Anse Royale

Les Cannelles

Anse Royale

Bird I.

Denis I.

Aride I. Curieuse I.

Baie Lazare

SEYCHELLES

Praslin I.
Cousin I.

Anse Takamaka

Quatre Bornes

Anse Forbans

North I.

La Digue

Anse Intendance

Silhouette I.

Frigate I.

N

MADAGASCAR

Mahé I.

0 ————— 30 km

Police Bay

Area: 308 sq km
Population: 72,000 (1989 estimate)
Capital: Victoria (Mahé island)

160

The Seychelles are the only mid-oceanic group of granite islands in the world. They comprise 115 islands. Of these 41 are granite, with luxuriant foliage and coconut palms. The remaining 74 are mostly low-lying coral atolls, with no population, sprawling over a wide area of ocean – the furthest 705 miles from Mahé. The largest and best known atoll, Aldabra, has unique flora and fauna and is the last refuge of the giant land tortoise of Seychelles in its natural state.

Clear, clean seas lap the shores of the granite islands, which are bordered by distant reefs outlined with white foam. The coastlines of white sandy beaches are indented with bays and lagoons, while inland, exotic trees and shrubs cover the hilly landscape and dark granite rocks loom up like rugged watchtowers. The flora, bird and marine life are fascinating and unspoilt, creating a paradise for naturalists.

Above all, the Seychelles are ideal for those in search of a holiday destination where they can relax, unwind and enjoy the simple pleasures of nature and watersports in a remote and beautiful setting.

The Land and The People

Most of the Seychellois live on Mahé. It is a mountainous island, 17 miles long by three to five miles wide, and lies four degrees south of the equator. On it stands the smallest capital city in the world, Victoria.

All the granite islands, including the second largest, Praslin, lie within a radius of 40 miles of Mahé. Each has some specific natural feature to recommend it, and already six can offer varied accommodation.

The Islands lie 990 miles from the East African port of Mombasa, and 580 miles from Madagascar. They were uninhabited until the French arrived in 1770. Most of the population are Creoles, mixed descendants of early French settlers and African slaves. There are also numbers of Indians, Chinese and Europeans.

The country is now diversifying its economic base, concentrating particularly on industrial fishing.

Culture

Though French rule prevailed for a relatively short time at the end of the 18th century, the culture of the islands remains more French than British. The predominant language is Creole, which is French-based but with many words and constructions derived from English, Arabic and African languages. Since 1979 the Seychelles is busy reviving its own national culture.

The islanders' handicraft reflects their rich marine inheritance – tortoiseshell, shark's teeth, mother-of-pearl, fish scales, coral – and the exotic vegetation, with flowers fashioned from coconut fibre, raffia-work, leaves of pressed cinnamon, and the islands' pride, the famous Coco-de-Mer nuts.

History

The Seychelles were uninhabited, though not unvisited, until settled by the French, starting in 1770. At first, economic activity consisted only of catching tortoises and felling trees, but the administration later discouraged the reckless explolitation of the islands' resources, and agriculture was developed.

During the Napoleonic Wars, Seychelles changed hands several times; the islands were finally ceded to Britain in 1814.

The original population of French settlers and their servants and slaves was substantially augmented during the 19th century, due to the landing on the islands by the British Navy of ex-slaves who had been freed from slave-ships. There was also a slow increase in the number of settlers, principally of French origin from Mauritius, but also Indians and Chinese.

The political development of Seychelles was, until recently, very slow. During the 19th century the islands were administered from Mauritius; Seychelles only became a separate Crown Colony in 1904. There were no elections until 1948, when minority elected representation on the Legislative Council was granted but with an electorate of only 2,000. Independence was achieved on 29 June 1976, with James Mancham, leader of the Seychelles Democratic Party (SDP) as President, and Albert René, leader of the Seychelles People's United Party (SPUP), as Prime Minister. Seychelles thus has a colonial history of 206 years. On 5 June 1977 René became President after a coup overthrew Mancham in his absence. The SPUP, renamed the Seychelles People's Progressive Front (SPPF), was declared the sole political party in June 1979. The SPPF is committed to socialism but has so far taken a very moderate line. A coup attempt by South African mercenaries in November 1981 was crushed after heavy fighting. René was re-elected for a further five year term in May 1984.

Economy

Like many 'island paradises', the Seychelles are far from idyllic for many of their inhabitants. The economy is beset by the problems of unemployment and poverty inherited from the colonial past. Much of the land is uncultivable and the vast potential for the development of a fishing industry has so far been largely neglected. Food production has never been adequate and is even less so since the recent influx of tourists began. Copra and cinnamon, the Seychelles' traditional exports, have declined sharply in recent years, and there is a huge trade deficit. The economy is heavily dependent on foreign aid and investment.

The opening of the international airport in 1971 caused an upsurge in tourism and it has developed into a major industry. In 1978 close on 65,000 visitors were recorded. From 1971 considerable effort and money have been devoted to improving infrastructure, primarily on the main island of Mahé, but also, to a lesser extent, on the nearby islands of Praslin and La Digue.

Tourist accommodation has been provided and modern facilities installed. However, tourist policy emphasises the overriding need to protect the natural beauty of the islands and an upper limit has been put on the number of tourists.

Whilst the Government encourages the growth of tourism it is equally committed to reviving agriculture, improving social services and raising living standards. It has instituted a low-cost housing scheme, free medical care and a price freeze on staple foods. The expansion of the fishing industry was a major priority in the 1985-89 development plan, while oil prospecting is also underway.

Wildlife

The Seychelles are the home of dozens of the world's rarest birds. Individual islands like Bird, Cousin and Aldabra are already bird sanctuaries, and other places such as Praslin, where the black parrot lives, and La Digue, home of the paradise flycatcher, are specially protected. These birds and other rare species attract ornithologists and scientists from all over the world. There are also huge numbers of more common tropical birds including the lovely fairy tern – as many as 10,000 live in Cousin alone – egrets and the fruit-eating flying fox (which is a large bat).

Big game fish abound in the deeper waters – barracuda, tuna, kingfish, marlin, sailfish and bonito. Bottom fishing is also excellent, the most common local fish being bourgeois, job, vieille and parrot fish – the first two making the best eating. The Government has banned spearguns but encourages goggling and scuba diving.

The coral reefs and underwater plateaux around the granite island group are truly spectacular and unspoiled. Sharks do not venture inside the reefs or in the coastal waters and lagoons. The swimmer can spend hour after hour wandering through intricate and ever-changing subterranean scenery watching a thousand varieties of tropical fish.

The prolific plant life is as much of an attraction as the birds, fish and giant land tortoises – some of which have been known to live for a century and a half. There is a broad range of tropical fruits and vegetables, including delicious mangoes, guavas, coconuts and *fruit-a-pain.* The Coco-de-Mer grows only on the islands of Praslin and Curieuse. The tall palm trees can live up to 800 years, the nuts take 25 years to mature and the fruit seven years to ripen.

It is an offence under the Protection of Shells Regulations both to collect shells from protected areas and to disturb them in their natural environment. This includes turning over live coral, causing it to die. Any offence under the regulations is punishable by a large fine and imprisonment. The areas protected under the Protection of Shells Regulations are as follows: on Mahé, from Rat Island southwards to Pointe au Sel and from North East Point northwards to the northern boundary of the Carana Beach Hotel site;

the islands of Cousin, Curieuse, St Anne, Cerf, Cashée, Long, Moyenne and Round; on Praslin, from and including Anse Boudin eastwards to Pointe Zanguilles; on La Digue, from the lighthouse at La Passe northwards to Gross Roche.

The protected areas are not only the foreshores and the reefs but also the sea for a distance of 400 metres from the nearest point on the low-water line.

Beau Vallon beach on Mahé Island

General Information

Government

Republic. The president and National Assembly are to be elected every five years. The ruling party is the Seychelles People's Progressive Front (SPPF).

Languages

English and French are the official languages. The first language of most Seychellois, however, is Creole.

Religion

Roman Catholics (90%), Anglicans (8%).

How to Get There

By air: Seychelles International Airport is on Mahé. Services are provided by the following international carriers – Aeroflot, Air France, Air India, Air Seychelles, Air Tanzania, British Airways, Kenya Airways.
By sea: Several cruise ships and cargo vessels call at Mahé, but there is no regular schedule.

Entry Regulations

All visitors require a valid passport. Requirements change from time to time, so visitors are advised to check with an airline or travel agent before departure.

Entry visas are not generally required of visitors, except for certain specified countries outside the British Commonwealth. Visitor Passes are granted on arrival and are valid initially for one month (which may be extended to 12 months). Visitors must be in possession of onward or return tickets, valid travel documents, sufficient funds for their stay and evidence of acceptability at their next port of entry, and may also be required to submit proof that they have suitable accommodation for the length of their stay. Those without onward or return tickets may be required to deposit a sum not exceeding Rs.4,000 with a senior Immigration Officer who will then proceed in buying them a ticket, or they may do so themselves upon arrival. The holder of a Visitor's Pass may not accept employment without permission in writing, from the Principal Immigration Officer, PO Box 430, Victoria, Mahé.

Customs Regulations

Used personal effects are exempt from import duty; they must, however, be declared. Firearms, air pistols, air rifles and spear fishing guns are prohibited.

Visitors may take in free of duty (but must declare) a maximum of 125 cc of perfume, a quarter litre of toilet water, 200 cigarettes or 50 cigars or 250 grammes of tobacco, a litre of spirits and a litre of wine.

Climate

Average temperatures throughout the year range from 24°C to 29°C. The wettest months are from December to February; the hottest, March to April; the coolest, June to September; and the most pleasant, May, June and October. The annual rainfall is 230 cm. There are sudden squalls, but the islands lie outside the cyclone belt so high winds and thunderstorms are rare.
What to wear: Life is very informal, so all that is needed is the lightest of casual clothes and sportswear, canvas shoes for exploring coral reefs, a sun hat and dark glasses. Something warm is useful if the wind turns cool at night. It is suggested that something more than a bikini or swimsuit be worn in Victoria town.

165

Health precautions

There are no poisonous snakes, malarial mosquitoes or dangerous wild animals, but it is advisable to take an insect repellant and sting relief ointment with you. Sunburn and seasickness are the ailments most commonly encountered.

Banks and Currency

Foreign currency and travellers cheques are best exchanged at one of the banks in Victoria. There are also facilities at the main hotels and a banking service at the airport.

Barclays Bank, PO Box 167, Victoria, Mahé

Bank of Credit and Commerce International SA, PO Box 579, Victoria, Mahé

Banque Français Commerciale, PO Box 122, Victoria, Mahé

Habib Bank Ltd, PO Box 702, Victoria, Mahé

Standard Chartered Bank Ltd, PO Box 241, Victoria, Mahé

Currency: Seychelles Rupee (SR), divided into 100 cents.

(See currency table, page 9).

Business Hours

Banks: Monday-Friday 0830-1300; Française Commerciale Monday-Friday 0830-1500; Saturday 0900-1130

Offices: Monday-Friday 0800-1200 and 1300-1600

Shops: Monday-Friday 0800-1200 and 1330-1700

Post Office: Monday-Friday 0800-1200 and 1300-1600; Saturday 0800-1200

Public Holidays

New Year, 1/2 January
Good Friday, 13 April 1990
Easter Sunday, 15 April 1990
Easter Monday, 16 April 1990
Labour Day, 1 May
Liberation Day, 5 June
Independence Day, 29 June
Assumption Day, 15 August
All Saints' Day, 1 November
Feast of Immaculate Conception, 8 December
Christmas Day, 25 December

Transport

By road: There are over 550 cars available for hire on Mahé and a limited number on Praslin. It is wise to make advance reservations, particularly in high season. Conditions of hire and insurance cover should be carefully checked.

There are also about 135 taxis on Mahé and Praslin. Their fixed rates are laid down by the government. Buses run at regular intervals between the rural areas on Mahé and Victoria from 05.30 to 19.00 hours. Visitors should try riding in the traditional camions (found only in Praslin) which are decorated with bright flowers and palm fronds.

By air and sea: Several schooners and motor cruisers offer a regular service between Mahé, Praslin and La Digue. Air Seychelles have daily flights between Mahé and Praslin, and Mahé to Bird Island and Denis Island.

Embassies

China PR: Cemetry estate
France: Arpent Vert, Mont Fleuri
U.K.: Victoria House, Victoria, tel: 23055
U.S.A.: Victoria House, Victoria, tel: 23921
Libya: Villa Laurel, Mont Fleuri
USSR: Mountain Rise, Bel Air, tel: 21590

Accommodation and Food

Most of the hotels, guest houses, holiday apartments, chalets and lodges in the Seychelles are on Mahé. Apart from the large and small hotels, there are also more than 20 guest houses on Mahé, as well as self-catering apartments and villas.

Praslin has 10 hotels and lodges. There are three hotels on La Digue and one or two small lodges or chalets on Bird, Denis, and Poivre. There is also one island for private hire – Chauve Souris Island.

The facilities are modern (or, on the smaller outer islands suitably rustic). The resort hotels have air-conditioning, as do many of the guest houses. Prices are sometimes high at the larger hotels and fairly moderate at guest houses. Camping and nude bathing are not allowed.

The guest house can have delightful specialities, such as the Bougainville (south Mahé), essentially French and well known for its excellent food, the Casuarina at Anse-aux-Pins on the edge of the ocean, and Sunset and Glacis, two smaller inexpensive guest houses by the sea. For those who prefer the hills, Abbéville offers a retreat near la Misère Pass.

There are many good restaurants, mainly in the hotels, but also independently run and offering a variety of Creole specialities. Enticing seafoods, meat, chicken, curries and international cuisine – French, Chinese, Italian, Swiss, German – are all available at various restaurants. There is also a commendable meal exchange system, so that you can vary your choice of eating places. Creole barbecues at the hotels are popular and tasty and offer a wide selection of local dishes, particularly at Mahé Beach, Beau Vallon Bay and the Reef hotels.

Self-caterers can take advantage of the availability of fresh fish, lobster and octopus, coconuts and herbs, and a wonderful array of tropical fruit. Most hotels have bars and other restaurants usually offer wines and Seychelles beer, which is good. All spirits are imported. There is also a coconut cocktail and a delicious fresh lime crush. Some recommended restaurants include Fisherman's Cove, Coral Strand, Auberge Louis XVII, Le Corsaire, La Marmite, La Sçala, Marie Antoinette, La Sirène and Sundown. Seychelles Hotel School with a restaurant on Mont Fleuri Road, en route to the airport, is well worth patronising for an excellent meal. The Seychelles tourism division produces a restaurant and hotel guide for visitors.

Hotels

NAME	ADDRESS	TELEPHONE	TELEX	FAX
MAHÉ				
Auberge Club	Danzilles, PO Box 526	47550	SZ 2323	47606
Beau Vallon Bay	Beau Vallon, PO Box 550	47141	SZ 2237	47606
Barbarons Meridien Beach	Port Glaud, PO Box 626	78253/78310	SZ 2258	78484
Coral Strand	Beau Vallon, PO Box 400	47036	SZ 2215	47517
Equator Grand Anse	Béolière, PO Box 526	78228	SZ 2277	

[Hotels]

Fisherman's Cove Meridien	Bel Ombre, PO Box 35	47252/47436	SZ 2296	
Northolme	Glacis, PO Box 333	47222	SZ 2355	47606
Plantation Club	Valmer, PO Box 437	7117	SZ 2370	71636
Reef	Anse aux Pins, PO Box 388	76251	SZ 2231	47606
Sheraton	Port Glaud, PO Box 540	74851	SZ2245	71571
Sunset Beach	Glacis, PO Box 372	47227	SZ2344	
Vista do Mar	Glacis, PO Box 622	47351	SZ 2318	

PRASLIN

Archipel	Anse Gouvernement	32040/32242	SZ2345	
Chateau de Feuilles	Pointe Cabris	33316	SZ 2255	
Chauve Souris Island Lodge	Chauve Souris Island, Praslin	32200	SZ2246	
Cote D'or Lodge	Cote d'or	32200	SZ 2246	
Flying Dutchman	Grande Anse	33337	SZ 2236	
Indian Ocean Fishing Club	Grande Anse PO Box 543	33324/33457	SZ 2201	
Maison des Palmes	Amitié	33411	SZ 2326	
Paradise	Anse Volbert	32255	SZ 2251	
Praslin Beach	Cote d'Or Praslin	32222	SZ 2250	47606

[Hotels]

Village du Pecheur	Cote d'Or, PO Box 586	32030	SZ 2394	32185

LA DIGUE

Island Lodge	Anse la Réunion	34233/32	SZ 2292
Gregoire's Island Lodge	Anse la Réunion	34233	SZ 2292

GUEST HOUSES

MAHÉ

Coco d'or	Beau Vallon, PO Box 665	47331	SZ 2325
Residence Bougainville	Anse Royale, PO Box 378	71334	–
Pension Bel Air	Bel Air Victoria, PO Box 116	24416	SZ 2310
Le Tamarinier	Bel Ombre	47611/47429	–
Carefree	Anse Faure, PO Box 403	76237	–
Auberge Louis XVII	La Louise, PO Box 607	44411	SZ 2259

BIRD ISLAND

Bird Island Lodge	Bird Island, PO Box 404	21525	SZ 2334

ISLETTE ISLAND (just off Mahé's SE Coast)

Islette	Port Glaud, PO Box 349	78229	–

SILHOUETTE ISLAND

Silhouette Island Lodge	Silhouette Island	24033	SZ 2396

Mahé

The largest island, where 90% of the population lives, Mahé is the centre of the tourist industry. Much of it is surrounded by a coral reef and the warm, blue waters are both safe for swimming and clean. Skin-diving, deep sea-fishing, sailing, water-skiing and the less demanding pursuits of sun-bathing and picnicking are all available in one of the world's most spectacular and lovely tropical settings.

Victoria, the capital and port, on the north east side of Mahé, is the only town of any size. It is a quaint, rather ramshackle place, the central point of which is a statue of Queen Victoria and a miniature Big Ben. The clock chimes twice, once on the hour and again a few minutes later in case the sleepy islanders missed the first strike. Indian and Chinese shops with wide verandahs and tin roofs line the main streets. Local handicrafts such as baskets, straw hats, carved fishbone, tortoise-shell and exotic sea-shells can be bought at reasonable prices.

Victoria is the business centre of the islands, and possesses all the normal services like banks, a tourist information office, travel agents and airline offices and a post office.

A little out of town, on rising ground with the magnificent mountains of Morne Seychellois and the Troi Frères soaring above, is State House – a classic white-painted colonial mansion with wide verandahs, green lawns and cool colonnaded interiors. Botanical gardens, which boast a rare and fine orchid garden, and a museum are on view to the public.

Entertainments: The night life is vibrant yet unsophisticated, and there is much to be enjoyed. The resort hotels generally offer something different every evening – barbecues, dances and films – and the local folk singers and dancers wander nightly from one hotel to another. A speciality is the Camtolet music, and dancers demonstrating the Seychelles Contredanse and the rhythmic Sega. Several hotels have nightclubs – Mahé Beach, Coral Strand and Vista do Mar and, less sophisticated, the Katiolo Club at Anse Faure near the airport. There are also cinemas in Victoria.

Sports: Warm, crystal-clear seas with protective coral reefs and white sandy beaches are ideal for swimming, goggling or snorkelling, scuba diving, underwater photography, water-skiing and wind surfing; all can be enjoyed in safety. Equipment is available for hire.

The marine life is prolific and snorkelling offers a spectacular underwater world. Marine National Parks and strict conservation laws protect the natural life of the sea and spear-fishing is strictly forbidden. Simple precautions when snorkelling; wear canvas shoes or flippers and never reach into a crevice with a bare hand. Also check the location of restricted areas where shelling is prohibited.

Fishing is a great sport in the Seychelles. Game fishing is relatively new but a variety of deep-sea fishing boats can be chartered for a day or a week of angling. Line fishing is also possible from the shore and can be enjoyed throughout the year.

There is an active Yacht Club in Victoria where visitors can usually arrange a temporary membership. Mini-sails and canoes can be hired. Power boats, cabin cruisers and yachts are available for charter. The Tourism division has a detailed list or Marine Charter Association, PO Box 469, Victoria. Tel: 222126.

Mahé also has facilities for golf, tennis, squash and horseriding and there are many picturesque walks on Mahé and other islands.

Shopping: Local handicrafts include basketware, table mats and straw hats. Jewellery is made from mother of pearl, green snail shells, coconuts, seeds and tortoiseshell. The Coco-de-Mer is a favourite and unique purchase. They may be in their natural state or highly polished and, as they are so large, some are halved to make salad bowls. Other handicrafts are made of bamboo, shark's teeth, raffia, fish-scales and vanilla pods. You can also buy bundles of cinnamon sticks. These products are on sale at the Home Industries Shop (opposite GPO), Home Craft Centre (Pirate's Arms) and Airport Souvenir Shop. There is also a duty-free shop in Victoria where you can buy local handicrafts, watches and cameras. In Victoria and at the larger resort hotels there are boutiques which offer a good variety of local tie-dye and 'batik' cotton beachwear.

Tourist Information: Kingsgate House, Victoria, Mahé, tel: 22655. Ministry of Tourism, PO Box 56, National House, Victoria, Mahé, tel: 22041.

Other Islands

Praslin, home of the world-famed Valée de Mai, lies two hours from Mahé by boat or 15 minutes by air. It is the second largest island. The main interest for the visitor is the botanical splendour of the Valée, home of the Coco-de-Mer palm with the large, double nuts. There are thousands of trees, some reaching to 102 feet. The beaches are lovely, swimming safe and snorkelling excellent. There is a hotel, lodges and guest houses.

La Digue, where the rare Black Paradise Flycatcher breeds in the woods, is considered by many to be the most beautiful of all the islands. There are conducted ox-cart excursions or a bicycle may be hired for local sightseeing. The island is tranquil, rural and unspoilt. Creole cuisine is a speciality. La Digue is two to three hours by boat from Mahé and measures three miles wide by two long.

Denis Island is a must for game fishermen. There are daily fishing excursions, and good snorkelling off the beach. It is 50 miles from Mahé (20 minutes by air). Turtles breed on this richly vegetated island and there is a hotel with chalets.

Bird Island, 60 miles from Mahé (six to eight hours by sea; 30 minutes by air), is best known for the one-and-a-half million Sooty Terns which nest there. It is a great draw for ornithologists and fishermen, too, as it is a particularly good area for deep-sea fishing. There is comfortable accommodation and good food.

Cousin is about two-and-a-half hours by boat from Mahé. It is a paradise for the ornithologist, as thousands of sea birds nest and breed there. It is owned and administered by the International Council for Bird Preservation.

Aride has the greatest concentration of seabirds, with the world's largest colonies of Lesser Noddy and Roseate Tern. Two hours by boat from Mahé.

Silhouette, the third largest island in the group, is two hours by boat from Mahé.

St Anne, Cerf, Round and Moyenne are situated in the Marine National Park, close to Victoria. Glass-bottomed boats are available for morning and afternoon excursions.

Moyenne is owned by a British ex-journalist, Brendan Grimshaw who welcomes tourists several times a week and serves them with a delicious Creole lunch after a 45 minute walk round the island. The day trip is combined with fish-viewing from a specially constructed boat with glass panels in its keel. It allows clear observation and photography of a myriad of tropical fish.

Thérèse, a two-and-a-half hour cruise from Victoria around Mahé's northern coast, has long sandy beaches and is pleasant for walking.

SOMALIA

Somalia, officially known as the Somali Democratic Republic since the 1969 military coup, has so far remained virtually untouched by the tourist wave spreading over Africa. Although it has the second largest coastline on the African continent – stretching for nearly 3,200 km along the shores of the Indian Ocean, around the Horn of Africa and along the Gulf of Aden – facilities for the tourist are largely lacking. The National Agency for Tourism has recently, however, embarked on a hotel programme and on improving facilities in the game parks.

Those who do visit the country will find people who are warm and friendly, beaches which are unspoilt and wildlife which is colourful and varied.

The Land and the People

Somalia is a hot, arid country, with a nomadic population, and scenery ranging from mountains in the north, through flat semi-desert plains, to the sub-tropical region of the south. Separated from the sea by a narrow coastal plain, the mountains gradually slope south and west to the central, largely waterless, plateau which occupies most of the country. While there are some ports, notably Mogadishu, Kismayu and Marka, good natural harbours are rare. A coral reef runs from north of Mogadishu to the Kenyan border in the south but sharks still get through and are dangerous causing a number of fatalities each year. The beaches are among the longest in the world, with many rare shells, including the Marginalis cowrie.

The only two perennial rivers, the Juba and the Shebelle, both rise in the Ogaden region of Ethiopia. Most of the agricultural land lies on the banks of these two rivers. Much of the interior – waterless and with little vegetation – is of little use and remains isolated, although an ambitious road programme will open up the remoter regions.

Somalia experiences little change in the seasons, except in the areas above 1,600 m. Most of the country is uniformly hot, with temperatures in the northern coastal towns rising to 42°C between June and September. The coastal regions are generally hot and humid while the interior is hot and dry. Rainfall is generally higher in the south, varying from 30 to 50 cm a year.

The population is concentrated in the coastal towns, in the northern areas with the highest rainfall and in the south near the two rivers. A large nomadic population is lightly scattered throughout the interior. Since the 1974 drought the Government has persuaded many nomads to settle as farmers of fishermen in new communities.

A tall, lithe people, the Somalis form a cultural, linguistic and religious

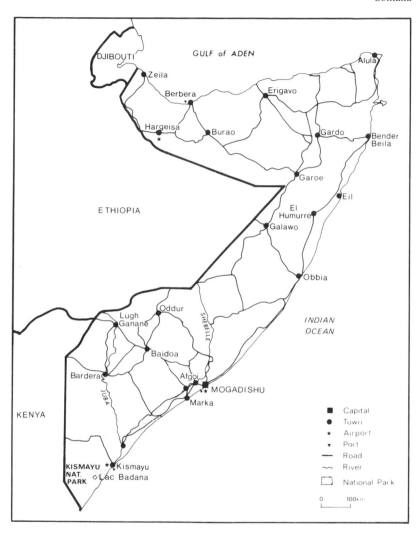

Area: 637,657 sq km
Population: 6.0 million (1989 estimate)
Capital: Mogadishu

unit, with Islam the dominant religion for over a millennium. The Somali language, a member of the Cushitic group, is now the official language. It was unwritten until 1972 when a Latin orthography was chosen.

All educated Somalis also speak Arabic and either Italian or English or both. Possibly because Somali was not traditionally a written language, it has a rich literature of narrative poetry of exceptional quality.

Somali craftsmen are renowned for their gold and silver jewellery, finely woven cloth and baskets from the Benadir region. Meerschaum ivory and wood carvings are also produced.

Traditional dance, music and folk songs still flourish. Ritualistic dances are performed to placate evil forces, diseases, crop failures, marauding wild animals and foreign invaders, while recreational dances celebrate happy events, including the coming of the rains, the harvest, marriages and births, the arrival of important visitors and the frequent traditional feats.

The *istun-ka* festival is a stick fight between groups of gaily dressed men from opposite banks of the Shebelle River at Afgoi, 32 km from Mogadishu, which commemorates the traditional contest used to decide which group would get the best part of the river's water during the dry season.

Poetry and drama have both seen considerable revival since independence and performances are given regularly in Mogadishu's National Theatre.

The International Somali Trade Fair and African film festival is held from 29 September to 12 October (this is biennial event).

History

The origins of the Somalis – the 'Black Berbers' of early Greek and Arab writers – date back thousands of years into the very earliest history of the Horn of Africa. Rock paintings and cave inscriptions in the northern region, such as those at Gaanlibah and Gelweita, near Las Khoreh, date from early Stone Age. As early as 1500 BC, the port of Mogadishu was known to the Egyptians, who called the country the 'Land of Punt'. Mogadishu also traded with the Phoenicians and supplied most of the frankincense and myrrh to the pre-Muslim kingdoms of the Arabia peninsula. In the 12th and 13th centuries Mogadishu's trading links extended to Thailand and China, as well as East Africa and the Middle East; while Berbera, on the north coast, Marka, a small seaport south of Mogadishu, and Zeila, now a ruined city near the Djibouti border, were also major trading centres.

Islam reached Somalia in the 7th century from Saudi Arabia across the Gulf of Aden. By the 13th century, Zeila was not only the capital of a powerful city-State but also one of the acknowledged centres of Islam. The ruler of Zeila in the mid-16th century beat back joint Portuguese-Ethiopian attacks, capturing the Abyssinian highlands.

The Sultanate of Oman – which had extended its control over Zanzibar and the East African coast and as far east as Pakistan – took control of southern Somalia. Britain, having established a base in Aden early in the

19th century, announced a protectorate over northern Somalia in 1927, while the French later occupied the port of Djibouti, which they controlled. The Omani-Zanzibari dynasty, which had occupied Mogadishu in 1871, sold its area to Italy in 1889. In the same decade, between 1881 and 1886, Britain extended its control in the north by more treaties with local chieftains. In 1898, Italy occupied its colony.

A major rebellion against colonial rule broke out in the south east corner of the British Protectorate in 1899, led by a famous religious leader whom the Europeans called the 'Mad Mullah of Somaliland' – who is venerated by Somali nationalists today – Mohammed Abdille Hassan. The resistance campaign lasted until the Mullah's death in 1921. Joint operations by Ethiopia, British and Italian troops – which included the first use of aircraft for military purpose in Africa – eventually cornered him in a remote area, but failed to destroy his movement. It eventually disintegrated shortly before his death under the impact of a smallpox epidemic.

With the advent of the Italo-Ethiopian war in 1935, Italy overran Ethiopia. It occupied the Somali Protectorate in 1940, during the Second World War, and all Somalis, except those in northern Kenya and Djibouti, were placed under one administration. After the defeat of the Italians in 1941-42, the British military continued this administrative pattern for some years. The great powers could not agree on the future of Italy's former colonies, and these rapidly became mere pawns in a wider diplomacy. In 1949 Italy was granted its former Somali colony by the United Nations on a ten-year trusteeship basis.

In 1959 with the preparation for independence of the Italian trusteeship territory, the British also came under pressure in the northern territory. The two territories became independent within 5 days of each other, in June and July 1960. They subsequently united to form the Somalia Democratic Republic. At that time there was no *de jure* border separating the latter from the Ogaden region in Ethiopia, inhabited almost entirely by Somali speaking nomads. To date, the 'provisional administrative line' established by Britain, Italy and Ethiopia at the time of the establishment of the Italian trust in 1949 is still all that exists. Repeated United Nations efforts to secure a demarcation between Ethiopia and Somalia between 1950 and 1960 show that the UN did not believe that the provisional administrative line was a *de jure* border.

A series of multi-party Governments succeeded each other in the new Republic, but the administration proved unable to curb increasing levels of corruption and inefficiency, and on 21 October 1969 the army led by Major-General Mohammed Siyad Barre took power in a bloodless coup. The government, which was centralised under a 'Supreme Revolutionary Council', pursued socialist policies, placing great emphasis on self-help schemes. A single party was formed, the Somali Socialist Revolutionary Party (SSRP).

From 1970-77 Somalia, from having been largely Western-oriented in foreign affairs, turned for aid and advice towards the Soviet Union and other eastern bloc countries, but tension soon developed between the Somali ambition to reunify the Somali lands on the one hand, and revised Soviet policies in the Horn on the other. In 1974 Somalia joined the Arab League and pressure on Somalia for political realignment increased.

The constant tension in the Ogaden region was aggravated by the failure of the Ethiopian government to act in time to prevent catastrophe during the 1974 famine. As the former Imperial Ethiopian administration collapsed it was the Somali government aided by the Soviet Union which responded to the crisis over her borders. However, in May 1977, the Soviet Union, in a change of political alignment, affirmed its support for the Ethiopian revolution, and began supplying arms to Ethiopia on a substantial scale, causing deep resentment among all Somalis. This led to the outbreak of the Ogaden war in July 1977. Somalia invaded the Ogaden and by the end of the year Ethiopia retained control only of the cities of Harar and Dire Dawa.

When the Soviet Union continued to arm the Ethiopian forces, Somalia withdrew all military facilities given to the Soviet Union and expelled all Soviet military and civilian advisors. Massive military aid from the Soviet and Cuban forces enabled Ethiopia to reoccupy the Ogaden in the following months and to defeat Somalia by March 1978.

These events have had predictable results – the Western Somalia Liberation Front has returned to guerrilla warfare which continues with harsh reprisals on the part of the Ethiopians. This has led to the present critical refugee situation within Somalia. There are over half a million refugees in camps and at least as many again roaming around the countryside. One person in four in Somalia is now a refugee from Ethiopia.

Severe drought in the northern regions has made the position ever worse and food shortages are affecting the whole country. The extra burden of feeding the hundreds of thousands of refugees is becoming an intolerable strain on an already fragile economy.

Following the party congress in January 1979, a new draft constitution was passed for public referendum and was approved in August 1979 by 99% of the votes cast. This constitution is the basis for a People's Assembly which holds office for five years and which elects a President for a six year term. In January 1980, President Mohammed Siyad Barre was unanimously re-elected by the country's new People's Assembly for a further six years. In November 1984 the Assembly passed constitutional amendments which transferred all effective power to the President. On 23 May 1986 Barre was badly injured in a motor accident but he recovered and resumed control. An invasion of northern Somalia by the Somali National Movement guerrillas, in May 1988 disrupted the north of the country, where troubles persist.

Economy

Somalia is a country with few natural resources and over 60% of the population are nomadic pastoralists, herding their camels, sheep and goats in the interior. Its principal export is livestock on the hoof, and skins to the Middle East, especially Saudi Arabia. Next in importance is the banana crop, grown in the riverine areas in the South. The bulk of the crop has traditionally gone to Italy but is increasingly being directed to Somalia's Arab neighbours.

The agricultural sector is limited to the cool areas west of Hargeisa and between the rivers Shabelli and Juba in the South. Apart from the bananas, the produce is all for domestic consumption. Several development schemes are in progress, perhaps the most important of which is the sugar development near Kismayu. This will allow Somalia to export sugar as well as satisfying her domestic demand, currently met by imports. The fishing industry is also being developed, with a fish canning plant in Las Khoreh on the Red Sea coast and a number of fishing communes being established all round the coasts. Manufacturing industry is very limited; alcohol and perfumes are produced in Jowhar and there is a textile and clothing factory in Bal'ad to the north-west of Mogadishu.

Continuing drought and the influx of refugees led to fresh appeals for international assistance in March 1986.

Wildlife

Lying astride the division between the near-desert and the bush territory of East Africa, Somalia has a wide selection of wildlife. The fauna has remained relatively undisturbed by development. The greatest profusion of wildlife is in the south near the two rivers, and includes elephant, rhino, hippo, giraffe, zebra, hartebeeste, gazelle, the greater and lesser kudu and the smaller antelope species. Animals in the northern and drier areas include the rare oryx and the wild ass.

National Parks

Somalia has three game parks and ten games reserves. The game reserves fall into three categories: absolute reserves (Lac Badana, Gedka-Dabley, Mogadishu and Mandere); controlled game reserves (Borama, Bush-Bush and the Juba left bank areas) and partial game reserves (Jowhar, Beled Weyne and Bulo-Burti areas). The **Kismayu National Park** in the south-west contains the widest variety of animals, including all the species common to East Africa and also many rarer species such as Soemmering gazelle, the Speke gazelle and the Somali dibtag. The game park north of Hargeisa in the mountainous area bordering the Gulf of Aden has such rare animals as the wild ass and klipspringer. A new national park was recently opened within easy reach of the capital. Roads are passable to the absolute reserves of Lac Badana and Gedka-Dabley. A number of parks and reserves can be reached from Kismayu and Mogadishu. Lodges are being constructed at Lac Badana and Bush-Bush.

General Information

Government

Somalia is a socialist state with a single party, the Somali Socialist Revolutionary Party (SSRP).

Languages

The official language of the country is Somali, using a written form with a Latin script since 1972. Arabic, English and Italian are also widely used by educated Somalis while Swahili is spoken in the southern coastal towns.

Religion

Islam. Most Somalis are Sunni Muslims.

How to Get There

By air: Somalia is served by the following international airlines: Alitalia, Aeroflot, Al Yamda, Kenya Airways and the Republic's own airline, Somali Airlines. Visitors arriving at Mogadishu Airport will need to take a taxi into town.
By rail: There are no railways in Somalia.
By sea: Mogadishu, Kismayu, Berbera, Marka are the main ports. A new port with modern shipping berths is being built at Mogadishu.

Entry Regulations

A visa is necessary for the visitor to Somalia and this is obtainable at Somali Embassies abroad. It is important that a visa be obtained *before* entering Somalia.

Certificates of inoculation against yellow fever and cholera are essential. Vaccinations against typhus, typhoid and tetanus are advisable, but not essential.

Customs Regulations

No customs duty is exacted for normal personal effects. Duty will be charged on any commercial items.

Visitors staying in the country for three months or less may import or export any amount of foreign currency. Import and export of Somali shillings is restricted. On arrival one has to pay 5s for a foreign currency declaration form and 5s for a counter-declaration form on departure.

Visitors should note that exchange of currency except through a bank or authorised hotel is prohibited in the Republic. An exchange control form is issued to visitors on arrival and should be filled in each time foreign currency is exchanged during the visitor's stay.

Climate

The nomadic cycle of movements follows the climatic pattern of four seasons: the *jilal* starts around January and is the harshest time, when vegetation dries up and the search for water begins in earnest. *Gu*, the first rainy season, generally lasts from March to June. August is the start of the dry season of *hagaa* when dust clouds are everywhere and the heavier monsoon winds blow. The second rainy season starts around September. This is called *dayr* and lasts till December.
What to wear: Dress is informal and lightweight. There is no objection to bikinis on the beach.

Health Precautions

Somalia is virtually free from such disease as yellow fever, smallpox and sleeping sickness but malaria is endemic and a prophylactic should be taken for a fortnight before the visit, during the visit and for a fortnight after.

Banks and Currency

Central Bank of Somalia, PO Box 11
Mogadishu
Commercial and Savings Bank of
Somalia, PO Box 203, Mogadishu
(branches in all major towns)
Currency: Somali shilling.
(See currency table, page 9).

Business Hours

Banks: Saturday-Thursday 0800-1130
Government Offices: Saturday-Thursday
0800-1400
Offices and Shops: Saturday-Thursday
0900-1300 and 1600-2000.

Public Holidays

New Year's Day, 1 January
Labour Day, 1 May
Eid al-Fitr*, 26/28 April 1990 (and two
following days)
Independence of Somaliland, 26 June
Independence Day for the Somali
Republic, 1 July
Eid al-Arifa*, 3/6 July 1990 (and two
following days)
Hijra*, 23 July 1990
Ashoura*, 2 August 1990
Anniversary of the 1969 Revolution,
21-22 October
Prophet's Birthday*, 2 October 1990
The dates of the Muslim holidays marked
with an asterisk, are only approximate as
they depend on sightings of the moon.

Embassies in Mogadishu

Algeria: PO Box 2850
Bulgaria: Via Trevis, PO Box 119
China PR: PO Box 548, Via Scire
Uarsama
Czechoslovakia: Km 4, PO Box 1167
Egypt: PO Box 74
France: Corso Primo Luglio, PO Box 13
Germany DR: PO Box 987
Germany FR: Via Muhammad Habi, PO
Box 17

India: Via Mogadishu, PO Box 955
Iran: Via Nazione Unite
Iraq: Via Lenin, PO Box 641
Italy: Via Alta Jiuba, PO Box 6, tel:
20544
Kenya: Km 4, PO Box 618, Via Mecca,
tel: 80857
Kuwait: Via Lenin, PO Box 1348
Nigeria: Villa Haji Fara
Pakistan: Corso Somalia, PO Box 339
Saudi Arabia: Via Mecca, PO Box 603
Sudan: Via Hoddor
Syria: Via Mcdina, PO Box 986
UK: Via Londra, PO Box 1036
USSR: Via Repubblica PO Box 607
USA: Via Primo Luglio, PO Box 574, tel:
20811
Yemen Arab Republic: Via Berbera
Yemen, People's Democratic Republic:
Corso Republica, PO Box 493
Yugoslavia: Via Mecca, PO Box 952

Transport

By air: Somali Airlines connects all major
towns in a network of regular internal
flights.
By road: There are restrictions on travel
outside Mogadishu. It is advisable to
check with the authorities on arrival.
There are good roads from Mogadishu to
Burao in the North and Baidoa in the
West. Further sections of road linking
Burao, Hargeysa and Berbera, and from
Mogadishu to Kismayu are under
construction.

Travellers wishing to see more than the
main towns, and their surrounding within
a 150 km radius, will probably need to
use the Somali Airlines internal services.

Improvements to roads to the Game
Parks in Lac Badana and Gedka-Dabley,
as well as the construction of suitable
landing strips, are being undertaken.
Car hire: In the larger cities there are taxi
scrvices. In Mogadishu, in addition to the
regular saloon-car taxis there are little
'Bee-taxis' constructed around a motor-
scooter which do a brisk trade in the city.

In Mogadishu, the visitor with an international driving licence can hire a drive-yourself at reasonable cost. Taxis can also be hired by the hour. It is advisable to fix the tariff beforehand.

Accommodation and Food

Hotels everywhere are run down and of a poor standard even in Mogadishu and Hargeysa. Other accommodation facilities are in Berbera, Borama, Burao, Afgoi, Marka and Kismayu, with usually at least one reasonable commercial hotel. There is also a system of Government rest houses in many places which provide four to ten beds. Accommodation facilities are provided in the national park south west of Kismayu and the one north of Hargeysa.

There are good restaurants in the larger towns, particularly in the capital, which serve Somali, European and Chinese food. The lobsters, prawns, squid and other fish are excellent.

Mogadishu

Lying alongside the Indian Ocean, Mogadishu offers a mixture of Somali and Italian influences. The old quarter of the capital, Hamar Weyn, retains signs of the city's former status as a major trading port for the region with an Arabic influence visible in the buildings. One major mosque, Fakhr-Din, dates from the 13th century, and another, Sheikh Abdul Aziz, is of unkown age.

Narrow alleys bustle with traditional craftworkers in gold, silver and cloth. Tourists can order their own jewellery designs in gold, silver and ivory in the smith's shops, where the prices remain relatively low.

The National Museum of Somalia, in the former palace of the Sultan of Zanzibar, is worth a visit. The building has beautifully carved doors and inside is some fine silverwork and a maritime room. The Museum is generally open from 0900 to 1300.

Mogadishu's beaches are one of its main attractions but sharks are now plentiful and swimming can be dangerous.

Hotels: Five hotels are available. The newest, largest, and most luxurious is the **Uruba Hotel** which has its own swimming pool and private beach. Also of high standard are the **Juba**, the **Shabelli**, the **Croce del Sud** tel: 23201, telex: 745 and the **Hotel Rugta Taleh** (motel suites). The Croce del Sud is located in the business centre in the city.

Restaurants: Eating out is not luxurious, but cheap and fairly good. There are a number of Italian restaurants, as well as places offering local specialities.

The restaurant **Azan's** next to the **Shabelli** hotel has a rooftop restaurant Terraza with a panoramic view over the rooftops of the city and offers excellent Italian and International cuisine. Also well worth a visit are the open-air restaurant of the **Croce del Sud** hotel, the Chinese restaurant **Ming Sing** and the **Cappuccetto Nero.** In all these restaurants lobster, crab and fresh tuna are especially good, as are Somali bananas, mangos and papaya. The restaurants of the **Uruba** and **Juba** hotels serve good international food and during the month of Ramadan are the only places allowed to serve food during daylight hours. The visitor to Somalia should also try the delicious traditional Somali meal of roast kid and spiced rice, especially good at the Shabelli hotel restaurant.

Entertainments: Night-clubs with local bands playing European and African music include the **Lido** and **Azan's.**

Sports: Visitors may join the Anglo-American Beach Club which offers swimming and inexpensive food. The Golf Club is a popular social rendezvous.

Tourist Information: The National Agency for Tourism, PO Box 533, Mogadishu, tel: 2031.

Other Towns

Capital of the former British Protectorate, **Hargeysa** (population 100,000) is situated in the highlands of the north. It has a modern airport and hotels of European standard. Some international flights stop at Hargeysa, which is a livestock trading centre.

Tourists should make their arrangements with the National Agency for Tourism for visits to other cities, for example the smaller town of **Afgoi,** an agricultural centre, and the old seaport of **Marka,** both near the capital, **Berbera,** the seaport on the northern coast, and **Kismayu** on the southern coast near the Kenyan border.

Kismayu airport, after modernisation, is now superior in passenger facilities to Mogadishu and Kismayu also boasts the best hotel in Somalia, the **Waamo Hotel** which is set in attractive parkland, complete with monkeys and ostriches and which offers accommodation in ethnic styled chalets. The hotel is situated just outside the town and there is a frequent bus service to the town centre. The Government hopes to make Kismayu into a major centre for the national parks in the south. Visitors to Kismayu can arrange safaris beforehand with the Ministry of Tourism in Mogadishu or save the latter's commission by organising trips directly through the state tourist office in the Waamo Hotel. Kismayu's architecture displays evidence of both Portuguese and Arab styles.

Somali shopkeeper

ALAN HUTCHISON

SUDAN

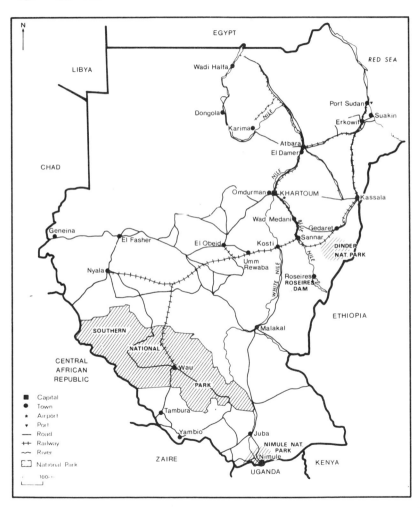

Area: 2,505,813 sq km
Population: 24.6 million (1989 estimate)
Capital: Khartoum (including Omdurman)

Sudan has a special appeal to all adventurous travellers. Its huge size embraces a bewildering variety of communities, climatic regions, types of terrain, vegetation and wildlife. But the sheer vastness of the country has its drawbacks for the modern tourist and business visitor. Communications outside Khartoum are often difficult and slow and few of the accommodation facilities outside the capital are up to international standards. Moreover Sudan is periodically hit by shortages of such essentials as petrol and it is as well to ask about travel conditions in advance of any intended visit.

For the visitor to Khartoum or Port Sudan with a tight schedule it is also advisable to make advance reservations for the first-class hotels. Second and third class hotels exist but an expansion of the country's accommodation facilities is necessary to meet the growing tourist and business traffic. It should also be stressed that travel to Juba, and the south generally, is still not a simple matter and precise information should be requested before journeying.

For all this, any trouble taken to explore the Sudan will be amply rewarded, both by the warmth and hospitality of the people, and by the rich experience of journeys along the Nile, to the Dinder National Park, or the coral reefs of the Red Sea.

Africa meets the Middle East

The Sudan may be divided into four geographical regions. The desert region, covered by the Libyan and Nubian deserts, lies in the north and extends south to Khartoum. The Nile River Valley runs through the centre of this area and there is some vegetation at the scattered oases. The steppe region from Khartoum to El-Obeid in central Sudan is covered by short, coarse grass and bushes. The Kordofan plateau lies 500 m above most of the area. The Savannah region is south of the steppe. The equatorial region stretching across the south of the country consists mainly of a shallow basin traversed by the Nile and its tributaries. In the centre lies the Sudd, an enormous marsh over 120,000 sq km. Mount Kinyeti rises 3,480 m on the border between Sudan and Uganda.

The country's special geographical and ecological factors combine to provide a rich variety of flora and fauna.

The Sudanese are of Hamitic and Negro origin, though in the North there has been much intermingling with the Arabs and the people there are traditionally nomadic or semi-nomadic. In the Southern Region the Nilotic peoples predominate. The Southern Region unlike the North, which is largely Muslim and Arab, is much more African in culture.

The Sudanese like to think of their country as a meeting point for the Middle East and Africa and they often speak of it as being a bridge between Africa North and South. The Sudan is very rich in tribal culture and folklore: each tribe has its systems of belief, style of living, handicraft and folkdances, musical instruments, hand carving and weaving.

Antiques

About 160 km north of Khartoum is the Shendi area where monuments dating back to the ancient Meroitic Kingdom are found. They include the antiquities of Naga, Masawarat and Bajrawiya as well as churches and monasteries from the period when the Sudan was a Christian country (6th to 14th century).

North of Shendi, and half-way between the Egyptian border and Khartoum in the middle of the Nile loop, is the town of Karima near the Barkal Mountain, site of the ancient Napata Kingdom, centre of the first Sudanese Empire which ruled the whole of ancient Sudan and Egypt during the 25th dynasty. The temple of the God Amun is well preserved. In the Kuru area, a few miles from Karima, are the pyramids of the Kings of Napata. Across the river are the pyramids of Nuri. All these areas can easily be reached by rail, air or road from Khartoum.

History

The history of Sudan, especially the region north of Khartoum, was bound from ancient times with that of Egypt. In 750 BC the first Sudanese kingdom of Napata flourished near the Barkal Mountain and its Cushitic kings also ruled over Egypt. Meroe, near present-day Shendi, was the second of these ancient kingdoms, famous for its iron works which exported iron to other parts of Africa. The medieval kingdoms of Nubia, Maquarra and Abodia – which flourished in northern Sudan – were converted to Christianity during the sixth century. The next important phase came with the penetration of the Arabs and Islam. The 16th century saw the rise of the kingdoms of the Fung, Darfur, Tagali and other minor dynasties. During this period Arabisation and Islamisation of the northern parts was completed, but the south has been largely unaffected by these influences.

Although little is known about the history of the south during this period, it is certain similar kingdoms to those which existed elsewhere in Africa at the time also existed there.

In 1820 the country was conquered by Egypt and the Turko-Egyptian regime was established. In 1881 Muhammed Ahmed al-Mahdi led a successful revolt against the Turko-Egyptian rulers. Britain occupied Egypt the same year but forces under General Gordon failed to arrest the Mahdi's revolt and they were defeated in 1886. Khartoum was captured by the Mahdi whose Islamic state lasted for 13 years. Control of the Nile waters became a British colonial priority and in 1898 the Mahdists were defeated by British-Egyptian forces in the battle of Omdurman.

From then until 1956 Sudan was ruled by the Condominium Administration – a supposedly joint Egyptian and British Administration which in reality accorded Britain political domination. The colonial administration established railways, a modern system of education, the important Gezira peasant cotton scheme and a central system of government.

Following the July 1952 revolution in Egypt, the British agreed to demands for Sudanese independence. The South which sought either separation or federal association with the north was disappointed by the rejection of its demands by the transitional government and the country was in the throes of civil war when Britain departed and Sudan became independent in 1956. A parliamentary system of government was established but it was overthrown in a military coup in 1958. This regime foundered in 1964 when its failure to end the increasingly expensive southern war prompted a popular revolt. Sadiq al-Mahdi, the great-grandson of Muhammed Ahmed came to power in 1966. From 1965-69 economic conditions deteriorated drastically and the civil war continued unabated. The ensuing political crisis encouraged another military takeover in May 1969. The coup was led by younger radical officers under Major-General Numeiry, who was elected President in September 1971. His major achievement was to reach agreement with the southern Sudanese rebels in March 1972, at Addis Ababa, which gave the south regional autonomy and brought to an end the war which had sapped the strength of the country for 17 years.

However after the signing of the Addis Ababa agreement there was only sporadic progress towards development in the South. Resentment at northern domination was fanned by difference of opinion about exploitation of considerable oil reserves in the South, and by lack of faith in government policies.

Numeiry's regime was populist in orientation and Sudan was to be 'democratic, socialist and non-aligned'. Foreign banks and trading companies were nationalised and the estates of wealthy members of the powerful Muslim sects were expropriated. Sudan's economic shortcomings, however, forced Numeiry to support more moderate economic policies. Furthermore, Saudi economic aid was accompanied by moves to adopt a more orthodox application of Islamic Sharia law. State-run football pools were abolished, prostitutes driven off the streets and bars periodically closed.

In the wake of prolonged riots in August 1979, caused by petrol and bread shortages in Khartoum, massive inflation and increased taxes on tobacco and alcohol, in March 1980 Numeiry called for fresh elections for both the national and regional assemblies after a radical shake up of his government.

Numeiry was re-elected to a further six years as President in January 1980, but he faced an increasingly difficult refugee problem as the 400,000 refugees in Sudan became a growing burden for the ever-more precarious economy.

By mid-1980 the links with Egypt had been drawn closer particularly in respect of economic co-operation and the pursuit of tourism. Ties became even tighter with the signing of the "Charter of Integration" on 12 October 1982. It is intended to bring the two countries together over a ten year period and to give a formal structure to existing co-operation.

Numeiry's unpopularity in the south grew with the imposition of the Islamic Sharia law in September 1983 and martial law in March 1984. A new southern rebel movement the Sudanese People's Liberation Army (SPLA) emerged in the south and proved impossible to dislodge.

In 1985 divisions opened up also in the north over the Sharia law and Numeiry's increasingly autocratic rule. There were strikes over increased prices of food and fuel. Professional men started a campaign of civil disobedience. The mounting tension led the army to intervene and depose Numeiry on 6 April 1985 when he was visiting the USA. A military government under Lt-Gen Swar el Dahab then took over. Sadiq el Mahdi became Prime Minister of a new civilian government in April 1986. Another military government under General Omar el Bashir seized power in July 1989.

Economy

Most of the country's foreign exchange is gained from export of a single main crop – cotton. Groundnuts, sorghum, gum arabic and livestock are also important export products.

Most Sudanese are directly involved in agriculture and pastoralism, however the country has not been able to realise its full potential in this field. Agricultural development has been held back by a lack of basic inputs. Currently the World Bank is leading a number of aid agencies in an ambitious programme to rehabilitate various agricultural schemes. Success depends very greatly on efficient irrigation. The most important project in this respect is the Jonglei Canal scheme. Also at an advanced stage is the Rahad River irrigation project designed to use water stored in the Roseires Dam on the Blue Nile to reclaim 820,000 acres of land.

The Gezira irrigated farming project is the world's largest farm under single management and its central importance stems from Sudan's dependence on cotton which accounts for about 50% of export earnings.

Sudan's construction industry is currently suffering from a lack of building supplies and cement in particular. Consequently, cement production in the country is receiving attention under the present development plan. Hotel construction is expected to be a major growth industry as there is a serious shortage of accommodation. At present Port Sudan, or the Red Sea, 784 km from Khartoum, is the only seaport. This leads to congestion and increased transport costs. The discovery and exploitation of oil in the south at the Unity field, was suspended in February 1984 when some Chevron oilmen were captured by the SPLA guerillas. The digging of the Jonglei canal was also stopped for the same reasons.

The economy virtually collapsed in the 1980s, with massive payments and budgetary deficits and escalating debt, despite a series of rescue attempts by the IMF, and foreign banks and Arab donors.

Wildlife

The full range of African wildlife is represented in the Sudan's reserved areas and national parks. It is possible to travel into the bush where elephants and buffaloes wander in big herds. Giraffe, zebras, lions, hippo and crocodiles can be found in the reeds and swamps with other species of wild animals and magnificent colourful birds. But please check in Khartoum on which parks are open.

Darfur is another area rich in game. There are more addax and oryx here than in any other part of Africa. The ibex, which is rare almost everywhere else, can still be hunted in the Red Sea Hills area.

The Dinder National Park is the best developed of the tourist areas and can be reached by road, rail and air from Khartoum.

National Parks

There are three game parks and 17 game reserves and sanctuaries.

Dinder National Park (6,100 sq km) is open to visitors from Christmas to the end of April. It is 512 km south-east of Khartoum and closer to Europe than any of the other more popular African big-game reserves. Visitors can stay in a specially built village with an attractive restaurant and bar area under spreading trees.

The visitor can expect to see many different types of animals and birds and a spectacular range of rolling savannah grasslands, sandy palm groves and tropical forest.

The most abundant animal species are the many types of antelope – the magnificent roan antelope, quite rare in most African game parks, the spiral-horned greater kudu, waterbuck, reedbuck, signa gazelle, oribi and bushbuck. There are also lion, giraffe, buffalo, warthog, several types of monkey, mongoose, fox and wild cat. The bird species include ostrich, eagle, vulture, guinea-fowl, pelican, bustard, crowned crane and large numbers of colourful smaller birds.

In the south are Nimule National Park (192 km south of Juba with its own holiday village in Gumeiza) and the Southern National Park (Bahr al-Ghazal Province – 18,400 sq km). In these two parks and in other parks of southern Sudan, amid gigantic trees and high waving grass, elephants roam in herds which occasionally number as many as 400. Among the swamp reeds hippo, crocodile and buffalo are plentiful, as well as giraffe, rhino, zebra, leopard, lion and various types of cat. There are many types of antelope as well as countless birds, butterflies and beetles.

General Information

Government

The constitution of April 1973 was suspended after the coup of 6 April 1985. Civilian government was restored on 26 April 1986.

Languages

Arabic, the official language, is spoken by about half the population. The majority of Arab speakers are in the centre and the north and in the major towns. English is widely spoken and is the language of the Government in the South. Nilotic, Nilo-Hamitic, Sudanic and Darfurian languages are also spoken. In total, well over 100 languages are spoken in Sudan.

Religions

Sudan is predominantly Sunni Muslim but there are also Christian communities. Traditional religions are more widespread in the south than either Christianity or Islam.

How to Get There

By air: Khartoum airport is served internationally by Aeroflot, Air France, Alitalia. Balkan Airways, British Airways, Egypt Air, Ethiopian Airlines, KLM, Kuwait Airways, Lufthansa, Libyan Arab Airlines, MEA, SAS, Saudi Arabian Airlines, Sudan Airways, Swissair, Tunis Air, and Yemen Airways.

The national carrier, Sudan Airways, connects Khartoum with Egypt, Germany, Greece, Jordan, Italy, Kenya, Kuwait, Lebanon, Qatar, Saudi Arabia UAE and the UK.

All passengers embarking on international flights from Khartoum must pay an airport charge. Taxis are available at the airport, which is about 10 minutes by car from the centre of Khartoum, on the eastern outskirts of the city. On request airlines sometimes arrange for passenger transport from hotels to the airport.

By air: Ships from various parts of the world dock at Port Sudan on the Red Sea, the country's only seaport.

By road: Motorists must apply for permission to drive through Sudan well in advance of the journey (three months' notice is advisable). Applications should be made to the Under Secretary, Ministry of Interior, PO Box 770, Khartoum, or any Sudanese Legation or Embassy, and should list names and nationalities of travellers, number, make and horsepower of vehicles, reason for journey, proposed route and ultimate destination. Motorists must have a tryptique or carnet de passage from a recognised automobile club, or must pay a deposit or provide a guarantee signed by a known resident of Sudan, a bank or a business firm. Vehicles must be insured.

Permission to motor in, or through, Sudan may not be granted for less than two vehicles travelling together, and drivers should enquire about the state of roads before starting the journey. In main towns and their environs roads are surfaced but most outlying roads are rough tracks with sandy stretches, requiring strong vehicles.

Entry from Ethiopia has been impossible for some years because of the state of emergency in Eritrea.

By river and rail: From Egypt by train from Cairo to Aswan High Dam, by Aswan High Lake steamer, with rudimentary accommodation, from Aswan High Dam to Wadi Halfa and from there by train to Khartoum. Accommodation on trains must be reserved in advance.

For further information contact the Sudan Tourist Office, 308 Regent Street, London W1R 5AL. Tel: 01-631 1785.

Entry Regulations

Visas are needed by all visitors and should be obtained in advance from a Sudanese diplomatic mission abroad; they are not obtainable at Khartoum airport. Passports must be valid for at least three months beyond the period of intended stay.

Transit visas are available on arrival for visitors from countries with no Sudanese representation, provided they hold the required documents and have a confirmed reservation for a connecting flight within 24 hours. These visitors may not leave the airport. Admission to Sudan and transit rights are refused to holders of Israeli passports, or passports containing a valid or expired visa for Israel or South Africa. If travelling from Egypt a visa must be obtained from Cairo.

Visitors staying in Sudan longer than three days must report to the police. For travel to the southern regions – Bahr al-Ghazal, Equatoria and Upper Nile, including Malakal, Wau and Juba airports – a special permit must be obtained from a Sudanese representative abroad, or from the Ministry of the Interior in Khartoum (which takes five days).

Inoculation against yellow fever and cholera is recommended.

Customs Regulations

Foreign currencies in unlimited amounts may be imported, provided these amounts are allowed by the country of origin. All foreign currency, including travellers' cheques and letters of credit, must be declared on entry and departure. Exchange should be made only at authorised exchange points – ie banks and certain hotels and travel agencies –

and entered on the declaration form, which needs to be shown on departure. Export of foreign currency by visitors is limited to the amount imported. Import and export of local currency is prohibited.

Customs may sometimes be levied on articles such as cameras, typewriters, firearms, etc, subject to refund if they are taken out again within six months. A guarantee signed by a bank or business firm or a known resident may be accepted in lieu of a deposit. Special permission from the Ministry of Interior is required for the import of firearms.

Climate

The best time to visit Sudan (climatically) is in winter – November to March. Sandstorms rage across the Sahara from April to September. There is little rain in the extreme north. In the central region rainfall averages about 15 cm a year, most of it confined to July and August. In the south the annual average is about 100cm and the rainy season lasts from May to October. Summers are hot throughout the country, with temperatures ranging from 27°C to 46°C. Winter temperatures are around 16°C in the north and 27°C in the south.

In Khartoum the coolest month is January and the hottest June.

What to wear: Lightweight clothing is essential for most of the year but light woollens and a coat are needed in the winter. A raincoat will be necessary during July and August. Dress is almost always informal. Sunglasses are advisable.

Health Precautions

Precautions against malaria are advisable, although Khartoum itself is free of the disease. The water supplies of major towns are safe to drink. Swimming in slow-moving or static fresh water is not advisable as bilharzia is endemic.

Banks and Currency

Bank of Sudan, PO Box 313, Khartoum
Bank of Credit and Commerce International, PO Box 5, Khartoum
Bank of Khartoum, 8 Gamhouria Ave, PO Box 1008, Khartoum
El Nilein Bank, Parliament Street, PO Box 466, Khartoum
National Bank of Abu Dhabi, PO Box 2465, Khartoum
Sudan Commercial Bank, Kasr Avenue, PO Box 1116, Khartoum
Unity Bank, Barlaman Ave, PO Box 408, Khartoum
Citibank, Tel: 76640
Currency: The Sudanese pound (£S) divided into 100 Piastres. (See currency table, page 9).

Business Hours

Weekly closing day Friday.
Banks: Saturday-Thursday 0830-1200.
Government offices: Khartoum Saturday-Thursday 0630-1400; other towns Saturday-Thursday 0800-1400.
Central Telegraph Offices: 24 hours daily, including holidays.
Shops: Saturday-Thursday 0800-1300 and 1700-2000 (Friday 0800-1130).

Public Holidays

Independence Day, 1 January
National Unity Day, 3 March
Easter (Christians only) 15 April 1990
Ramadan begins*, 26 April 1990
1969 Revolution Day 25 May
Eid el-Fitr*, 26/28 April 1990
Eid el-Adha*, 3/6 July 1990
Hijra (Muslim New Year)* 23 July 1990
Prophet's Birthday*, 2 October 1990
Christmas (Christians only), 25 December
The dates of the muslim holidays, marked with an asterisk, are only approximate as they depend on sightings of the moon.

Embassies in Khartoum

Algeria: 31 Street
Belgium: Sharia Al Mek Nimr, No 4
CAR: Africa Road, tel: 45691
Chad: Street 17, PO Box 1514
China PR: 93 Street 22, tel: 222036
Denmark: Sharia el Gamhouria, tel: 80489
Egypt: Mogram Street, PO Box 1126
Ethiopia: 6, 11A Street 3, PO Box 844
France: 6H East Plot 2, 19th Street
Germany FR: 53 Baladiya Street, Block 8, tel: 77990
Italy: 39th Street, PO Box 793, tel: 45326
Jordan: 25, 7th Street, tel: 43264
Kuwait: Africa Ave, tel: 81525
Lebanon: 60 Street 49, tel: 45002
Libya: Africa Road 50, PO Box 2091
Morocco: St No 1, tel: 43223
Netherlands: PO Box 391, tel: 77788
Niger: Street 1, PO Box 1283
Nigeria: PO Box 1538, tel: 79120
Qatar: Street 15, tel: 42208
Saudi Arabia: Central Street, PO Box 852
Somalia: St 23-25, tel: 44800
Spain: Street 3, PO Box 2621, tel: 45072
Switzerland: New Aboulela Bldg., PO Box 1707
Syria: 3rd Street, PO Box 1139, tel: 44663
Tanzania: No 6 Square 42, tel: 78404
Turkey: 71 Africa Road, tel: 73894
Uganda: Excelsior Hotel, room 408/410
United Arab Emirates: Street 3
UK: New Aboulela Bldg., PO Box 801, tel: 70767
USA: Abdel Latif Avenue, PO Box 699, tel: 74700
Yemen Arab Republic: Street 35, tel: 43918
Zaire: Gamhouria Avenue, PO Box 4195, tel: 42424

Transport

Official permits are required for most journeys in the Sudan; they can be obtained from the Registry Office, Khartoum. You should also register with the police in each town you spend the night.

By air: Sudan Airways domestic service is subject to frequent change. Visitors are advised to check until the moment of departure. For reservations tel: 80871. Khartoum – Port Sudan is the most reliable. Flights to Juba, Kassala, El-Obeid, Malakal, Wau, Dongola were operating at the time of publication.

National Agricultural Organisations (Air Taxi) supplies a two weekly DC3 service to Nyala and operates single-engined charter throughout Sudan. Booking office at Khartom Airport and opposite the Farouk Mosque. For rates, tel: 75207.

By rail: Sudan has the longest railway network in Africa. The trains are comfortable and clean (first class) and are a good way to see much of the country and its people. They are, however, extremely slow. Three different classes are available plus an extra, *mumtaza*, which is excellent. There are trains to Port Sudan, Wadi Halfa, El-Obeid, Nyala, Wau, Roseires and Kassala. Sleeping cars and catering services are available on the main routes. Students' reductions are available on application to the Ministry of Youth in Khartoum.

By road: Although major work is underway to modernise roads, conditions are generally poor outside towns. Motorists should make inquiries about road conditions and administrative restrictions in the places they intend to visit. Roads in the north are often closed during the rainy season (July-September). In the south a number of roads are open throughout the year, but surfaces are poor. Sudan has very few tarred roads. A complete spare-part kit should be taken on any long journey.

Cars can be hired in the main towns. Auto Rent (PO Box 816, Khartoum) can provide chauffeur-driven vehicles for businessmen. Traffic drives on the right.

Khartoum's yellow taxis can be hailed in the street. They are not metered and fares should be arranged before the journey is undertaken. It is not necessary to tip the driver. There are also collective taxis which can be found in Khartoum market place.

Buses run between the main towns, and leave from the central market place (there is one in each of Khartoum's 'Three Towns').

By road-lorry: Lorries rumble throughout Sudan and are a cheap means of travel for the hardy visitor. For information on lorries, tel: 71882. Hitchhiking is not recommended.

By river: The River Transport Corporation (tel: 35654) operates a Nile steamer service.

Dongola-Karima (Sunday-Thursday)
Karima-Dongola (Monday-Thursday)
Kosti-Juba (alternate Wednesday) Juba-Kosti (Sunday).

The Dongola – Karima trip takes two days and is suitable for tourist travel. Trains from Khartoum are timed to meet the steamers (five).

At present, the southern service is more geared to local travel and cargo. Conditions are rough. You must take food and water. Downward voyages take 11 days, from Juba about eight days, depending on the river.

The River Transport Corporation is building four new 270-passenger steamers for the Kosti-Juba service. The first began operations in 1980.

Old river steamers may be hired for cruises in Khartoum.

Accommodation

There are a limited number of high standard hotels in Khartoum and Port Sudan. Elsewhere there are rest houses, with variable standards and permission must be obtained in advance to use them. There are plenty of cheap hotels in the main towns, although proprietors may be unwilling to take foreigners unless they do not mind sharing a room. There are youth hostels in Atbara, Ed Damazin,

El-Obeid, Kadogli, Khartoum and Port Sudan.

The restaurants in the Khartoum and Port Sudan hotels serve international cuisine. There are a few Greek and Middle Eastern restaurants.

Sudanese dishes served in small restaurants usually consist of *fool* – bean and bread and meat, and *dura* – cooked millet or maize. If you are invited into a Sudanese home you will be regaled with much more exotic fare.

Tipping: Hotels 10% of the bill; restaurants 10%.

Fishing on the Nile near Khartoum

Khartoum

Khartoum is generally known as the 'Three Towns' capital, ie Khartoum, Omdurman and Khartoum North. Omdurman is considered to be a national capital, Khartoum the commercial and administrative capital and Khartoum North the industrial capital. The three towns lie at the junction of the Blue Nile and the White Nile. Omdurman is joined to Khartoum by the White Nile bridge; the Shambat bridge joins Omdurman to Khartoum North and the Burri bridge joins the eastern extension of Khartoum to Khartoum North across the Blue Nile.

After its destruction in 1885 Khartoum was rebuilt on modern and spacious lines with huge colonial buildings, but old houses with shuttered windows, narrow streets and colourful market-places can still be found.

Particularly noteworthy from an

Hotels

NAME	ADDRESS	TELEPHONE	TELEX
KHARTOUM			
Acropole	PO Box 589	72860	–
Ambassador	PO Box 1808	72974	–
Araak	PO Box 1957	74826	22251
Excelsior	PO Box 272	81182	22361
Friendship Place	PO Box 148 Baladia Park	78294	26017
Grand Hotel	PO Box 316	72782/5	22436
Green Village	PO Box 2360	73949	20407
Hilton International	PO Box 1910	74100/78930	22250
Meridien	PO Box 1716 Qasr Avenue	75970/7	22499
Oasis	PO Box 272	81137/39	22361
Sudan	PO Box 1845	80811	22594
Take Hotel	PO Box 732	76912	–
PORT SUDAN			
Red Sea Hotel	PO Box 105	2813/4	–
Tagog Hotel	PO Box 609	–	–
Sudan Palace	PO Box 414	–	–
WAD MEDANI			
Wad Medani International	PO Box 213	392	–
JUBA			
Juba Hotel	Juba	2811/3310	–

historic and artistic point of view is a visit to the well organised National Museum. This museum contains archaeological treasures dating back to 4000 BC and earlier. A visit to the Natural History Museum is worthwhile to see the extensive collection of birds found in the Sudan. Near the river front is a zoo where the visitor can view animals or merely stroll on the lawn.

Among the other attractions in Khartoum are the Central Market; the Sunken Forest, a picnic spot and an interesting place for bird lovers; Tutti island (a ferry service leaves from opposite the Friendship Hall); wrestling on the banks of the Blue Nile at Burri on Friday afternoons.

Omdurman

Omdurman is rich in traditional Sudanese architecture: flat-roofed, baked mud or clay houses, city walls, narrow street of dark little shops where some of the finest Sudanese handicrafts can be found. Omdurman was built by the Mahdi when he began he siege against Gordon in Khartoum, and it became the capital of the Mahdi's empire. It was captured in 1898 when Kitchener led the British and Egyptians against the forces of the Khalifa.

Major attractions are the Mahdi's tomb and the Khalifa House, now a museum (open 0830-1330 except Monday). It contains interesting memorabilia of the Battles of Khartoum and Omdurman, letters from the Mahdi and General Gordon, photographs, pistols, uniforms and other relics. A camel market is held daily outside Omdurman at Hai el-Arab. There is a small boat-building industry by the Nile at Abu Rof. At 1630 pm on Friday Dervishes dance in the Hamad el-Nil Cemetery; other sects dance on weekdays in Omdurman. There is no charge.

Travel agents in Khartoum offer conducted tours of Omdurman which are advisable as sightseeing is difficult alone. A permit is required for photography, which makes little difference and visitors are warned to exercise caution.

Omdurman has long been the meeting place of all the peoples of Sudan; the Jaaleen, Shaigiyya, Danagla, Rubatab and Mahas of the north live side by side with the Baggara and Fur of the west and the Shilluk and Dinka of the south.

Restaurants: Besides the luxury facilities offered by bigger hotels – Grand, Hilton, Sahara – the following are popular restaurants.

Al Bustan, Khartoum 2, cnr. Africa Rd/Mek Nimr South, tel: 73138.

Barbari, Sh Zubeir Basha.

Bimbo, Parliament Street.

Blue Nile Cafe, Sh En Nil, near Burri railway bridge, tel: 34865.

Casablanca, Parliament St.

Escrabie, Sh 47 Khartoum 2.

St James, Gamhouria St.

Entertainments: National Theatre, Nile Avenue, Omdurman, tel: 51549 – the season is 1 October to 30 June. The **Hilton** open-air night club is popular. There are several cabarets and cinemas.

There is a sailing club and a nine-hole golf club, and the Cultural Centre has a good library and facilities for tennis and swimming. Golf and tennis are also available at the Hilton.

There are also a number of interesting Nile cruises. Launches with capacity for 15 persons can be hired: 24 hours' notice is required.

Additional entertainments are **Hamad Floating Casino,** Nile Avenue, Khartoum; **Blue Nile Cafeteria,** Nile Avenue, Khartoum; **Ali Abdel Latif Stadium,** Omdurman; and **Youth Stadium,** Khartoum; **Jimmy's Night Club,** Khartoum. **Shopping and markets:** The souk in Omdurman sells a variety of gold jewellery, basketware and traditional crafts. Basketware and spices are sold in the souk in Khartoum. Curio shops in Khartoum central sell decorated gourds, beads, cheap silver jewellery and ivory artifacts. Visitors are urged not to buy cheetah skins as the slaughter of cheetahs is forbidden by the world wildlife act.

Tourist Information: Tourism and Hotels Corporation, PO Box 7104, tel: 74031, telex: 22203, cable: Hababkum, Khartoum. There are regional offices in Port Sudan and Nyala. Travel Agent: Sudan Travel and Tourism Agency, PO Box 769, tel: 72119.

Port Sudan

Sudan's port city replaced the old-established city of Suakin at the beginning of the 20th century. It is a bustling commercial centre, with well-stocked shops and a market. Port Sudan also has some splendid houses and gardens.

The 'marine gardens' with their exquisite coral and tiny fish can be visited in glass-bottomed boats. There is sailing in the harbour, swimming in a choice of pools and tremendous scope for fishing (barracuda, grey cod, shark, etc.).

Port Sudan is a base to visit the Red Sea coral reefs which are renowned for excellent diving (spear-fishing is prohibited). Diving holidays are possible at Sanganeb, 2½ hours by boat.

Suakin lies 56 km south down the excellent new highway. Although most of its coralstone houses have crumbled beyond repair, Suakin is a small jewel, highly recommended for a day's visit. There are no amenities and visitors should take food and drink from Port Sudan. Suakin is a coral islet linked to the mainland suburb of el-Geif by a short causeway. El-Geif is a functioning settlement of fundamental economic

Suakin

Old man of Suakin

activities associated with visiting nomads like the Hadendowa, the Bani Amir and the Rashyda. Both places are easily explored on foot.

Erkowit is a summer resort in the Red Sea Hills, inland from Suakin and Port Sudan, offering relaxation among beautiful mountains which rise to 1,200 m above sea level. It has a good hotel with easy access from the railway station.

Wad Medani

Tourists interested in agriculture can make a day trip from Khartoum to Wad Medani, capital of the Gezira area in the

Blue Nile province. The trip has more significance during the growing period as cotton fields line the roadside. The ginneries can be visited. The headquarters of the Sudan Gezira Board at Barakat are most attractive and have pleasant rest house facilities. Tours leave Khartoum early and do not return until night which is tiring for elderly travellers. Some tours spend a night in Wad Medani and visit the Sennar Dam the following day.

Other Places of Interest

Sudan's archaeological areas stretch along the banks of the Nile north of Khartoum to Wadi Halfa. The monuments of Bajrawiya, Naga, Musawarat, El Kuoru, Nuri and Merowe are among the most fascinating in the whole area.

Dongola, in northern Sudan, is not for the fastidious and pampered traveller. Although there are no hotels, there is a special house next to the satellite station where unexpected guests will be welcomed and found accommodation with Sudanese family.

West and south of Khartoum lie the Nuba mountains, an area rich in folklore. The main town is El-Obeid, the largest market for gum arabic in the world. Further west is Jebel Marrah, a huge mountain rich in vegetation and natural beauty. There are waterfalls, volcanic lakes and springs (some cool, some warm, some hot). The rest houses in the region include that at Suni near the summit.

The Southern Region is characterised by green forests, open parkland, waterfalls and treeless swamps with birds and wild animals.

Much of the deep South is affected by the civil war and advice should be taken before travelling in the area.

Tribesmen from Western Sudan

TANZANIA

Tanzania is a large country, beautiful in parts, rich in wildlife and the scene of mankind's earliest habitats. Its Government, under President Ali Hassan Mwinyi, has three main priorities: building an egalitarian non-racial society, leadership of the 'Front Line States' in their struggle for equality in Southern Africa, and the protection of the natural environment. Whilst having a more enlightened and successful wildlife policy than neighbouring Kenya, Tanzania is fighting a losing battle against soil erosion and tree felling.

It is the only country in the world where the Government has set aside almost one-quarter of all the land as national parks, game reserves and forest reserves. At the time of independence in December 1961 there was only one national park – the Serengeti. Today there are 12.

The visitor to Tanzania should be advised that there are certain restrictions imposed for security reasons. It is not permitted to photograph police stations, prisons, party offices, army camps and major installations such as bridges and dams. If these restrictions are violated, one is likely to be arrested by an ordinary citizen and escorted to the local police station.

Travel to villages off the main routes is not exactly prohibited; however, to avoid any difficulties, it is advisable to obtain official written permission. This may be done through the Ministry of Information in Dar es Salaam, but may not preclude questioning again on reaching the villages.

Plains, Lakes and Mountains

Situated just south of the equator, Tanzania (which also includes the Indian Ocean islands of Pemba and Zanzibar) is East Africa's largest country – larger than France, West Germany, Austria and Switzerland combined. Over 53,000 sq km of the total area are covered by inland water. Most of the lakes were formed by the Rift Valley, which is one of the world's most remarkable geographic features.

There is still volcanic activity in the neighbourhood of the Rift Valley. Ol Donyo L'Engai, in the eastern Rift Valley, last erupted in 1983. Kilimanjaro, Africa's highest mountain at 5,895 m, is quiescent although there have been recent rumblings and there are continuous vents of steam emitting from the ice-filled crater. One of the best views of Kilimanjaro and the nearby Mount Meru can be gained while landing at Kilimanjaro International Airport, on the road between Arusha and Moshi, in the Sanya Juu Plains.

The Tanzania mainland is divided into several clearly defined regions. The coastal plain, which varies in width from 16 to 64km, is hot and humid. In the north, the Masai Steppe, 213 to 1,067 m above sea level, is semi-arid with

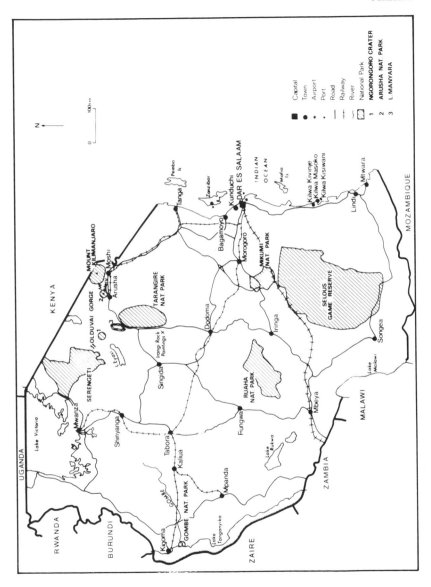

Area: 945,087 sq km
Population: 25.5 million (1989 estimate)
Capital: Dar es Salaam (proposed change to Dodoma)

199

small hills and occasional mountains. The southern area towards Zambia and Lake Malawi is a high plateau.

The high altitude of the greater part of Tanzania counteracts its tropical location. Its climate and vegetation are not 'tropical' in the usual sense, except along the lush coastal belt. Savannah and bush occupy more than half the country. Desert, semi-desert and arid lands account for the remainder.

Tanzania is the home of 120 different peoples, without any single dominant group; this has given the country a stability lacking in many neighbouring States. Most groups are Bantu-speaking and are thought to have entered Tanzania from Zambia and Zaire around 100 BC, mixing with and absorbing the earlier inhabitants – the Hadzapi (Wakindiga) and Sandawe, an extension of the Xhosa peoples of southern Africa who speak a 'click' language. A second group, now living around Mbulu in the north, speak a similar language to the Cushitic group in Ethiopia. A third group (including the Masai) who migrated from the north, are Nilo-Hamitic.

The German colonial authorities encouraged Indian immigration to provide workers for the building of the railways. Many subsequently went into the construction business, or set up as traders.

The population of the Zanzibar islands is almost entirely Muslim. They are a mixture of peoples originating from the East African mainland – Shirazis, who are the descendants of the early settlers from Persia, Arabs from the Gulf States, and Comorians from the Comoro Islands.

History

Early times: In the Rift Valley between Kenya and Tanzania is the famous Olduvai Gorge where the remains of Nutcracker Man (Zinjanthropus) were found. Here his later descendants made some of the first stone hand-axes in the world. At that time there were more lakes along the valley and greater rainfall made it lusher than it is now, although it was still open grassland abounding in game. Stone Age hunters also occupied the highlands to the south, and in the Kondoa district there are over 1,000 of their rock paintings, vivid naturalistic portrayals of human and animal life.

During the first millennium AD, Bantu speakers began to come in from Zaire, south and north of Lake Tanganyika. They brought the knowledge of iron-working and pottery-making and absorbed the hunters and gatherers into more settled communities.

In Roman times, Rhapta (perhaps at the mouth of the Rufiji River) was already known as a trading village where ivory was sold. At Pemba Island men searched for turtle shells in boats sewn together and driven by matting sails. Soon the mixture of Arabs and Bantu-speaking Africans became known as Swahili, from the Arabic word for 'coast' and formed an aristocracy governing a number of separate city-States on islands and peninsulas along the seashore.

By the 10th century they had been joined by Persians and people from even farther east, bringing with them the Muslim religion. The Swahili began to build houses, mosques and palaces of stone, and their foundations can still be seen at Kilwa. By the 13th century Kilwa surpassed all the other towns, since it gained control of the gold trade from Zimbabwe in Rhodesia.

The arrival of the Portuguese in the Indian Ocean, although it did not lead to political domination, slowly strangled the commercial life of the Swahili cities, and many of the inhabitants eventually turned to subsistence farming on the nearby mainland.

In the interior, the poor soils and drainage supported only a sparse population, ruled for the most part by chiefs who exercised both religious and political power over small groups of villages.

During this period, two Nilo-Hamitic groups moved in. The first, arriving perhaps about 1500 AD, were a Kalenjin people whose language is still spoken by the Pokot; then in the 18th century came the Masai. They were not interested in farming but settled on the pastures of the Masai steppe and raided their neighbours for cattle – they believed God had intended cattle only for the Masai.

The 19th century brought trade, with Arab and Swahili caravans dealing in ivory, rhinoceros horn and coconut oil. Later there was also gold and copper. The caravans widened their range as the demand abroad increased for ivory, and for slaves to work the new clove plantations introduced in Zanzibar by the Imam of Oman, Seyyid Sayed, and for export to Persia, Egypt, Turkey and even farther afield. After establishing trading centres at Unyanyembe (Tabora) and Ujiji they pressed on north into Uganda and by mid-century west into Zaire.

In the meantime Ngoni invaders had swept up from South Africa under their leader Zwangendaba, who died on the Fipa plateau in about 1845. His followers split up into small groups: some settled, for example in Songea, and others became mercenary bands (*ruga ruga*) who would fight for any chief. The lawlessness of these times and the advent of guns caused some societies to disintegrate, but others, like the Hehe or Mirambo's Nyamwezi, united in a combined defence.

German influence in the area began in 1884 when Dr Karl Peters negotiated with the tribal chiefs for their land. In 1890 the coastal strip was acquired by Germany on payment of £200,000 to the Sultan of Zanzibar. The mainland territory was declared a Protectorate of German East Africa and Zanzibar became a British Protectorate under the Anglo-German Agreements of 1886 and 1890.

The years from 1888 to 1898 were difficult for the Germans as they tried to establish themselves over the territory. They built a railway and tried to encourage both settler plantations of sisal and rubber and peasant cash-cropping in cotton. The soil was unsuitable however and the attempt had disastrous results which led to a major trans-tribal rebellion against the Germans, known as the Maji Maji rising (1905-6), which is still vividly remembered for its bloodshed and the succeeding famine.

When the British defeated Germany in the First World War, German East Africa was allotted to Britain under a League of Nations mandate as a Trust Territory to be governed until deemed fit to rule itself. The name was changed to Tanganyika, with the present day countries of Rwanda and Burundi in the west being split from the colony and given to the Belgians to administer. The British retained the German practice of using Swahili as the lingua franca of local government business. This contributed to the linguistic unity enjoyed by modern Tanzania, which is virtually alone in this respect in sub-Saharan Africa.

Independence came in 1961 after a peaceful and remarkably united campaign by TANU (Tanganyika African National Union), led since 1954 by Julius Nyerere who was widely admired for his exposition of African socialism. Since independence the most important events in Tanzania have been the Arusha Declaration of 1967 which proclaimed the policy of 'socialism and self-reliance', and the *Mwongozo* (party guidelines) of 1971 which ostensibly sanctioned vigilance against the self-enrichment of Government and Party leaders.

In the meantime Zanzibar erupted into riots against the Arab sixth of the population who held great bureaucratic power. The conflict ended in 1964 with the dispossession of the Arabs, 5,000 Arabs killed and the rise to power of an Afro-Shirazi alliance, led by Sheikh Abeid Karume and consisting of Shirazi, long resident on the island, and mainlanders. This radical Government joined in April 1964 with Tanganyika to form the United Republic of Tanzania although Zanzibar retained its own administration as well as its own party. After Karume's assassination in 1972, President Aboud Jumbe was appointed to head the Government.

In 1977 the two political parties of Tanzania and Zanzibar joined forces and merged to form a new party, Chama Cha Mapinduzi (CCM – Party of the Revolution), with Nyerere as its first chairman. A new constitution was introduced on 26 April 1977 retaining many features of the previous dual administration of the Republic. Tanzania was the major force in deposing President Amin of Uganda in April 1979.

After repeated warnings, President Nyerere at 63, finally carried out his promise to resign and handed over to Ali Hassan Mwinyi on 5 November 1985. Nyerere, who had ruled Tanzania since 1961, continued as Chairman of the CCM party.

Mwinyi, formerly President of Zanzibar, was elected as the sole candidate for the presidency after strong competition from other fancied contestants. Joseph Warioba, the former Justice Minister and Attorney General became first Vice President and Prime Minister.

Economy

Under colonial rule Tanganyika was turned into a typical export economy, poorer than most and overshadowed in British East Africa by the greater prosperity of Uganda and Kenya. There was virtually no modern industry and the development of communications was closely tied to the extraction of cash crops, particularly of coffee and cotton, for export.

After independence the two Development Plans of 1960-63 and 1964-9 drawn up by foreign 'experts' both failed. This was one of the main causes of the Arusha Declaration in 1967 with its commitment to 'Socialism and Self-Reliance', which resulted in the nationalisation of banking, insurance and the major means of production and distribution, and also in the voluntary formation of *ujamaa* (communal) villages. Severe drought and the international recession in 1974-75 caused serious economic problems compounded by the villagisation campaign which failed dismally on a voluntary basis. In 1973 Nyerere ordered compulsory villagisation and a series of massive operations began in which millions of peasant families were moved to new village sites. The principal aim of this strategy was to raise the productivity of labour in household agriculture by concentrating the peasantry into administratively and politically accessible units but it failed to increase agricultural production.

At present, there are major programmes underway for intensive maize, rice, and sorghum production and the extension and improvement of key export crops such as coffee, tobacco and cotton, many of which are financed by the World Bank.

In the industrial sector, a redirection of government policy involved the encouragement of private enterprise for the first time since the 1967 Arusha Declaration. District Development Corporations have been encouraged to promote joint ventures with local businessmen and a number of foreign firms have been invited to re-establish operations in the agro-industrial field although the government's policy of self-reliance remains firm. The core of industrial activity is the processing of local agricultural products – textiles, brewing and cigarettes. Iron and steel production is being developed with Chinese assistance.

Serious efforts are being made to improve tourist facilities and the construction of additional hotel accommodation is underway. Plans were approved in early 1979 for a large road project in southern Tanzania which will greatly improve communications.

After several years of debate, Tanzania finally decided to curb private medical practice as from June 30 1980.

Tanzania is presently facing its most serious economic crisis since independence. In recent years export prices declined, oil prices soared, and drought severely affected agricultural production. President Nyerere was forced to make an urgent appeal for food aid to avoid a famine. Foodstuffs were imported, imports were drastically cut and the visitor to Tanzania immediately noticed the severe shortages of consumer goods (flour, rice, sugar and cooking oil). Tourist hotels, however, have a special licence to import food and alcohol.

High inflation and declining real incomes over the past two years have taken their toll. President Mwinyi began to take tentative steps to liberalise the economy on his assumption of power, in November 1985.

Wildlife and National Parks

Points to remember: Firearms and domestic pets are prohibited in the parks. Leave radios behind. Blowing horns or chasing animals will only make them more timid, and if you drive fast you will also frighten the animals and see very little. The speed limit is 50 km per hour but you will see much more if you drive at 25 km per hour.

Remember that, of all the animals, the big cats can be the most dangerous because they can see you *in* the car. All other animals only see the vehicle.

The five year ban on big game hunting has been lifted although licencing is now on a seasonal basis only. Big game hunting is supervised by the Tanzania Wildlife Corporation.

The Northern Parks

Arusha National Park: The park is situated 32 km east of Arusha on the Arusha-Moshi road; within it are to be found three distinct areas – Ngurdoto Crater, the Momela lakes and the rugged Mount Meru. Altitudes range from 1,600m at Momela to nearly 5,000 m at the summit of Meru.

This is a park with a difference – it has no lions. Neither are there tsetse flies nor mosquitoes, but there is a wealth of wildlife, including the colobus monkey, bushbuck, buffalo, red forest duiker, hippo, rhino, reedbuck, waterbuck, elephant, giraffe and leopard. Birdlife, especially waterfowl, is abundant and during October and May there are many northern migrants. The lush, green rain-forest contains ancient cedar and podocarpus trees.

Visitors may not go down into Ngurdoto Crater but may view the wildlife on the crater floor from lookout points on the crater rim. The area has been set aside as a reserve within a reserve, and it has been decided that here there should be no interference whatsoever from man.

The best times to visit the park are the months of July through March, with December as the best month of all.

Accommodation: There is no hotel in the park yet, but it can be easily visited from Arusha where there are several comfortable hotels. Just outside the park gate, comfortable accommodation is offered in thatched rondavels at the Momela Lodge, PO Box 535, tel: 4622.

Camping is allowed on Meru Mountain, where there are sites at 1,600 m, 2,200 m and 2,600 m. Clean, safe water may be drawn from nearby mountain streams and firewood can be gathered. All sites should be booked in advance through the Park Warden, Arusha National Park, PO Box 3134, Arusha.

Tarangire National Park: The Tarangire National Park in northern Tanzania forms the dry season retreat of much of the wildlife of southern Masailand and is therefore at its best during the months of June to October inclusive, with September probably the best month of all.

Accommodation: Tarangire tented Safari Camp, PO Box 1182, Arusha, tel: Arusha 3625. The camp is located on the banks of the Tarangire River, and overlooks a drinking place for animals. Each tent has a private toilet and shower, and there are dining hall, bar and shop facilities.

Camping is permitted on application to the Park Warden. Campers must be completely self-sufficient, except for water and firewood. contact Tanzania National Parks, PO Box 3134, Arusha.

Lake Manyara National Park: Lake Manyara is 128 km from Arusha on a road part tarmac and part all-weather, but good all year round. The ride is through the stark landscape of the Masai Steppe.

For the adventurous this park offers a close-up view of animals that are rarely found in any other park. It is famous for great herds of buffalo, sometimes over 400 strong, and for lions. The birds of Manyara too are spectacular – the varied vegetation and the extensive mud-flats, reedbeds and marshlands provide ideal feeding grounds for countless resident and migratory species. The most profuse and lovely of these are the thousands of flamingoes that, during certain times of the year, form a solid line of shimmering pink stretching many miles down the lake.

Accommodation: Lake Manyara Hotel, 100 rooms with private baths. The hotel is 10 km from the park gate on the very edge of the Rift Wall, 300 m above the park, and commands an incredible view. There is an airstrip for light aircraft. Information from Tanzania Tourist Corporation, PO Box 2485, Dar es Salaam.

Camping: Sites are available near the park entrance, but campers must bring their own food and drinking water, and must be completely self-sufficient. Mosquito nets are essential.

Ngorongoro Crater: Ngorongoro is the largest intact crater in the world (there are five damaged ones that are larger) and was an active volcano some eight million years ago. Technically it is a caldera: the cone collapsed and slid back into the volcano, leaving a crater 17 kms in diameter. Its floor is 160 sq km in extent, and the rim of the crater, where all the hotels are located, is 2,286 m above sea level. From the rim down to the crater floor is 610 m and only four-wheel-drive vehicles are allowed down. The crater rises high above the Serengeti plain, and from it six mountains over 3000 m are always in view.

Over 30,000 animals live in the crater, from the smallest gazelle – the dik-dik – to the elephant. During the spring months this is an important migratory point for flamingo, and the lake edge is covered with hundreds of thousands of them, giving the impression of pink foam. Ngorongoro has an invigorating climate, enabling hours of game viewing.

The Ngorongoro Crater burial mounds were the site for some of the earliest archaeological finds in East Africa.

Accommodation: Ngorongoro Wildlife Lodge, located on the rim of the crater, 75 rooms with private bathrooms. All rooms are heated. For information and reservation: Northern Circuit Reservations, PO Box 3100, Arusha.

Ngorongoro Crater Lodge: for further information: Ngorongoro Crater Lodge Ltd., PO Box 751, Arusha.

The Ngorongoro Forest Lodge; provides more modest, but comfortable accommodation; for further information: Ngorongoro Forest Lodge, PO Box 792, Arusha.

Camping is allowed inside the crater, and in the conservation area. Campers must be fully self-supporting, even with water. There is no tsetse fly at the higher levels and no mosquitoes.

Serengeti National Park: The Serengeti National Park contains over one and a half million animals – the largest and most spectacular concentration of plains animals anywhere in the world.

The park is 14,700 sq km in area, and Tanzania's largest. The altitudes range from 900 to 1,830 m. Seronera Lodge lies at 1,520 m. The driest months are June-December, and heavy storms may be encountered in April and May, though the roads usually dry quickly. Midday temperatures are around 27°C but drop to 16°C at night, so warm clothing is necessary.

The annual migration, usually in May or June, of wildebeeste and zebra from the central plains to permanent water in the west and north is a truly remarkable sight. The wildebeeste over 500,000 of them – with their unending grunting 'hee-haw' sound, mill around in the southern part of the park making the horizon hazy with dust. Suddenly two break away and start running, and the whole herd moves after them in single file. They might only move half a mile and then stop, or they might keep moving till they disappear from view. They mill about in this fashion for several months until suddenly they begin the migration, followed by thousands of zebra. Then the great herds move steadily westwards in a long stream, sometimes several miles long. The migration then breaks into two parts. One group goes west, often outside the park, where poaching is a problem, and then turns north-east. The second group heads straight north and continues until it reaches the Masai Mara reserve in Kenya. The two groups join up there and turn around to head south again, back to the central plains.

There are two types of lion in the Serengeti – the sedentary lions who stay around Seronera in the centre of the park, and the migratory lions which follow the great herds on their trek.

Olduvai Gorge lies just outside the park boundaries, about 40 km north-west of the Ngorongoro Crater. At Olduvai in 1959 Dr and Mrs Leakey, world-famous anthropologists from Kenya, unearthed a skull one and three-quarter million years old.

Accommodation: Lobo Wildlife Lodge, 75 rooms with private bathrooms. This is a boldly designed lodge, 64 kms north of the park centre, built into the faults and contours of a massive kopje, with the swimming pool dug out of the rock and filled by a waterfall. For information: PO Box 3100. Arusha. Tanzania or Box 2485 Dar es Salaam, Tanzania.

Ndutu Safari Lodge, on the shores of Lake Lagaja near the south-eastern corner of Serengeti National Park has 12 double rooms with private bathrooms and 21 double tents with ample shower and toilet facilities. All rooms and tents have an unrestricted view of the lake and vast plains beyond. In the evenings one can sit around a large bonfire, relax and listen to the African night.

Seronera Wildlife Lodge, 75 rooms with private bathrooms. Situated right in the heart of the Serengeti National Park the lodge is strategically placed to see the annual migration of the game through the Serengeti to the eastern shores of Lake Victoria. Booking through TTC, Box 3100, Arusha, or Box 2485 Dar es Salaam.

Camping: There are nine camping sites within four kms of Seronera. No camping is allowed elsewhere in the park. Campers must provide entirely for themselves and may not use the lodge facilities.

For information and reservations contact: Tanzania National Parks, PO Box 3134, Arusha.

The Southern Parks

Mikumi National Park: The park lies in a horseshoe of towering mountains – the Uluguru range rises to 2,750 m – and forested foothills which almost enclose the flood plain of the Mkata River. This plain lies 550 m above sea level. The climate is influenced by the monsoons, so the days are hot and the evenings cool.

Mikumi has a large concentration of buffalo, elephant and lion. Giraffe can be seen in herds of over 50, and lions are often found in prides of 20 or more. One of their favourite resting places is the hangar at the airstrip. The new Uhuru Railway now marks the boundary of this park with the Selous Game Reserve to the south.

Accommodation: Mikumi Wildlife Lodge. The lodge is beautifully constructed from local *mninga*, *podo* and bamboo and is situated on a cliff overlooking a lake. Bookings through TTC Reservations, PO Box 2485, Dar es Salaam, tel: 23491.

Mikumi Wildlife Camp. The hut camp is 300 m off the main road and the accommodation is comfortable and pleasant. There is a spacious and cool thatched bar with an adjoining dining-room. Booking through Oyster Bay Hotel, PO Box 1907, Dar es Salaam.

Camping: The only camp site in the park is situated 4 km from the entrance gate. Camping is not permitted elsewhere and campers must be self-supporting.

The Ruaha National Park: The Ruaha is the second largest national park (12,950 km) after Serengeti, and July to November are the best months to visit it. Elephant are probably its greatest single attraction. They may be seen congregating in huge herds along the bank of the Great Ruaha River. Apart from elephant and a wide variety of smaller animals, the park is best known for sighting and photographing greater and lesser kudu, sable and the rare roan antelope. The birdlife is rich and interesting too.

Accommodation: There is no lodge as yet in the park, but the town of Iringa offers a choice of two comfortable hotels.

Camping: Camping is permitted at a variety of unspoiled places. Parties must be completely self-supporting.

There is a do-it-yourself camping unit near the Park Headquarters at Msembe consisting of two rondavels on the bank of the Ruaha River. Piped water, firewood, beds and bedding are provided.

Bookings should be made in advance to: Park Warden, Ruaha National Park, PO Box 369, Iringa.

Gombe National Park: Located on the eastern shore of Lake Tanganyika, 16 km from Kigoma, Gombe National Park is famous for its population of wild chimpanzees.

Because of the research still being carried out by scientists and the tameness of the chimpanzees, visitors are restricted in this park, and only 20 people are allowed in at a time.

For information on visits to the park, contact: The Director, Tanzania National Parks, PO Box 3134, Arusha, Tanzania.

Selous Game Park: One of the largest parks with beautiful country, most of which is inaccessible by road, but which offers unique water habitats which can be viewed on boat safaris, and on guided walking safaris through very dense vegetation. There are four camps, each with its own airstrip. Two of the camps offer accommodation in insect-proof tents with private shower and flush toilets; the other two have permanent buildings and a higher level of facilities. Contact the Tourist Corporation for details.

Hunting is now allowed between July and December. For details contact Tanzania Wildlife Corporation, PO Box 1144, Arusha.

Cheetah and cubs

TANZANIA HC TOURIST OFFICE

General Information

Government

Single-party rule by the Chama Cha Mapinduzi (Party of the Revolution). The President is elected every five years by universal suffrage.

Languages

KiSwahili is the lingua franca and the official language. English is widely spoken and there are also many local dialects.

Religion

Christianity, Islam, traditional and Hindu.

How to Get There

By air: Besides the national air line, Air Tanzania, Tanzania is served by numerous international airlines: British Airways, Aeroflot, Air France, Ethiopian Airlines, Kenya Airways, KLM, PIA, SAS, Sabena, Swissair and Zambia Airways. International airports are Dar es Salaam and Kilimanjaro.

By road: Tarmac roads connect Tanzania with Kenya and Zambia. From Lusaka in Zambia the Great North Road is tarmac all the way to Dar es Salaam. The main route from Rwanda is being improved and road links are being built from Mozambique.

Bus services do not operate across the borders. It is necessary to walk across the border and catch a bus on the other side – if one is lucky.

By rail: Dar es Salaam is linked to Lusaka in Zambia by the Chinese-built Uhuru (Tanzam) Railway.

By sea: Dar es Salaam is served by ocean-going freighters and passenger liners. Both Lake Victoria and Lake Tanganyika have steamer services. Two more passenger steamers were commissioned recently for Lake Victoria. For details contact: Tanzania Railways Corporation PO Box 9040 Dar es Salaam.

Dar es Salaam; also National Shipping Agencies Co. Ltd. (NASACO), PO Box 9082, Dar es Salaam.

Zanzibar government steamers run regular services to and from the islands.

Entry Regulations

Visitors to Tanzania from other Commonwealth countries, Scandanavia and Ireland do not require visas. Visitors from other countries should obtain a visa in advance of departure for Tanzania. In an emergency visas can be obtained at the port of entry, but this may entail delay, inconvenience and even deportation.

In countries where Tanzania has no diplomatic representation visas may be obtained by writing directly to: The Principal Immigration Officer, PO Box 512, Dar es Salaam. All temporary visitors must hold a visitor's pass.

Visitors must have an international certificate of vaccination against yellow fever. It is also advisable to have a certificate showing vaccination against cholera.

Motorists must be in possession of a permit or a *carnet de passage*, otherwise a deposit must be made, based on the duration for which their vehicles will be in Tanzania.

Customs Regulations

Tourists on a visit not exceeding six months' duration are granted duty-free baggage importation privileges in respect of all non-consumable goods for their own use.

Visitors over the age of 16 years are permitted one litre of alcoholic liquor and 250 gm of tobacco or equivalent cigars or 200 cigarettes, ½ litre of perfume or toilet water.

There is no limit on the amount of foreign currency one may bring into Tanzania. There are, however, strict exchange control laws. Visitors are required to declare the amount they have upon entering the country and are required to show receipts for money spent upon departure. Travellers' cheques may only be cashed at authorised dealers (banks, tourist hotels, etc.). At no time may they be cashed by a private individual. It is generally more advantageous to change foreign currency at banks since non-TTC hotels charge high commission.

When leaving Tanzania the visitor may not take out more than shs. 100 in Tanzanian currency. It is therefore advisable to have small denomination travellers' cheques. (There is an airport departure tax of shs. 200.)

Climate

Even though Tanzania lies in the tropics and is a land without winter, its climate is governed by its altitude.

Coastal strip: Temperatures vary from 24°C-27°C in the cool season (June-September) to 27°C-30°C during the hot months of December-March when the humidity is very high, though at night it drops considerably. Short rains in November last for three weeks. The long rains begin around April and last for six weeks, when there are periods of sunshine or just cloud cover; this is often a good time to visit Tanzania (April-May) as rates are reduced and hotels are less crowded.

The Central Plateau (800-1,200m): The plateau covers much of the country, and is warm and dry (average 27°C) in the daytime and cool at night.

The Highlands: (1,600-2,200 m): This is a semi-temperate zone, pleasant in the daytime and quite cool at night.

What to wear: Dress is generally informal. However, men should not wear very tight trousers and probably not shorts – especially if visiting the *ujamaa* villages and women should wear skirts covering the knee or trousers, but not shorts, except on the beach or in resort areas. Warmer clothing is recommended for evenings, especially from June to September. It can be very cold at the higher altitudes, and you may need a warm jersey.

The strength of the direct sun can be deceptive at these higher altitudes. So whether you are coming to the parks or the beaches it is wise to bring sunglasses, suntan oil and a hat. Insect repellents are advisable. Carry these with you as they are not easily purchased locally.

Health Precautions

Malaria is prevalent throughout Tanzania except at altitudes over 1,600 m. It is advisable to begin taking a prophylactic two weeks before arrival and for two weeks after departure. Most tourist hotels are either air-conditioned or furnished with mosquito nets, but if you intend camping nets are essential.

All urban centres have hospitals, while many rural areas have clinics and dispensaries.

Most inland watercourses and dams are infected with bilharzia, so it is not recommended to swim in lakes and rivers. The ocean is of course free of it. The majority of game lodges have treated swimming pools (see under individual parks). The water in all urban and tourist areas is chemically treated and safe. It is wise however to bring some medication for dysentery.

For a modest fee visitors to East Africa can take out a limited membership of the Flying Doctor Service of East Africa. If injured or ill, the service will fly you out of the bush to an urban centre for treatment. For further information contact: The Flying Doctor Service, Kilimanjaro Christian Centre (KCMC), PO Box 3010, Moshi, Tanzania.

Banks and Currency

Banks of Tanzania: PO Box 2939, 10 Mirambo St, Dar es Salaam
National Bank of Commerce, PO Box 1255, Dar-es-Salaam, tel: 28671.
Currency: Tanzanian shilling divided into 100 cents.
(See currency table, page 9)

Business Hours

Banks: Monday-Friday 0830-1200; Saturday 0830-1100
Government Offices: Monday-Friday 0730-1430; Saturday 0730-1200
Offices: Monday-Friday 0730-1430
Shops: Monday-Saturday 0800-1200 and 1400-1715

Public Holidays

Zanzibar Revolution Day, 12 January
CCM Day, 5 February
Good Friday, 13 April 1990
Easter Monday, 16 April 1990
Union Day, 26 April
May Day, 1 May
Eid el-Fitr* 26/28 April 1990
Peasants Day, 7 July
Eid el-Haj*, 3/6 July 1990
Maulid*, 2 October 1990
Independence Day, 9 December
Christmas Day, 25 December
The dates of the Muslim holidays, marked with an asterisk, are only approximate as they depend on sightings of the moon.

Embassies in Dar es Salaam

Algeria: PO Box 2963, 34 Upanga Rd
Australia: PO Box 2996, NIC Bldg, Mirambo St
Belgium: PO Box 9210, NIC Bldg, Mirambo St
Canada: PO Box 1022, Samora Machel Av.
China PR: PO Box 1649, 2 Kajificheni Close/Toure Drive
Cuba: PO Box 9282, 313 Upanga
Denmark: PO Box 9171, Bank House, Samora Machel Ave
Egypt: PO Box 1668, 24 Garden Ave
Finland: PO Box 2455, NIC Investment House, Samora Machel Avenue
France: PO Box 2349, Bagamoyo Rd
German DR: PO Box 2083, 65 Upanga Rd
German FR: PO Box 9541, NBC Bldg, Maktaba, City Drive, tel 23286
Italy: PO Box 2106, 316 Lugalo Rd, tel: 29961
Netherlands: PO Box 9534, ATC town terminal Bldg
Nigeria: PO Box 4214, 3 Bagamoyo Rd
Norway: PO Box 9012, Extelcoms Hs, Samora Machel Ave
Rwanda: PO Box 2918, 32 Upanga Rd
Somalia: PO Box 2031, 31 Upanga Rd
Spain: PO Box 842, IPS Bldg, tel: 23203
Sudan: PO Box 2266, "Albarakat", 64 Upanga Rd
Sweden: PO Box 9274, Extelcoms Bldg, 9th Floor, Samora Machel Ave
Switzerland: PO Box 2454, 17 Kenyatta Drive, tel: 67801
Syria: PO Box 2442, 276 Upanga East
USSR: PO Box 1905, 73 Kenyatta Drive, tel: 67039
UK: PO Box 9200, Maktaba St, tel: 29601
USA: PO Box 9123, 36 Laibon Rd
Yugoslavia: Upanga Rd, tel: 21520
Zaire: PO Box 975, 438 Malik Rd
Zambia: PO Box 2525, 442 Malik Rd, Upanga

Transport

By air: Air Tanzania, launched in 1977 to replace the defunct East African Airways, has introduced regular services to all main towns. These are reliable and efficiently run, but are cancelled if there is a below average pay load. It is best to check with the town airline office before leaving for the airport. Foreigners must pay for air tickets in foreign currency. There is a $10 airport tax.

All national parks have air strips and there are two charter companies operating single- and twin-engine aircraft to take you to any town or bush strip in the country. Contact Tanzania Air Services, PO Box 364, Dar es Salaam, tel: 22032 and 29974: Tim-Air Charters, PO Box 804, Dar es Salaam, tel: 27128.

By road: Tanzania has a good network of tarmac and all-weather roads connecting all major points. A few all weather roads are suitable for saloon cars provided they are fitted with heavy-duty shock absorbers and extra spring leaves. Even then these roads become impassable to all except four-wheel drive vehicles during the long rains in April and May. Traffic drives on the left.

An inexpensive bus service exists throughout the country, but is unreliable in both frequency and ability to complete the journey. Tanzania Railways (Station Road, tel: 26241) operate bus services from Dar es Salaam to Morogoro, Iringa, Mbeya Port, Tunduma and Njombe and from Iringa to Arusha and Moshi.

The Automobile Association of East Africa, Cargen, Corporation House, Maktaba Street, PO Box 3004, Dar es Salaam, telephone 21965 has reciprocal facilities in East Africa with the AA and RAC in Britain.

Car Hire: Self-drive car hire is extremely expensive. Hiring a Landrover can cost as much as £30.00 per 100km.

In Dar es Salaam: Tanzania Safari Tours Ltd., PO Box 20058, tel: 63546: Subzali Tours and Safaris, PO Box 3121, tel: 25907: National Tours Ltd, PO Box 9233, tel: 20681.

In Arusha: State Travel Service, PO Box 1369, tel: 3300; Subzali Tours and Safaris, PO Box 3061, tel: 3681; United Touring Co. Ltd., PO Box 3173, Tel: 3727.

By rail: It is possible to travel to most of

Tanzania railways: an excellent way to see the country

TANZANIA HC TOURIST OFFICE

the major towns by train. There is a choice of first, second or third class. Good value. Restaurant cars unpredictable so it is advisable to carry your own food. Further information is available from Tanzania Railways, PO Box 9040, Dar es Salaam.

Useful Phrases

Hello	*Jambo*
Please	*Tafadhali*
Thank you	*Asante*
Goodbye	*Kwaheri*
Welcome	*Karibu*
Tea	*Chai*
Coffee	*Kahawa*
Milk	*Maziwa*
Good	*Nzuri*
Bad	*Mbaya*
How much (does it cost)?	*Ni shillingi ngapi?*
Where is the lavatory?	*Wapi choo*

Accommodation and Food

Tanzania has many excellent hotels. The cheaper establishments are not very comfortable, but adequate.

Tourist hotels are very expensive in terms of local salaries, few of even the better-off Tanzanians can afford to stay in them. However, in every town there are local guest houses, many of the better class ones used, for example, by Tanzanian civil servants travelling on business. They are respectable and clean although washing facilities are communal. Breakfast is not provided. There are also cheaper guest houses, often the off-shoots of local bars and therefore frequently very noisy. Prices of guest houses are higher in the larger towns, but in general the quality can be assessed from the quoted tariffs. Both due to the fact that new guest houses open every year, and owing to the large number of existing ones, we have not included an individual listing in this guide. Guest houses are not bookable in advance, and

if you like to read in the evenings, it is suggested you carry a 60 watt light bulb with you! If you are interested in seeing more of how Tanzania works and less of tourist hotels, this is a good alternative way of travelling.

The food served in most hotels tends to be roasts, steaks and seafood. It is generally good and in Dar es Salaam there are one or two excellent restaurants, including Indian and Pakistani, but in the major Government-operated tourist hotels the quality is variable.

To get good Tanzanian traditional dishes, one has to be invited to a Tanzanian home – the food then is superb.

When on the road, and far from any tourist centres, one can eat at local *hotelis*, which are often rather scruffy, but serve good, hot, very sweet tea, and tasty local snacks. The larger establishments of this kind also serve substantial stews with rice.

Tanzania produces three wines – Dodoma Sweet, Dodoma Red which is variable in quality, and Dodoma Rosé which is usually quite pleasant. A good selection of imported wines, spirits and liquors are available, but no imported beer. Tanzania produces four types of beer, all very good.

There is a Government levy of 10-12½% on accommodation charges in all hotels.

Tipping: Should be discouraged. Many of the game parks and some hotels make a service charge. Tips should NOT be offered in Zanzibar.

Dar es Salaam

Dar es Salaam – meaning 'Haven of Peace' – nestles around one of the prettiest ports and harbours in the world, and the town stretches northward along the Indian Ocean coast. It is not at all a modern metropolis like Nairobi or Abidjan, though a few skyscrapers are

Hotels

NAME	ADDRESS	TELEPHONE	TELEX
DAR ES SALAAM			
Continental	PO Box 2040	22481	
Embassy	PO Box 3152	30006	41021
Kilimanjaro	PO Box 9574	21281	
Mawenzi	PO Box 3222	27761	
Motel Afrique	PO Box 2572	30134/36	41570
Motel Agip	PO Box 529	23511	41276
The New Africa	PO Box 9314	29611	41061
The Oyster Bay	PO Box 2261	68631	
Twiga	PO Box 1194	22561	41249
Skyways	PO Box 21248	27601	
Moderately priced hotels			
Airlines Hotel	PO Box 227	20647	
City Guest House	PO Box 1326	22987	
De Luxe Inn	PO Box 84	20873	
Etiennes Hotel	PO Box 2981	20839	
Florida Inn	PO Box 2975	22675	
Luther House	PO Box 389	32154	
Palm Beach	PO Box 1520	22931	
Rex Hotel	PO Box 2040	21414	
Sea View	PO Box 542	22114	
YMCA	PO Box 767	–	

[Hotels]
Beach Hotels

Africana Vacation Village	PO Box 2802	47369	
Bahari Beach	PO Box 9312	47101	41185
Kunduchi Beach	PO Box 9313	47621	41061
Mafia Island Lodge	PO Box 2, Mafia	Mafia 23491	41061
Silversands Sea Resort	PO Box 20318	47231	

ARUSHA

Equator	PO Box 3002	3127	42125
Mount Meru	PO Box 877	2711/2712	42065
Mount Meru Game Lodge	PO Box 659	Usa River 43	
The New Arusha	PO Box 88	3241	42034
New Safari	PO Box 303	3261	
Tanzanite	PO Box 3063	Usa River 32	
YMCA	PO Box 658	27658	
Hotel 77	PO Box 2485	27658	41061

DODOMA

Dodoma Hotel	PO Box 239	–
Dodoma Inn	PO Box 411	23204/21021

IRINGA

Kilimanjaro Guest House	–	–
White Horse Inn	PO Box 48	–

MBEYA

Mbeya Guest House	PO Box 153	–
Mbeya Hotel	PO Box 80	–

[Hotels]

MOROGORO

Acropol	PO Box 78	–	
Mikumi Wildlife Lodge	PO Box 2485	23491	41061
New Savoy	PO Box 35	23491	41061

MOSHI

Coffee Tree Hostelry	PO Box 184	2787
Moshi Hotel	PO Box 501	3071
YMCA	PO Box 865	2362

MWANZA

New Mwanza Hotel	PO Box 2485	41061

SERENGETI/LAKE MANYARA

Lobo Wildlife Lodge	PO Box 2485 Dar es Salaam	23491	41061
Ngorongoro Wildlife Lodge	PO Box 2485 Dar es Salaam	23491	41061
Seronera Wildlife Lodge	PO Box 2485 Dar es Salaam	23491	41061
Lake Manyara Hotel	PO Box 2485 Dar es Salaam	23491	41061
Tarangire Safari Lodge			

TANGA

Mkonge	PO Box 1544	–
Palm Court	PO Box 783	–
Planter's	PO Box 242	–
Seaview	PO Box 249	–
Splendid	PO Box 397	–
Tanga	PO Box 625	–

USUMBARA MOUNTAINS

Lawns Hotel	PO Box 33, Lushoto	–
Oaklands Hotel	PO Box 41, Lushoto	–

[Hotels]		
ZANZIBAR		
Africa House	PO Box 317	–
Hoteli ya Bwawani	PO Box 670	–
Zanzibar Hotel	PO Box 390	–

For accommodation in the National Parks see under Wildlife and National Parks in text.

starting to rise.

Most of the streets are narrow and winding with low buildings, many dating back to the Arab period. In German times, the architecture consisted of squat two-storey square buildings with very high ceilings and verandahs around the outside – very practical in the tropical heat. There are examples of these all along the harbour front.

The main street, Samora Machel Avenue, is filled with curio shops, banks, airline offices, chemists, Government Ministry buildings, embassies and clothing stores. There are usually several dozen freighters and a few passenger ships in port, and occasionally an old Arab dhow from the Persian Gulf calls, following the downward monsoon. The fast and graceful *ngalawas* bring in their daily catch to a large open-air fish market just at the entrance to the harbour. *Ngalawas* are sail boats made of dugout canoes with out-riggers.

Some places of interest are the Village Museum which has a collection of traditional Tanzanian architecture from all over the country; the National Art Gallery where one can buy the very best of Makonde carvings; the National Museum on Shaban Robert Road has an interesting collection of chiefs' stools and photographs of the Kilwa ruins.

Kunduchi ruins, 25 km north of the city, has examples of 15th- and 18th-century tombs, mosques and houses. Msasani Village, 8 km from Dar es Salaam is a fishing village with tombs dating from the 17th to 19th centuries.

Mafia Island, a fisherman's paradise, is situated only 40 minutes' flying time south-east of Dar es Salaam. Fishing varies from rock, bottom and surf to trolling along the ocean shelf and around the many islands.

Two charter companies operate between Dar es Salaam and Mafia Island. The main fishing season is from September to March.

Restaurants: There are very few restaurants outside the hotels in Dar es Salaam. Those at New Africa, Twiga, Oyster Bay and Agip Motel are the best.

Entertainments: The **Kilimanjaro Hotel** is the only place with a nightclub and cabaret. There are seven cinemas, all air-conditioned; and one drive-in cinema. There is also a lively **Little Theatre** at Oyster Bay.

There are many local clubs where Tanzanian, or even better, Zairean jazz is played. **Margot's,** near the Motel Afrique, is central, but rather disreputable; near the University there are **Mlimani Park,** the **Mpeakaniere Tours and Hunters,** the **Safari Resort,** and many smaller ones. The music is not to everyone's taste, and rather loud, and

217

DAR ES SALAAM

there is usually only beer to drink, but this is where young Tanzanians prefer to spend their weekend evenings.

Sport: Sports and sailing facilities can be arranged from hotels or private clubs, where temporary membership can be obtained.

Shopping and markets: The city centre is lined with shops that sell everything from amethysts and avocados to zebra skins and Zanzibar chests, and they will ship to any part of the world.

There are two main markets: Kariakoo and Ilala where you can buy inexpensive fresh vegetables, meat, fish – dried and fresh – tobacco, household items, carvings, African drums, old brass and copper, carved chess sets, Bao boards, jewellery and large wooden salad bowls carved from one piece of ebony, teak or *mninga*. *Kitenge*, the local cloth, is much in demand and one is unlikely to find much in Dar es Salaam although markets in small upcountry towns often have quite a good selection.

Tourist Information: For all enquiries regarding tourism or safari travel – **The Tanzania Tourist Corporation,** IPS Building, Independence Avenue, PO Box 2485, Dar es Salaam, tel: 27671-4.

Tanzanian child

Kilwa Ruins

There are actually three settlements all bearing the name of Kilwa. The oldest, Kilwa Kisiwani – Kilwa on the Island – resisted the Portuguese until they finally gave up trying to take it from the Arabs in the 15th century. Kilwa Kisiwani is the most rewarding of the Kilwas. It has ruins of a Portuguese fort, a 13th century mosque and a 14th century house of gargantuan proportions, with a swimming pool and amphitheatre, unique in this part of the world. The island is reached by hiring a local canoe from Kilwa Kivinje – Kilwa of the Casuarina Trees – built on the mainland. It was probably founded about 1830 and has a fine market built by the Germans but in Arab style. The newest, and still very small, is Kilwa Masoko – Kilwa of the Markets – built as an administrative centre and situated on a peninsula.

Kilwa can be reached by road about five months in the year, but the best way to get there is by charter aircraft. Alternatively it can be reached by the regular NASACO ship which stops at Kilwa en route to Mtwara and has some second class cabins which are moderately comfortable. There is no tourist hotel in Kilwa but there is a small, somewhat scruffy, local guest house in Kilwa Kivinje. It is advisable to take food from Dar es Salaam because there is frequently nothing at all in the shops in Kilwa.

The Northern Circuit

This circuit is the most popular with visitors. Here are the famous Serengeti plains, Kilimanjaro and the Ngorongoro crater. There are entry fees to all parks.

Arusha

Arusha, a lovely city with an extravagant display of flowers and blooming trees, was the headquarters of the now defunct East African Community, but is still a thriving city. Its altitude is 1,380 m on the

219

slopes of Mount Meru. It is in an important area producing coffee, wheat, sisal, pyrethrum, sugar, textiles and dairy products. It also manufactures plastics, radios, the world-famous meerschaum and briar pipes.

Arusha is the starting place for safaris into the parks of northern Tanzania – Serengeti, Manyara, Ngorongoro Crater, Tarangire, Olduvai Gorge and Arusha National Park. There are many shops and services catering for photographic and hunting safaris.

The city is reached by tarmac road – 680 km from Dar es Salaam, 272 km from Nairobi – or by rail.

Camping: Lake Duluti, 11 km from Arusha and one and a half km off the tarmac road to Moshi, has a camping/caravan site on the shore. Application for use of the site should be made to PO Box 602, Arusha.

Moshi

The town is overshadowed by the imposing presence of Kilimanjaro. Situated at 900 m it is the heart of Tanzania's coffee growing region. This is very lush and fertile volcanic country and 40% of Tanzania's wheat is grown on the slopes of the mountain.

The new Kilimanjaro International Airport – capable of handling all types of aircraft, including jumbo jets – is on the Sanya Juu plains between Arusha and Moshi with a tarmac road connecting it to

both towns. The area is being developed to take large package-tour groups on charter flights from Europe to East Africa's game parks.

Mount Kilimanjaro

The climb up Kibo to Gillman's Point on the crater rim generally takes five days – three up and two down. No special equipment is needed but it is essential to have very warm clothing, gloves, boots, a sunproof hat, dark glasses or goggles and protective lotion for the face. For Uhuru Peak, a further 600 m, an ice axe and Alpine climbing rope should be carried. For Mawenzi, the smaller peak, it is necessary to have both alpine equipment and considerable climbing experience. For both these climbs advanced Alpine experience and the hire of professional mountain guides are essential. There are no readily available mountain rescue teams on either peak.

The best months for climbing the mountain are January, February, September and October when there usually is no cloud cover. However, it can be climbed any other month except April and May during the long rains.

There are four huts on the mountain run by Tourism Division, namely Mandara Hut (formerly Bismark) at 3,000 m above Marangu; Horombo Hut (formerly Peters) at 4,100 m below Mawenzi; Kibo Hut at 5,000 m on the west side of Mawenzi. Mandara hut can

Safari in the Serengeti

accommodate 24 climbers; Horombo Hut 31 climbers; Kibo Hut 18 climbers and Mawenzi 4 climbers. Water is available at Mandara Hut and Horombo Hut but not Kibo Hut, the last water point being a mile above Horombo Hut. Firewood is available near Mandara Hut, but is scarce near Horombo Hut and unobtainable near Kibo Hut.

All intending climbers should be aware that guides and porters are essential even to Gillmans Point. Organised climbs with food and staff can be arranged at some cost through the Marangu or Kibo Hotels. It is advisable to book well in advance. Slightly cheaper and more rough and ready safaris can be organised through the Kilimanjaro Mountain Club, PO Box 66, Moshi. Alternatively, climbers can bring their own supplies and hire staff and equipment (arctic sleeping bags and extra trousers) at the park gate, which is very much cheaper. The climb is well worth trying even if one doesn't make it to the top; there are fascinating changes in ecosystems and a wonderful sense of peace.

Accommodation: Marangu, on the eastern slopes of the mountain and 32 km east of Moshi, has two comfortable lodges. They are both able to organise mountain climbing safaris.

Marangu Hotel, PO Box 40, Moshi, tel: Himo 11. Good food, camping sites.

Kibo Hotel, Private Bag, Moshi, tel: Himo 2.

Kilimanjaro National Park Hostel at the entrance to the park. Bunk beds with clean sheets and lots of blankets. Bring your own food which resident cook will prepare for a small fee.

Osirwa Safari Cottages: PO Box West Kilimanjaro, tel: West Kilimanjaro 542, or contact Osirwa Safari Cottages, 9 Upper Grosvenor Street, London W1, tel: 01-499 4850.

The cottages, situated 80 km from Moshi on the spectacular wheat farms on the north-west slopes of Kilimanjaro, are well equipped and at 1,950 m have

sweeping views of Masailand, the Amboseli Game Reserve and Kilimanjaro.

The Southern and Coastal Circuit

This circuit is not as well known as the northern, but there is a variety of scenery which the north does not offer – 800 km of untouched white beaches on the Indian Ocean, exotic Zanzibar, the great Selous Game Reserve and the Mikumi National Park.

Bagamoyo

Once the capital of Tanganyika, Bagamoyo was the last mainland halt for the slaves before they left, first for the Zanzibar slave markets, then to be scattered around the world.

During the 19th century it was also the starting point on the mainland for many of the explorers from Europe. The chapel in which Livingstone's body rested for the last time on the African continent is still there, and so is the Old Customs House, the ruins where the slaves were kept, and a small German fort. Quaint gas-lamps still adorn the streets, and some of the houses have Zanzibar-carved doors, often over 100 years old.

Bagamoyo, 64 km north of Dar es Salaam can only be reached by road, unless you are adventurous and want to hire a *ngalawa* and sail up the coast to it.

Morogoro

This important agricultural centre at the foot of the Uluguru mountains is 288 km west of the capital on an all-tarmac road. It can also easily be reached by railway. The town lies at 500 m and has a population of 39,000. It has an airport.

Dodoma

Dodoma, in the very centre of Tanzania, is harshly arid. The town lies 1,133 m above sea level, 512 km west of Dar es

Salaam, which it is designated to replace as Tanzania's capital. It is on the central railway line. The 84,000-acre Kongwa ranch, a source of excellent beef and high quality breeding cattle, lies in this region. The very promising Dodoma wine industry started by the Fathers at Bihawana Mission is also located here.

In the neighbourhood of Dodoma are many *ujamaa* villages of the Wagogo peasants who broke away from their traditional life in the early 1970s. These villages show the beginnings of a vast agrarian revolution.

The Stone Age Kondoa Irangi rock paintings can be seen 176 km north of Dodoma on the Arusha road.

Iringa

Iringa (population 46,000) is 502 km south-west of Dar es Salaam on the main Tanzania-Zambia road. Because of its altitude (1,635 m) it is relatively cool. It is within easy reach of the Ruaha National Park. It is a farming centre and tobacco is the important crop.

Mbeya

Mbeya (1,737 m, population 20,000), 875 km from Dar es Salaam and only 114 km from the Zambian border is a very pleasant town located on the edge of the

Southern Highlands. It is the last stop on the Tanzam railway before the Zambian border.

Zanzibar

Only 20 minutes' flight from Dar es Salaam, Zanzibar is one of the world's most beautiful islands. The gateway to Zanzibar – the airport – is surrounded by coconut plantations and the visitor can still see the house near the dhow harbour where Livingstone lived while fitting out his last expedition to the mainland. Another reminder of the past is the house of the notorious slave trader Tippu Tip.

The Anglican Cathedral Church of Christ stands on the site of the great Zanzibar slave market, while on the sea-front the palace of the former sultan and the towering Beit-el-ajaib (The House of Wonders), the largest building in Zanzibar, are vivid reminders of the island's long and colourful history. To enjoy the old town to the full the visitor should go on foot, to see the buildings with their handsome carved doors. Many of them have been allowed to deteriorate, but some are now being restored.

To see the island you can take a taxi, but the Government tours are recommended. The guides are very good and a

Mangapawani Beach on Zanzibar

GERRY BEVINGTON

A dhow in the water off Zanzibar

two-hour ride takes in a great deal.

Recent history of Zanzibar

The revolutionary regime which won power in 1964 virtually closed the island to tourism for several years, but under the more restrained leadership of the Presidents who followed, some of the old tranquillity has returned.

When Shaikh Abeid Karume (who was assassinated in 1972) and his Revolutionary Council came to power they set about righting some of the injustices of the previous regime. The large Arab plantations were broken up, with 18,000 plots of three acres each going to peasant families. New housing schemes were undertaken for workers who previously lived in mud and wattle huts. They now receive free education, medical care and modern housing and pay very little for electricity and water.

The island depends upon cloves for foreign exchange and has one of the highest per capita incomes in Black Africa. Efforts are being made to diversify the cash economy through the production of tobacco, pepper and other spices. Zanzibar also produces yams, pineapples, bananas and millet.

Note of caution: All visitors to the island must conform to Zanzibar's rules on dress, which are very strict, as the Zanzibaris are devout Muslims. Women must at all time wear dresses that do not expose the knees, even when sitting; shorts on men and women are strictly forbidden, as are tight-fitting trousers or any see-through clothing on both sexes. Advice to men – if your hair is longer than 5cm tie it up and wear a hat or, as the rules say, 'you will receive a free haircut'. Women visiting the island generally buy a few lengths of *kanga* in Dar es Salaam and wear them as wrap-around skirts.

Visas

All visitors to Zanzibar must contact the Principal Immigration Officer, Zanzibar, or the Friendship Tourist Bureau of Zanzibar, PO Box 216, Zanzibar, directly. Visas are usually issued at the airport, however.

UGANDA

Uganda's tourist industry collapsed with the advent of Amin. In the aftermath of his regime and the war of liberation, successive governments have attempted to repair the ruined economy and disrupted transport system, but the state of the country remains dire. In the capital, Kampala, shops are boarded up and scant food is to be had in the markets. Conditions in the north are even worse. Travel is difficult, with roads in decay and some risk of attack by bands of marauders. It will be some time before Uganda can restore its tourist industry.

The present situation denies the tourist one of the finest experiences Africa can offer, for Uganda is a spectacularly beautiful country, with mountains, lakes, rivers and fine game parks, a temperate climate and – political situation permitting – an exceptionally friendly and hospitable people.

The Land and the People

Uganda has almost every conceivable variety of scenery – lush tropical forest and tea plantations on the slopes of the Ruwenzori's snow-capped peaks; arid plains of the sparsely populated Karamoja; the lush, heavily populated Buganda; the rolling savannah of Acholi, Bunyoro, Toro and Ankole; the fertile cotton area of Teso.

The heartland skirts Lake Victoria, which is the size of Ireland. The White Nile, flowing out of the lake, traverses much of the country. Few African countries are so well-watered; this makes survival comparatively easy for many of the fourteen million inhabitants whose staple diet is the green banana (*matoke*), or in other areas, millet-bread, cassava and sweet potatoes. There is ample fish in the lake and Nile, and large herds in the cattle country.

The south is green and heavy with banana plantations fronting the hills. 500 km north the harsher ribs of the land show through the thinner soil. Here the shorter grass burns off more easily in the harder dry season.

Lake Kyoga forms the northern boundary for the Bantu-speaking peoples who cover much of East, Central and South Africa. In Uganda they formed powerful kingdoms, notably Buganda in the central area, west of Kampala; Bunyoro to the north as far as Lake Albert; Toro, around Fort Portal near the Ruwenzori mountains; and Ankole in the south west. These, together with Rwanda and Burundi, were the famous Interlacustrine Kingdoms, in existence for some 600 years, and isolated until the 18th century from all non-African influence. The people within each kingdom are typically stratified into a pastoral aristocracy (called the Hima or Tutsi, who may

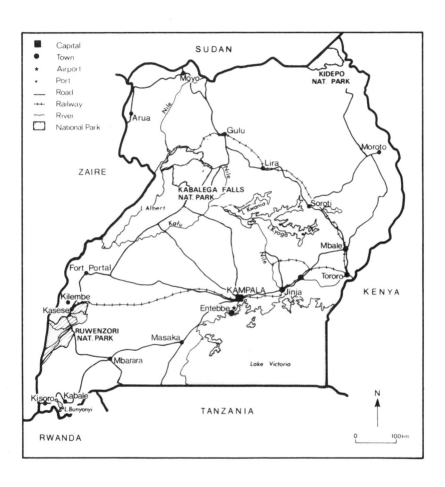

Area: 236,860 sq km
Population: 16.7 million (1989 estimate)
Capital: Kampala

possibly have come originally from southern Ethiopia, speaking Cushitic languages) and a majority of peasants. There were smaller kingdoms too in Eastern Region, the main peoples there being the Bantu-speaking Basoga and Bagisu.

In the north live the Langi near Lake Kyoga, and the Acholi between them and the Sudan border. Both speak River-Lake Nilotic languages. East of them are the Teso and the desert-dwelling Karamojong who are Plains Nilotes, related to the Masai of Kenya and Tanzania. In the far north west of Uganda are the Central Sudanic Lugbara people. In the far south west in the Ituri forests are pygmies.

History

Uganda is a particularly fertile country, and as a result has attracted migrations throughout its history. The first migrants were the Bantu from the west, followed by northern Nilotic peoples and Hamitic pastoralists from the north east.

Much of the country's history has been marked by tensions among the southern Bantu peoples, especially the four major kingdoms of Buganda, Bunyoro, Toro and Ankole, and between the Bantu and northern Nilotic groups. After the scramble for Africa this north/south tension was exploited by the British as colonial rulers, and has dogged post-independence politics ever since.

The Bantu kingdoms engaged in successive wars, rivalries and shifting alliances from the fourteenth century onwards. Initially the Banyoro were dominant, but from the eighteenth century the Baganda began to emerge as the most powerful of the kingdoms, with a highly centralised autocracy.

In the nineteenth century, Arab traders and Muslim missionaries made contact with the Baganda. They were followed in the 1860's and 1870's by European explorers and missionaries, both Catholic and Protestant, from Britain, France and Germany. The Baganda rulers were suspicious of missionaries and persecuted their converts.

The Anglo-German treaty of 1890 gave Uganda to the British, who made it a Protectorate in 1893. Kabaka (King) Mwanga of Buganda was deported, and in 1900-1903 new agreements with the four major kingdoms consolidated the customary British practice of indirect rule: increased powers for the chiefs, privileged status for the four kingdoms and a special relationship with the Baganda fostered regional and tribal divisions and ensured that the powerful anti-imperialist currents in Uganda remained disorganised for another half-century.

In general, British policy was successful; the feudal ruling class was well served, and the new African administrative stratum found security in the civil service, local government, teaching and the church. The British-officered army was recruited among the 'martial' but 'obedient' northern Langi and Acholi. Although Europeans and Asians monopolised production and commerce, there was no widespread seizure of lands, and Africans were encouraged to grow cash crops like coffee and cotton, and to develop their own co-operatives for marketing them.

Nevertheless, the privilege of Whites and Asians, and the time-honoured imperialist custom of fixing artificially low prices for African agricultural produce brought sporadic manifestations of popular discontent.

The British, abroad as at home, had a long tradition of assuaging unrest with political concessions, and set up a Legislative Council in 1921 – but without African appointments until 1945.

No Ugandan nationalist parties developed until the early 1950's – in a period when Baganda separatist aspirations reached a new peak with the demand for independence in 1953 and the consequent deportation of the Kabaka to Britain for two years. At this time the British first permitted indirect election of Africans to the Legislative Council.

It was not until 1962 that a fully elected National Assembly replaced the Legislative Council, and after a second election the same year, Uganda achieved independence under Dr Milton Obote.

Obote's regime was based on a shaky alliance with the Kabaka under a British-influenced federal constitution which, by granting virtual autonomy to Buganda, all but encouraged friction between nationalists and feudal rulers.

In 1966 Obote finally used his army, under Col Idi Amin, to crush the Kabaka, who escaped to Britain where he subsequently died. This precedent for military intervention was followed by a new unitary constitution, an attack on feudal structures and a substantial move to the Left, including a 60% government stake in major companies by 1969.

Tribal, religious and personal rivalries centred increasingly on Amin, who pre-empted his own arrest in January 1971 by seizing power while Obote was out of the country. He gained initial support from the West and the Israelis, and consolidated his position by a combination of shrewd alliances, brutal repression and publicity stunts.

The Israelis were expelled and foreign policy re-oriented towards the Pan Islamic bloc, bringing aid from Arab countries. The economy was 'Africanised' in 1972/73 with the expulsion of Asians and the nationalisation of British interests. The army was expanded and local government militarised. The Langi and Acholi, tribes favoured by Obote, were massacred in their thousands; Amin's own Kakwa people were promoted, and the Baganda appeased. Muslims were favoured over Christians.

A poorly organised invasion of Uganda by Tanzania-based exiles was crushed in 1972, as was an attempted counter-coup in 1974. As the economy went into decline Amin became increasingly dependent on the army, but even its loyalty could not be guaranteed once the collapse of coffee prices after 1977 deprived it of luxuries.

Amin's 1978 invasion of Tanzania, which harboured the deposed Obote, provoked a counter-invasion by the Tanzania People's Defence Force with an alliance of Ugandan exile groups, which combined into the Uganda National Liberation Front (UNLF) in March 1979 at a conference at Moshi, Tanzania, convened by President Nyerere. The Moshi Declaration proposed a new Ugandan constitution in which the supreme body would be a 30-person National Consultative Council (NCC).

Kampala fell to the UNLF forces in April 1979 and the conservative Professor Yusufu Lule was elected President by the NCC. He lasted only three months before being forced to resign in June.

Lule was succeeded by Godfrey Binaisa, a lawyer. His policies differed little from Lule's, but he was a more adroit politician. In May 1980, however, he was overthrown by the UNLF's Military Commission led principally by pro-Obote men.

Bitterly contested elections, supervised by the United Nations, were held on 10 December 1980 and Obote was narrowly returned to power, amidst claims of ballot rigging and electoral malpractice. The security situation in the country, particularly in areas of Buganda around Kampala, remained shaky and gave little encouragement to tourism.

Obote failed to create a peaceful or prosperous nation and his regime was marked by massacres of his opponents and violence against civilians. But it was tribalism in the army that finally brought him down, when Acholi army officers under Lt.Gen. Tito Okello seized power in July 1985. The military government tried to bring conflict to an end, but it could reach no permanent agreement with the guerrillas of Yoweri Museveni's National Resistance Movement. Ultimately there was no basis on which the two groups could share power and Museveni finally took Kampala and was sworn in as President on 29 January 1986. He restored order in the south and west of the country, but a number of new guerrilla movements sprang up in the north and east and led to years of fighting and depopulation.

Economy

Before the 1971 coup, Uganda was practically self-sufficient in food products and had a small but rapidly growing local industrial sector. Under Amin, 90% of the population reverted to subsistence farming, tourism ceased, as did industrial development, production of coffee and sugar slumped and foreign trade was severely disrupted.

In July 1979 the new Finance Minister announced that the economy was in 'total ruins', with an overall deficit of £757.2m, including balance of payments, external commitments and foreign currency reserves. With an absence of investment, widespread and increasing unemployment, a dearth of technocrats (65% fled or were killed by Amin) and a flourishing 'black' economy, the new government air-lifted 2,000 tons of coffee to ease the immediate foreign currency situation, and proposed as emergency measures a moratorium on all debt repayments, the establishment of a Compensation Commission and an Aid Conference to attract assistance.

In the aftermath of the Amin regime four successive governments failed to repair the ruined economy and much time was lost in political wrangling. The 1980 elections gave some hope and the economy partially recovered. Foreign funds from the IMF, World Bank, Britain, the US and the EEC countries helped. Devaluation allowed shops to build up their stocks, while, local foodstuffs became available in the markets. But when Yoweri Museveni took power in January 1986 he was faced with the task of major economic reconstruction.

Wildlife

Uganda has a magnificent variety of wildlife, including several extremely rare species such as the white rhino, Bright's gazelle and Chandler's reed buck. Unfortunately the game parks have not been left untouched by the country's bloody excesses and many species have been severely depleted by soldiers toting automatic weapons.

National Parks

Uganda has three major parks and 16 game reserves. Many wildlife enthusiasts claim Uganda's natural beauty is the finest in the world.

Kabalega (formerly Murchison) Falls National Park: This well-known park takes its name from the magnificent falls on the Nile river. It is famous for the rare white rhino as well as other rhino, hippo, elephant and crocodile. It is also the habitat of over 400 bird species. Visitors stay at either Paraa Safari Lodge or Chobe Safari Lodge.

Ruwenzori (formerly Queen Elizabeth) National Park: This park is along the shores of Lake Edward and Lake George, which are joined by the Kazinga Channel, and provides breeding grounds for the hippo, elephant, buffalo, Uganda kob, waterbuck and topi, lion, leopard, giant forest hog, warthog, sitatunga antelope and chimpanzee. There is a vast array of waterbirds. Mweya Safari Lodge serves the park.

Kidepo National Park: This park covers about 1,450 sq km on the borders of the Sudan in north east Uganda. It is not as well known as the other two and consequently is often overlooked by visitors. The park has a variety of big game, but is perhaps best known for several rare species – the greater kudu, Bright's gazelle and Chandler's reed buck. It has the largest herds of elephant in Uganda.

General Information

Government

The government comprises members of the National Resistance Army and their political wing – the National Resistance Movement, who make up a 35 member council. They are led by President Yoweri Museveni. Elections aren't expected until 1988/89.

Languages

English if the official language. Swahili is also spoken, as are numerous local languages.

Religion

There are strong Christian communities, mainly Catholic and Protestant, and many Muslims. Traditionalist religions also flourish. The new constitution guarantees freedom of religion.

How to Get There

By air: A large number of international airlines including Air France, Kenya Airways, Uganda Airlines, Air Tanzania, Ethiopian Airlines, Sabena, Aeroflot and Air Zaire fly to Entebbe. On departure at Entebbe Airport there is an Airport tax of 1,000 Uganda shillings.

By road: The road approach to Uganda from Kenya is through Tororo; and from Rwanda and Zaire it is through Kisoro. The journey may be made in a tour company coach or by the air-conditioned buses of the Akamba bus company from Nairobi. They stop at the border posts of Busia or Malaba where connection can be made with the Beautiful Omni buses to Kampala.

By rail: Mombasa-Nairobi-Kampala railway line no longer operates a through service to Uganda, but stops in Kenya.

Entry Regulations

No visas are required for members of the Commonwealth. Other nationalities need visas. However, everyone is advised to get an "entry pass" from a Uganda mission abroad. Visitors have to have onward tickets. Admission is refused to nationals of South Africa.

Yellow fever and cholera vaccination certificates are recommended.

Climate

Although Uganda lies on the Equator the temperature remains pleasant due to the altitude and low humidity level. Temperatures range from 26°C in the day to 15°C in the evening. The mountain areas become much cooler, and the top of Mount Elgon is often trimmed with snow. After the air-conditioning of Kampala's modern buildings it is refreshing to see the log fires and open grates in the Kabale area. Rain tends to fall more heavily in the March-May and October-November period.

Health Precautions

Tap water is not altogether safe, even in cities. It is wise to take a malaria prophylactic and vaccination against yellow fever is essential because it is endemic in Uganda. There is bilharzia in most lakes, but Lake Nabugabo in Masaka area and Lake Bunyonyi in the Kigezi hills are free of it. Medical facilities are not always readily available.

Banks and Currency

Bank of Uganda: PO Box 7120, 37-43 Kampala Rd, Kampala
Uganda Commercial Bank: PO Box 973,

12 Kampala Rd, Kampala
Bank of Baroda (Uganda) Ltd: PO Box 7191, 18 Kampala Rd, Kampala
Barclays Bank of Uganda Ltd: PO Box 2971, Kampala Rd, Kampala
Grindlays Bank (Uganda) Ltd: 45 Kampala Rd, PO Box 485, Kampala
Standard Chartered Bank Uganda Ltd: PO Box 311, Speke Rd, Kampala
Currency: Uganda shilling divided into 100 cents.
(See currency table, page 9).

Business Hours

Government Offices: Monday-Friday 0800-1230 and 1400-1700
Post Offices: Monday-Friday 0800-1230 and 1400-1700
Banks: Monday-Friday 0830-1230
Shops: Monday-Saturday 0830-1230 and 1400-1700

Public Holidays

Liberation day, 11 April
Good Friday, 13 April 1990
Easter Monday, 16 April 1990
Heroes day, 27 May
Eid al-Fir*, 26/28 April 1990
Independence Anniversary, 9 October
Christmas Day, 25 December
The dates of the Muslim holidays, marked with an asterisk, are only approximate as they depend on sightings of the moon.

Embassies in Kampala

Burundi: PO Box 4379, **China:** PO Box 4106, **Cuba:** PO Box 9276, **Egypt:** PO Box 4280, **France:** PO Box 7212, **Germany DR:** PO Box 7294, tel: 43693, **Germany FR:** PO Box 7016, **Ghana:** PO Box 4062, **India:** PO Box 7040, **Iraq:** PO Box 7137, **Italy:** PO Box 4646, **Kenya:** PO Box 5220, **Nigeria:** PO Box 2468, **North Korea:** PO Box 5885, **Rwanda:** PO Box 2468, **Somalia:** PO Box 7113, **South Korea:** PO Box 3717, **Sudan:** PO Box 3200, **Tanzania:** PO Box 5750, **UK:** PO Box 7070, tel: 57031, **USA:** PO Box 7007, **USSR:** PO Box 7022, **Yugoslavia:** PO Box 4370, **Zaire:** PO Box 4972.

Transport

All the main towns are connected by bitumen roads but most are in a state of disrepair. The main routes from Kampala radiate southwest to Masaka, Mbarara and Kabale, west to Fort Portal and Kasese; north to Masindi, Gulu and Kabalega Falls; east to Jinga, Tororo, Mbale and Soroti. Lira and Gulu can also be reached by heading north from Soroti; and Kasese can also be reached by travelling north from Kabale. Entebbe is linked to Kampala by a tarmac road.

Bus services operate between most parts of Uganda, but they are generally very full and rather unreliable. Taxis operate between most townships, but they are also overcrowded and sometimes erratically driven.

Accommodation and Food

Kampala has several hotels, and throughout the country the Government-owned Uganda Hotels Limited (PO Box 7173, Kampala) runs a network of hotels, but catering facilities have been disrupted by the shortage of sugar, salt, beer, soap, and many foods. Each National Park is provided with lodges, groups of *bandas* (cabins) and camping sites. Restaurants may be found in and around Kampala and all the State-owned hotels now serve local dishes. The most famous of these are *matoke*, a staple food made from bananas, maize bread and the chicken and beef stews which are eaten with it.

The national drink is Waragi, a banana gin, very popular among visitors as a cocktail base.

Hotel bookings at the hotels listed here can be made by writing to Uganda Hotels Limited or direct to the hotel of your choice. All visitors must settle their hotel bills in foreign currency.

Hotels

NAME	ADDRESS	TELEPHONE	TELEX
KAMPALA			
Colline Hotel	POB 7, Portal Ave	86212/86240	61325
Diplomat Hotel	POB 6968, Plot 971, Mugenya, Tank Hill	268311	61001
Fairway Hotel	POB 4595, Plot 3, Kafu Rd	234158	
Imperial Hotel	POB 7088, Nile Ave	59800	
Lion Hotel	POB 6751, 18 Namirembe Rd	43687/43490/ 43682	61332
Lunar Hotel	POB 16211, Gaba Rd	68196	61108
Nile Hotel	POB 7057, Nile Ave	58041	61090
Sheraton	POB 7041, Ternan Ave	244590	61517
Silver Springs Hotel	POB 734, Port Bell Rd	61301	
Speke Hotel	POB 7063, 7 Nile Ave	54553	
OUTSIDE KAMPALA			
White Rhino Hotel	PO Box 359, Arua		
Lake Victoria Hotel	PO Box 15, Entebbe	2644/5	
Mountains of the Moon Hotel	PO Box 36, Fort Portal		
Ruwenzori Tea Hotel	PO Box 53, Fort Portal		
Semliki Safari Lodge	PO Box 71, Fort Portal		
Chobe Safari Lodge	Private Bag, Gulu		
Crested Crane Hotel	PO Box 444, Jinja	21513	61150
Ripon Falls Hotel	PO Box 30, Jinja		

[Hotels]

White Horse Inn	PO Box 11, Kabale
Hotel Margherita	PO Box 41, Kasese
Mweya Safari Lodge	Private Bag, Kasese
Kisoro Travellers Rest	PO Box 15, Kisoro
Hilltop Hotel	PO Box 58, Kitgum
Lira Hotel	PO Box 350, Lira
Masindi Hotel	PO Box 11, Masindi
Paraa Safari Lodge	Private Bag, Masindi
Mount Elgon Hotel	PO Box 670, Mbale
Nganwa Hostel	PO Box 102, Mbarara
Moroto Hotel	PO Box 67, Moroto
Soroti Hotel	PO Box 397, Soroti
Rock Hotel	PO Box 293, Tororo

Kampala

Kampala, the capital, is set among hills, each dominated by a particular feature – the Anglican and Roman Catholic cathedrals, a mosque, and the palatial complex of the Old Kingdom of Buganda. The tree-lined avenues, with colourful flower-beds and waving palms, wind along valleys and up hillsides. Modern Kampala has a fine skyline and a fine mosque. Parliament Buildings and the National Theatre are fine architectural examples.

Kasubi Hill is the site of the Kabaka's Tombs; here are buried Mutesa I, Mwanga, and the late 'King Freddie', Sir Edward Mutesa II. They offer one of the finest examples of Buganda thatched buildings in the country. Strict observance of the customs of the tombs should be followed; it would be taken as a gross discourtesy if one entered the building without removing one's shoes.

Namugongo is the site of the Uganda Martyrs' shrine. The shrine is located 16 km out of Kampala on the Jinja road.

Entebbe

Entebbe is the gateway to Uganda for air travellers. Prior to independence in 1962 it was the seat of the Governor and most government departments were located there. Skirting the lakeside are the Botanical Gardens which offer a fine collection of tropical trees and plants. Although there is a fine beach it is most unwise to bathe in the lake because of bilharzia.

Please take advice before travelling to outlying parts of the country. Some areas particularly in the north and north east are controlled by the military and permission is needed to travel.

Fort Portal

Fort Portal is an ideal base for exploring the Ruwenzori Mountains. It lies 1,700 m above sea level and is the centre of the tea estates.

The town is within easy reach of the Ituri Forest – home of the pygmies – the hot springs of Bundibugyo, and the Toro Game Reserve. For climbing enthusiasts the Ruwenzoris offer Mount Speke, Mount Stanley, and Mount Baker, all over 5,000 m high. The vegetation of this area, equatorial forests with giant lush vegetation, gives one a very realistic picture of the Uganda of earlier years.

Jinja

Jinja is Uganda's second largest town and lies 80 km to the east of Kampala on the main route to Kenya. It is the country's main industrial area built around the Owen Falls dam and power station.

Kabale

Kabale, at 2,000 m above sea level, is Uganda's highest town. Trips to the lakes – Lake Bunyonyi, in particular – are worthwhile. The climate is naturally more variable at this height, and warm clothes will be necessary in the evenings.

Kisoro, nearby, is the starting point for climbing expeditions to Mounts Muhavura and Mgahinga. Seven lakes in the vicinity offer fishing and possible duck and fowl shooting. From Kabale you can drive north to Lakes Edward and George and the Ruwenzori Park. The road sweeps down from the mountains alongside the Kazinga Channel which links the two lakes. The view of the Game Park from Kichwamba on the escarpment is a photographer's dream. Kasese and Kilembe are the starting points for the game parks in the area.

Mbale

Mbale, Uganda's third largest town, is at the hub of the Eastern Region. Mount Elgon provides a beautiful backdrop to the fertile and lush countryside. Nkokonjeru is a steep hill which looms out of the plains to protect the town.

The Mount Elgon hotel is an ideal base for an ascent of the mountain, which offers a steep walk rather than a climb. The mountain, an extinct volcano, is 4,600 m high. The round trip to the summit takes three days. It is recommended both for easy climbing and for an interesting encounter with village life as you make your way up the slopes through coffee and matoke (cooking banana) plantations. In the rainy season the climb can be very difficult and local advice should be sought before you begin.

Mbarara

Mbarara is the headquarters of a large army camp. It is rather reminiscent of a Western movie set, an effect heightened by the large pair of Ankole cattle horns mounted on a plinth at the entrance to the town. It is the centre of a cattle ranching area, home of the famous Ankole cattle who have a hornspan of over one metre. The rolling hillside is a very direct contrast to the lush greenery of the Eastern Provinces. The town is a base for Lake Mburo Game Reserve with bushbuck, oribi, buffalo, lion and leopard.

Moroto

Moroto is the main centre of Karamoja – a dusty dry area. Its plains were rich with game before the poachers killed them.

The Karamojong are turbulent, tall, athletic people, very proud and still clinging stubbornly to their traditions. Only recently have they begun to wear clothes. They are cattle people and are frequently in dispute with Kenya border tribes over cattle raiding. These men still carry, and use, long spears; the women wear beautiful necklaces, bangles and bracelets. It would be foolish to roam around this area without a guide as bandits use automatic weapons.